321.23

SECRET
WASHINGTON D.C.

Sharon Pendana

JONGLEZ PUBLISHING

travel guides

We have taken great pleasure in drawing up *Secret Washington D.C.* and hope that through its guidance you will, like us, continue to discover unusual, hidden or little-known aspects of the city.

Descriptions of certain places are accompanied by thematic sections highlighting historical details or anecdotes as an aid to understanding the city in all its complexity.

Secret Washington D.C. also draws attention to the multitude of details found in places that we may pass every day without noticing.

These are an invitation to look more closely at the urban landscape and, more generally, a means of seeing our own city with the curiosity and attention that we often display while travelling elsewhere …

Comments on the guide or information on places we may not have mentioned are more than welcome and will help us to improve future editions.

Don't hesitate to contact us:

Jonglez publishing, 25 rue du Maréchal Foch,
    78000 Versailles, France.
    e-mail: info@jonglezpublishing.com

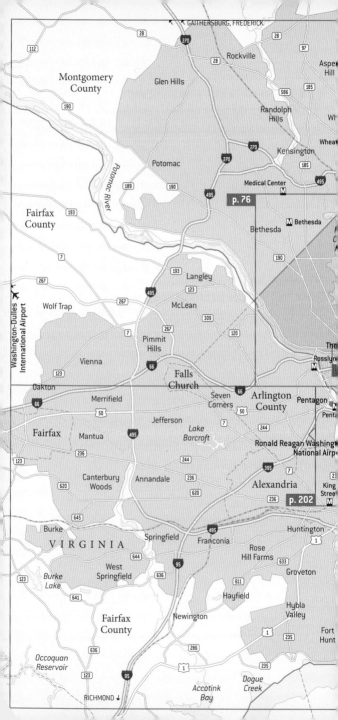

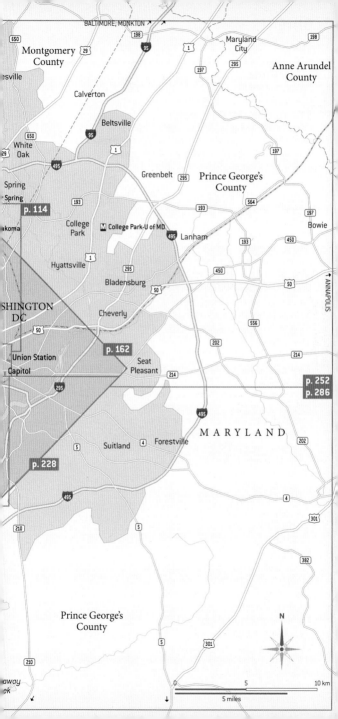

CONTENTS

NORTHWEST 1

NORTHWEST 2

CONTENTS

SOUTHWEST

SOUTHEAST

CONTENTS

GREATER WASHINGTON NORTH

GREATER WASHINGTON SOUTH

DOWNTOWN

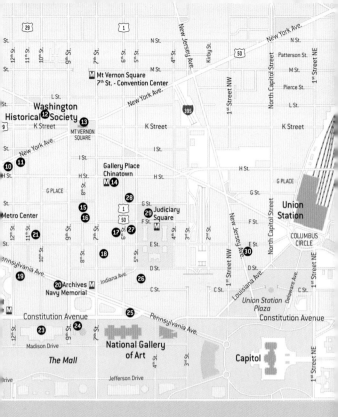

HAHNEMANN MEMORIAL ❶

1300 Corregidor Street NW
At Scott Circle (near the confluence of 16th Street, Massachusetts
Avenue, N Street and Rhode Island Avenue)
• Metro: Red Line to Farragut North or Blue Line, Orange or Silver Line to
Farragut West

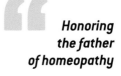

*Honoring
the father
of homeopathy*

On the eastern periphery of the traffic circle honoring Winfield Scott, the longest active duty general in American history, stands the city's only freestanding monument to a physician. The impressive memorial, a curving granite exedra bench with a portrait statue, honors the founder of homeopathy, Samuel C.F. Hahnemann. Bronze relief panels depict his life as a student, chemist, teacher and physician. The eye-catching central niche features a seated bronze sculpture of Hahnemann in thought, upon a pedestal inscribed *Similia Similibus Curantur* — "like cures like" — the main tenet of homeopathic medicine. Enlivening the domed recess is a vibrant glazed ceramic mosaic depiction of the cinchona plant (quinine), the bark of which caused malaria symptoms in Hahnemann, a healthy MD, while appearing to cure the disease in affected patients.

Now based in Fairfax, Virginia, the American Institute of Homeopathy was founded in New York in 1844, one year after Hahnemann's death. It is the oldest professional medical society in existence. Although Hahnemann had never set foot in Washington, the society petitioned for years to publicly commemorate the "Leader of the Great Medical Reformation of the Nineteenth Century," in the capital city. During his first term in office, President Grover Cleveland vetoed the idea, despite the fact that Hahnemann's influence had fostered the founding of the National Homeopathic Hospital in

Northwest in 1881. The homeopathy community persisted and raised funds to have architect Julius Harder and sculptor Charles Henry Niehaus design a memorial. Unveiled in June 1900 to the strains of the Marine Corps Band with President McKinley in attendance, it is a wonder that it was approved, considering the antipathy toward the homeopathic practice in America at the turn of the 20th century.

It was Dr. Hahnemann who rather derisively coined the term "allopath" to describe a practitioner of "Western" or evidence-based medicine, which countered the practice of the homeopath.

Two block-long Corregidor Street and its counterpart on the opposite side of Scott Circle, Bataan Street, situated near the Philippine Embassy, were named in 1961 in remembrance of the decisive battles precipitating the fall of the Philippines in World War II.

CHARLES SUMNER SCHOOL MUSEUM AND ARCHIVES ❷

1201 17th Street NW
• Open: Museum open Mon—Fri 10am—5pm; Archives 10am—4pm by appointment • Tel: 202-730-1421 for appointments
• Metro: Red Line to Farragut North

> *A fascinating timeline of the DC Public School system*

I n 1872, on the site of a humble schoolhouse established for black children just after the Civil War, prominent Washington architect Adolf Cluss designed a towering school of red brick. Named for ardent abolitionist Senator Charles Sumner, it was among the first purpose-built schools for African American children in the segregated DC Public School system (DCPS). With its central entrance clock tower and belfry, the stately structure hosted the first commencement ceremony for a graduating black high school class in 1877. Little over a century later, in 1978, with the school-age population of the area declining and the building deteriorating, Sumner School closed.

After restoration, the school, now known as the Charles Sumner School Museum and Archives, is one of the few remaining Cluss-designed buildings in the city. Standing across the street from the headquarters of National Geographic (pg.21), the repository of artifacts and the archives of DCPS invites visitors to roam the classrooms for an enlightening and often nostalgic look at public education in the District of Columbia through its ephemera and memorabilia. In an entry niche, a historical photograph of Randall Junior High School's class of 1954 stands out; the smiling young man in the first row is none other than Marvin Pentz Gay, Jr. before he went on to Motown fame as Marvin Gaye (pg.199).

On the second floor, in the Morgan Memorial Room, a sepia-toned 1895 portrait of Cadet Corps Lieutenant Alfred Sao-Ke Sze resides among other keepsakes of Central High School, once the pre-eminent public high school in the city. Sze arrived in DC from China in August 1893 as student translator of the Office of Legation. He excelled at the then whites-only Central High and would eventually become Chinese Ambassador to the United States. In gratitude, he endowed a schoolroom in honor of his English teacher Miss Ella M. Morgan with intricately carved Chinese furnishings and some of his personal effects.

Music history pervades the third floor. In the corridor, an antique hand-cranked upright music box holds a John Philip Sousa march. Paraphernalia displayed in a classroom documents Armstrong High School as an incubator for musical talent, from lyric soprano Madame Evanti to jazz legends Duke Ellington, Billy Eckstine, Jimmy Cobb, and John Malachi — great-grandfather of contemporary DC singer Carolyn Malachi.

From a "leatherhead" football helmet and copious championship plaques, trophies and medals, to the "state-of-the-art" 1928 electric stove from Francis Junior High, the museum and archive is a fascinating timeline of DC Public Schools.

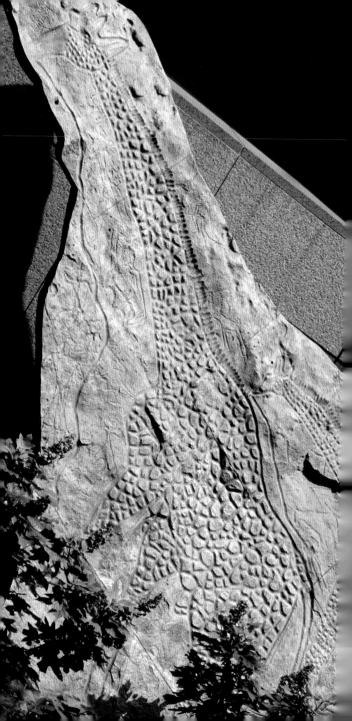

DABOUS GIRAFFE PETROGLYPH REPLICA ❸

National Geographic
1145 17th Street NW
• nationalgeographic.com
• 202-857-7588
• Metro: Red Line to Farragut North; Blue, Orange, or Silver Line to
Farragut West

**Secret
of the Stone Age
Sahara**

Bringing a bit of Saharan prehistory to the plaza at *National Geographic* headquarters, two giraffes amble along, nearly hidden in a landscaped nook; the pair a replica of the Dabous giraffe petroglyph of Niger, a nearly 20-foot Neolithic carving in a desolate stretch of the Sahara. Now home to nomadic Tuaregs, the region known as the Ténéré ("where there is nothing") was once, seven to ten millennia ago, lush with vegetation. The remarkable ruminants date to this era, obscured on a sandstone outcrop of the Aïr mountain range.

First encountered by Western eyes in 1987, the world's largest rock art carving (one of nearly 800 in the region) was surveyed by the Trust for African Rock Art (TARA) about ten years later. Recognizing the significance of the secret Saharan engravings, TARA partnered with UNESCO (United Nations Educational, Scientific and Cultural Organization) and the Niger Government to preserve, protect and secure the site, engaging Tuareg locals as caretakers.

The exemplary petroglyph, showing signs of deterioration, was placed on the World Monuments Watch list of the top 100 endangered monuments. With the support of the Bradshaw Foundation (dedicated to the study and preservation of the world's rock art) and the National Geographic Society USA, French restoration experts Mérindol in 1999 meticulously created a silicon polymer mold to replicate the carving for display worldwide. Cast in France, the first replica sits at the airport in Agadez, a 2-hour drive from Dabous. Lucky for us in the nation's capital, the second, a secret of the Stone Age Sahara, is within our city limits.

FROM THE STONE AGE TO THE INFORMATION AGE

The unknown Stone Age artists left an enduring legacy of rendering the majestic giraffe, the tallest living animal. Artist Shumba Masani, inspired by the giraffes of Zimbabwe, crafts towering (up to 9 feet tall) *Twiza* figures from aluminum cans. *Twiza*, the word for giraffe in the Shona language, translates to the poetic "one who grazes from the heavens." Take in Masani's menagerie to the strains of the *Mbira* (thumb piano) at Eastern Market on weekends.

RARE 1796 SOUVENIR WASHINGTON HANDKERCHIEF MAP

④

George Washington University Museum - The Textile Museum
Albert H. Small Washingtoniana Collection
701 21st Street, NW
- museum.gwu.edu
- 202-994-5200
- Open Monday 11 am - 5 pm, Closed Tuesday; Wednesday & Thursday 11 am - 7 pm, Friday 11 am - 5 pm, Saturday 10 am - 5 pm, Sunday 1pm - 5 pm
- Metro: Blue, Orange or Silver Lines to Foggy Bottom/GWU

> ***Eighteenth-century swag***

Among the treasures of the Albert H. Small Washingtoniana Collection at the George Washington University Museum and The Textile Museum is a rare surviving, late eighteenth-century souvenir, a handkerchief printed in 1796 in Boston with mapmaker Samuel Hill's 1792 engraving of Andrew Ellicott's *Plan of the City of Washington, in the Territory of Columbia.*

Despite President George Washington's dismissal of architect and civil engineer Pierre-Charles L'Enfant from his post as the designer of the new federal city in 1792, his successor Ellicott based the design upon the L'Enfant Plan. The handkerchief map, printed in red ink on cotton is embellished with a decorative border and symbolic flourishes--vignettes of Native Americans, indigenous foliage, and a sailing ship. As "an authentic plan of the Metropolis

of the United States," for prospective landowners as well as "a very handsome ornament for the parlor or counting room," it served a dual purpose. Most likely printed in connection with "the sale of lots in the new Federal Town," it holds a place in both American textile and advertising history, as it constitutes early American promotional swag.

Third-generation Washingtonian Albert H. Small generously donated his exceptional collection of nearly 1,000 manuscripts, books, newspapers, broadsides, photographs, postage stamps, paper currencies, prints and maps on his native Washington to GWU Museum in February 2011.

Among the extensive collection of maps, the rarest is "A Map of the Eastern Branch of the Potomac River" from 1790. Copied from a 1790 drawing by Maryland surveyor, John Frederick Augustus Priggs, and engraved by Daniel Bell, it was printed one year before George Washington selected the site for the new seat of government.

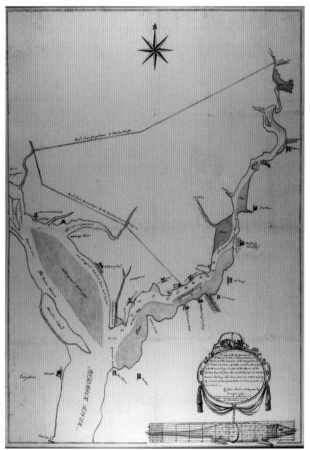

TIFFANY FAVRILE™ RED CROSS MEMORIAL WINDOWS ❺

American Red Cross National Headquarters
430 17th Street NW
• 202-303-4233
• Open: Wednesday and Friday for tours at 10 am and 2 pm by reservation only: tours@redcross.org; closed most federal holidays; ID required
• Metro: Blue, Orange, or Silver Line to Farragut West; Red Line to Farragut North

> **Largest suite of in situ Tiffany Favrile™ windows in a secular setting**

With a grudge against Louis Comfort Tiffany, irate incoming President Teddy Roosevelt ordered the removal of a resplendent Tiffany glass screen commissioned in 1885 for the White House entrance hall. But the Executive Mansion isn't the only game in town; nearby another white edifice, the National Headquarters of the American Red Cross, glistening in Vermont marble, holds a sublime tribute in Favrile™ glass from Tiffany Studios.

A welcoming docent guides you up a magnificent marble staircase, past Red Cross founder Clara Barton's journal and sewing kit among other effects and on to the Board of Governors Hall. Beyond the display of gifts presented to the organization, is a triptych of windows commemorating the heroic women who ministered to the fallen during the Civil War. Designed by Louis C. Tiffany, son of the famed jeweler, it was constructed of gem-like Favrile™ glass in his Tiffany Studios. Though Tiffany is often credited with developing the Favrile™ technique (embedding color into the glass rather than coating the surface) that honor belongs to Arthur J. Nash, his chief chemist.

The only surface treatment is in the delicately painted skin tones and encrusted glass stones. Upon close inspection, spot them in the horse's bridle and the flame of Saint Philomena's lamp. In the west panel, the martyred virgin saint of desperate cases is surrounded by representations of the virtues Faith, Hope, Charity, and Mercy. The east panel depicts Una, wife of the Redcrosse knight from Edmund Spenser's 16th-century allegory, *The Faerie Queene*. The roses flowing over her apron symbolize a generous spirit, and she is surrounded by Wisdom and Truth. The central panel depicts mounted knights in armor headed to battle, yet one kneels to aid a wounded soldier. Collectively the panels depict the spirit of the Red Cross.

Complemented by custom molding and designed specifically for the space it inhabits, it is the largest suite of *in situ* Tiffany Favrile™ windows in a secular setting. A 21st-century update brought the tableau to light. Says the docent, "When we renovated them in 2005, we put bulletproof glass outside and had them backlit so we could actually see them."

SAMUEL CHASE
LAWYER ★ ANNAPOL

CONSTITUTION GARDENS ISLAND ❻

1850 Constitution Avenue NW
• Open: 24 hours a day
• Tel: 202-426-6841
• Metro: Farragut West

The little-known park within a park

It's called Constitution Gardens — for the nearest avenue — but the celebrated document here is the Declaration of Independence. Across the wooden footbridge to the memorial honoring the signatories of that declarative statement of liberty, is a small island created in a man-made lake on national parkland from Potomac River infill.

In an earlier incarnation, the tidal wetland known as Potomac Flats was subject to flooding and sewage overflow from the city canal. The untenable stench and health hazards, as well as the need to enlarge the shipping channel, prompted an Army Corps of Engineers river-dredging project at the end of the 19th century that would increase the city's acreage by more than 600 and make way for Potomac Park. During World War I, the U.S. Navy and Munitions Department built there; temporary offices were ultimately demolished in the 1970s to create a 50-acre park within the greater expanse of the National Mall.

The Memorial to the 56 Signers of the Declaration of Independence, sequestered on a tiny pedestrian-accessible island, with lovely views of the park, lake and the world's tallest obelisk, opened in 1984. Its subtlety makes it one of the most overlooked memorials in the grand sweep of monumental Washington. Fifty-six angled pink granite markers, created by sculptor Joseph Brown and grouped by state, stand in unity, low to the ground, foundational. Each block honors a founding father with his name, occupation and hometown; pressed with gold leaf is an enlarged engraving of each signature. The markers stand perhaps in homage to the great price exacted for some signers — as their courageous declaration was, at the time, considered an act of treason toward King George.

On a bright, clear day, enjoy the gentle rustle of the willows and the gliding waterfowl on the lake — just watch your step for goose poop — nature reigns in both her grit and glory.

WILLOW WEEP FOR ME
An 1862 *Harper's Monthly* article says that Jack Custis, having been given a non-native salix Babylonia twig, planted it at Abingdon (see page 294), reputedly introducing the graceful weeping willow to America.

LABOR MOSAIC MURALS BY LUMEN WINTER ❼

AFL-CIO Headquarters
815 16th Street NW
• dclabor.org
• 202-637-5000
• Open: Monday to Friday 9 am – 4:30 pm
• *Labor omnia vincit* is in the lobby
• To view *Labor is Life*, contact Chris Garlock: cgarlock@dclabor.org
• Metro: Blue, Orange, or Silver Line to Farragut West

> **Hidden treasures of marble, Italian glass, and gold**

Washington is rich with prominent and remarkable mosaic tributes exalting saints in our many churches from the National Cathedral to the National Shrine and gods of myth like the astonishing *Minerva of Peace* at the Library of Congress. Within walking distance of the White House, two extraordinary mosaic murals honor not the supernatural, but rather ordinary working Americans.

Executed by skilled craftsmen to the exacting designs of Lumen Martin Winter, an accomplished mosaicist best known for his painted murals, the 15-by 71-foot mosaics adorn the lobbies of the AFL-CIO headquarters. They are hidden treasures of marble, Italian glass, and gold.

President Eisenhower attended the June 1956 dedication of the headquarters where the first mosaic, *Labor is Life* was unveiled. It takes its name from a passage from 19th-century philosopher and satirist, Thomas Carlyle: "Labour is Life: from the inmost heart of the Worker rises his god-given Force." Its central figures, a protective father, a seated mother and child reading, inspired the art on a US postage stamp issued that September in honor of Labor Day.

Building expansion nearly twenty years later created a north lobby and the need for additional wall art. Lumen Winter designed another labor-inspired mosaic even more beautiful than the first. Called *Labor omnia vincit*, a Latin phrase culled from the works of Virgil, it means "Work conquers all."

The first thing one sees upon entering the HQ is the glinting homage to labor above the interlocking hands of the AFL-CIO logo in the terrazzo floor. The *Labor is Life* mosaic, now sequestered from the public lobby beyond the security gate, is accessible only by escort. Chris Garlock of the Metro Washington Council AFL-CIO and creator of the DC Labor Map holds occasional tours.

JOE HILL'S ASHES

Convicted of murder based on circumstantial evidence, labor activist and Industrial Workers of the World (IWW) member Joe Hill, was executed in 1915 despite appeals by President Woodrow Wilson for clemency. His cremated remains were divided among 600 small envelopes to be scattered by his supporters. One, sans the ashes, is held at the National Archives, 7th and D Streets NW.

ALMAS TEMPLE ❽

1315 K Street NW
• almasshriners.org
• 202-898-1688
• Metro: Blue, Orange, or Silver Line to McPherson Square

> ### *Jewel box of K Street, Masonry's playground in the capital city*

An anomaly among the neutral office towers that surround it sits the Almas Temple, awash in rich, saturated color; a jewel box dwarfed by its skyscraping neighbor. The Alhambra-inspired structure is home to the DC chapter of the Ancient Arabic Order of Nobles of the Mystic Shrine (AAONMS,) now known as the Shriners and colloquially as "Masonry's playground."

A fun-loving Masonic auxiliary, the order was born in 1870 of a desire for fraternal fun and philanthropy in equal doses of kicking back and giving back. Western fascination with Orientalism at the founding of the order gives an Islamic bent to its architecture and customs without embracing the religion specifically. Brothers do however, greet one another with *Es Selamu Aleikum,* "Peace Be With You," and in reply, *Aleikum Es Selam,* "With You Be Peace," modifying the *salaam* of Islam.

In 1885, ten Scottish Rite Masons of DC (see page 133) and delegates of Baltimore's Boumi Temple convened to establish a shrine temple in the nation's capital. Chartered June 14, 1886, it was given as is customary, an Arabic name—Almas, "diamond." With its elaborate glazed terracotta and beautiful arched triptych, the 1929 Moorish Revival "temple" was placed on the National Register of Historic Places in 1966 and landmarked in DC in 1981. These designations saved it from destruction during late '80s redevelopment of K Street. The facade and some interior structures were dismantled, numbered and carefully reassembled a few yards west on the same block in 1989. Today the Almas brotherhood continues in charity and red-fezzed fellowship amid the splendor of polychrome tilework, some of the last of its kind in the District.

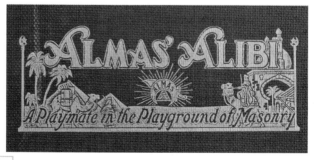

ROAD TO MECCA

Washington, DC hosted the 1923 Imperial Conclave of AAONMS worldwide members, a proud moment for the Almas Chapter. A grand 7-mile parade, "The Road to Mecca," was a spectacle of pomp and pageantry, ceremonial scimitars and signature fezzes along Pennsylvania Avenue, securing the District, as Leonard P. Steuart, Almas Illustrious Potentate proclaimed, the "nation's principal convention city."

NEARBY

FRANKLIN SCHOOL

Long considered the feather in the cap of German architect Adolf Cluss' many contributions to the built environment of Washington, the stately Franklin School anchors the western edge of Franklin Square, commanding the entire block. It became the model to which other succeeding schools aspired. Patinated by time and overlooked, the wall plaque near the corner of 13th and K Streets reveals a historic factoid. On June 3, 1880, from atop the building near the bust of electricity-loving Benjamin Franklin, Charles Sumner Tainter, an assistant to Alexander Graham Bell transmitted through their invention the photophone a wireless voice message via lightwave to Bell's 1325 L Street laboratory.

HANDWRITTEN LINCOLN EMANCIPATION BILL ❾

Lincoln Parlor of the New York Avenue Presbyterian Church
1313 New York Avenue, NW
• nyapc.org
• 202-783-5000
• Open: viewing Monday to Friday 9 am – 4:30 pm unless a meeting is
scheduled in the Lincoln Parlor
• Metro: Blue, Orange, or Silver Line to McPherson Square; Red Line to
Metro Center

> *Precursor to the Emancipation Proclamation*

In December 1951, the grateful son of Russian Jewish immigrants, Paramount Pictures president Barney Balaban, donated a historical document he'd bought at public auction. Not to the National Archives, the Smithsonian nor the Library of Congress but to a church. The draft of a compensated emancipation bill handwritten by President Lincoln on July 14, 1862, it was "one of the great documents of our American heritage," Balaban said. He felt "privileged to present" it "to the church in which Lincoln worshipped." Today that manuscript is proudly and permanently displayed in the Lincoln Parlor of the New York Avenue Presbyterian Church.

Though the bill didn't pass, it seems a bit of a dry run for what was to come when the president issued the Emancipation Proclamation, ending slavery in the United States on January 1, 1863.

The two-page Lincoln bill, held for years at the War Department, was bound for the incinerator when a custodian salvaged it. It remained in his family for decades. Though mounted in less than optimal archival conditions (slope, balance of gases and proper lighting) at the church, it is a tangible reflection of their mission of inclusion and social justice. This bit of Lincolnalia is but one of several nods to their former congregant at New York Avenue Presbyterian. His horse hitching post remains outside the entrance, and a stained-glass Lincoln window is installed above his family pew in the sanctuary.

NEARBY

NATIONAL MUSEUM OF WOMEN IN THE ARTS

Built in 1908 as a Masonic Temple, 1250 New York Avenue NW, was from the fifties to the early eighties a 535-seat movie theater. After extensive renovation, it opened in 1987 as the National Museum of Women in the Arts, the only museum dedicated solely to the work of women artists. Among its 4,500 works is the only Frida Kahlo painting in Washington, DC, *Self-Portrait Dedicated to Leon Trotsky*, 1937, an amorous memento of her clandestine affair with the Marxist revolutionary. Also in the museum collection is *Rainy Night, Downtown*, 1967, by DC native Georgia Mills Jessup, a descendant of the Pamunkey tribe whose ancestry goes back to the Powhatan Confederacy, the first people of this region.

OUR CHANGING SEAS I: A CORAL REEF STORY ❿
CERAMIC

American Association for the Advancement of Science
1200 New York Avenue NW
- aaas.org
- 202-326-6400
- Open: Monday to Friday 9 am – 5 pm
- Metro: Red Line to Metro Center

Shedding light on reefs at risk

A glimpse of artist and ocean advocate Courtney Mattison's astonishingly accurate replica of Scleractinian corals, anemone tentacles and other marine invertebrates brings awareness to the enchanted yet endangered garden of the sea—the coral reef. In their mission to increase public engagement with science and technology, the American Association for the Advancement of Science installed the 11 by 15 foot expanse of ceramic wonder in their lobby.

Mattison's *Our Changing Seas I: a coral reef story* is her Master's thesis project for Brown University Center for Environmental Studies with support from the Rhode Island School of Design ceramic studio. The large-scale wall installation is the culmination of her interdisciplinary study of how art can inspire marine conservation. While pursuing an undergraduate degree in sculpture and marine biology from Skidmore College, coursework at Australia's James Cook University allowed Mattison to indulge her life-long love affair with the sea in an epochal exploration of the Great Barrier Reef. "I create work that celebrates the exotic forms of ocean flora and fauna in concert with their biological complexity, diversity, and vulnerability," she says.

She hopes that by bringing something seldom-seen by the multitudes out of the water into broader public view she can "influence others to appreciate the fragile beauty of endangered coral reef ecosystems," garner interest in their conservation, and effect policy change.

Mattison's intimate scientific knowledge of these threatened sea organisms infused her painstaking process of hand-sculpting, refining with chopsticks and biology dissection tools, glazing and kiln-firing the pieces before creating the monumental assemblage. Both the clay and ceramic glazes used to recreate the reef share an elemental component, calcium carbonate with natural coral, lending authenticity to the work.

Illustrating the gradual degradation of a reef system, the lower third of the installation depicts a thriving coral reef, vibrant and diverse. In the middle third coral bleaching prevails and fewer varieties survive. Finally, green algae predominate at the top, shedding light on the effects of coastal development and its resultant pollution; overfishing and rising sea temperatures due to climate change. At the top corner, however, a red coral branch emerges optimistically from the algal muck. Symbolizing recovery, it is Mattison's "glimmer of hope."

HISTORIC GREYHOUND SUPER TERMINAL ⑪

1100 New York Avenue NW
1100newyorkavenue.com
View lobby museum during business hours; no photography allowed
• Metro: Red Line to Metro Center

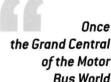

*Once
the Grand Central
of the Motor
Bus World*

The instantly recognizable logo at the threshold at 1100 New York Avenue - a greyhound galloping at full extension - is a tip-off to the building's former use. The Streamline Modern structure, now adaptively reused as the lobby to a behemoth high-rise, was once home to the Greyhound Bus Lines Washington Super Terminal. Dubbed the "Grand Central of the Motor Bus World," it is considered one of the finest of more than fifty Streamline-era Greyhound stations designed by William S. Arrasmith. The architect broke away from the "Greyhound Blue" enameled steel cladding of his earlier terminals, opting for stately Indiana limestone apropos to the city's preeminence as the nation's capital.

The site's oddly useful trapezoid shape allowed for sawtooth radial docking, a game-changing configuration that accommodated thirteen bus bays and boarding gates ensuring efficient traffic flow of buses and passengers. Adorning the walls of the central waiting rotunda, photo murals of scenic US destinations evoked the glamour of bus travel, as had the Greyhound-riding Claudette Colbert in the 1934 film *It Happened One Night*.

A public preview on March 25, 1940, with an orchestra and swing dancers, drew thousands. "Step through this new doorway to All America," Greyhound ads declared. "Come acquaint yourself with the special features and conveniences of this streamlined travel center." Amenities included air conditioning, lockers, a restaurant, barber, telegraph office, and several restrooms.

The hub of bus travel in Washington, the terminal retained its Deco flavor until a ghastly modernization in 1976 covered the signature ziggurat facade in asbestos paneling. A steadfast group of preservationists battled long and successfully to save the building, threatened with demolition, and restore its original facade.

Thanks to their efforts, the current owner has retained the original lobby and installed a well-executed informative exhibit of the historic bus bays, a look at 1940s innovation in travel. Life-sized casts of era-appropriate motorcoaches are docked exactly where they would have been during the terminal's operation.

Greyhound began in 1914 as a jitney for Minnesotan miners.

SALVAGED MASCARONS AT HENLEY PARK HOTEL   ⑫

926 Massachusetts Avenue, NW
henleypark.com
• 202-638-5200; Toll free 800-222-8474
• Metro: Green or Yellow Line to Mt Vernon Sq/7th St-Convention Center Station

> **A bit of Beaux-Arts Manhattan in Washington**

The National Cathedral doesn't have the lock on DC's gargoyles. In fact, the Henley Park Hotel, one of the most carefully preserved historic hotels in the city, has over one hundred of them, two of which, flanking a side entrance, are said to be modeled after the cigar-smoking architect and his bespectacled wife. Inside, discover four large architectural elements which bear the distinction of having been rescued from New York's Hotel Commodore before its razing in 2000. Salvaged patinated copper mascarons from the 1919 Warren & Wetmore-designed building hover above Henley Park's atrium restaurant, a bit of Beaux-Arts Manhattan in Washington.

The Tudor-style architecture lent the original, gentlemen-only 1918 building its name, Tudor Hall Apartments, once home to members of Congress and other dignitaries in the early 20th-century capital city. After a meticulous restoration and conversion to a posh hotel, Henley Park Hotel opened in 1982, its decorative stained glass monogrammed "T.H.," leaded glass windows, Mercer-tile lobby flooring, and medieval touches intact. Having once rimmed the roofline of the towering, iconic Commodore–functioning as antefixes (see pg. 54)– the era-appropriate verdigris mascarons are massive in scale and eye-catching in the Tavern at Henley Park. Visit to take a gander at the architectural treasures and stay for high tea, offered each afternoon.

A GOTHIC ARCHITECTURAL HOMAGE TO CHARLES LINDBERGH.

Adorning the porte-cochère of Alban Towers, a Gothic Revival luxury apartment building erected during the height of the late 1920's national fervor for aviation is a corbel carved with a man's head donning an aviator's cap and goggles. Though it doesn't appear to be Charles Lindbergh's visage, it is thought to be a nod to him and his historic 1927 nonstop solo flight from New York to Paris. The carvings at Alban Towers, which share a whimsical quality with those at the nearby National Cathedral (see pg. 82), are believed to have been executed by the stone carvers who worked on the Gothic church during the same era. 3700 Massachusetts Avenue, NW. Nearest Metro: Tenleytown/AU

Photographs

TO A YOUNG HISTORIAN

If Washington tonight were hid
In ashes as was once Pompeii,
Some one, as Bulwer-Lytton did,
Would sometime have a word to say.
And he would always seek, of course,
An excellent primary source.

On looking back to 1950
This future Toynbee, Beard, or Scott,
Would find that Jack's three books are nifty
And he would use them, like as not,
To see our town, as it appears
Across the intervening years.

So don't give up, Jack, gifts I bear,
Procured by this, your humble rhymer.
And all salute that noble pair,
Herodotus and John P. Wymer.
Littera scripta manet. Paucis verbis;
Nosce te ipsum. Ars longa, vita brevis.

JOHN P. WYMER PHOTOGRAPH COLLECTION ⓭

Kiplinger Research Library
Historical Society of Washington, DC
801 K Street NW
• dchistory.org
• 202-249-3955
• Check the website to confirm the temporary address
• Open: Tuesday to Friday 10 am – 4 pm by prior appointment; closed holidays
• Metro: Green or Yellow Line to Mt. Vernon Square/7th Street Convention Center; Red, Green, or Yellow Line to Gallery Place-Chinatown

> ❝ *Wymer's passion project, documenting Washington at mid-century*

From 1948 to 1952 with his trusty Pentax camera, Manor Park resident John P. Wymer, an unmarried California transplant, methodically documented for posterity the entire District of Columbia. Though well-traveled, he claimed he'd "never seen a more beautiful city than Washington." A statistician in the Division of Manpower and Employment Statistics for the Bureau of Standards, he gave up clement weather weekends and holidays for the endeavor. A one-man street view image gatherer long before Google was a thought, he took it upon himself to capture the city's built environment at mid-century. He noted that he wished to "convey some impression of how Washington looked to its inhabitants around 1950."

Neither a photographer nor cartographer, he created a map defining 57 areas within the District of approximately 6000 square feet each and set about to snap photos representative of the character of each neighborhood. Though he didn't set out to photograph people, if they happened to be on a block he was shooting, they too were recorded. He assembled fifty albums with 3972 images painstakingly captioned with the typewritten date and address. He typed a preface to each defined area and drew an accompanying map – not easy for a man with palsied hands. "We are really lucky to have received his collection. It's so comprehensive. It's an archivist's dream," says Laura Barry, of the Historical Society of Washington DC (HSW), the recipient organization

of the late Wymer's photographic bequest. The original books, not of archival quality, have deteriorated a bit and are now sheathed in Mylar, but all images and notations are now digitized, and the books reproduced.

HISTORIC ON LEONG CHINESE MERCHANTS ⑭ ASSOCIATION BUILDING

618 H Street NW
• Metro: Red, Green or Yellow Line to Gallery Place-Chinatown

An echo of old Chinatown

Long before the famed Friendship Arch staked its claim as the largest *paifang* (Chinese archway) outside of China, the On Leong Merchants Association led the charge in establishing a physical identity for the District's Chinatown. In 1932, following the displacement of the nearby earlier Chinatown, they acquired two 1850s buildings on H Street, merged them, and altered the facade with traditional Chinese architectural elements. It was the first such transformation in what had been a German immigrant enclave. Today as the restaurant Chinatown Garden, its entrance bears a historical plaque.

The Chinese presence in Washington began in 1851 when Chiang Kai settled on Pennsylvania Avenue near 4½ Street. Eventually, a block-long, mostly Cantonese bachelor community known as "Little China" emerged. Despite the limitations of the Chinese Exclusion Act of 1882, immigration continued (including families) expanding the self-sufficient Chinatown from 3rd to 7th Streets. Homes positioned along the inaugural parade route brought their residents extra cash for the prime views from their windows.

Benevolent associations and *tong* ("hall") societies commonplace in US Chinese immigrant communities offered mutual aid and protection. A branch of On Leong Tong formed in DC in 1912, incorporating on September 3, 1919. In the late 1920s, the city claimed Chinatown property for government

expansion and On Leong led the migration to nearby H Street. Replacing "Tong" with "Merchants Association," in their official name, they dispelled notions of opium dens and organized crime and helped foster an active business district that thrived despite periods of rampant Sinophobia.

The 1968 riots and the ensuing decline of downtown sent many fleeing to suburban Maryland and Virginia. Once again displacing remaining businesses and residents was construction of a convention center (now demolished) in 1980 and a huge arena in 1997. Designed with cultural sensitivity by Alfred Liu, Wah Luck House, erected in 1982 at Sixth and H Streets, created 153 apartment units for displaced seniors.

Today Chinatown is a bustling commercial district existing in a tipped balance of big brands bearing mandated signage in Chinese characters and the stalwarts of its heyday working to preserve over 150 years of cultural heritage in Washington.

Visit the Chinatown Community Cultural Center at 616 H Street for classes in Chinese Brush Painting, Gu Zheng (Chinese zither), Kung Fu and Tai Chi.

THE THRONE OF THE THIRD HEAVEN OF THE ⑮
NATIONS' MILLENNIUM GENERAL ASSEMBLY

Smithsonian American Art Museum
8th and F Streets NW
- americanart.si.edu
- 202-633-1000
- Open: daily 11:30 am – 7:00 pm; closed December 25
- Admission: free
- Metro: Red, Yellow, or Green Line to Gallery Place/Chinatown

Fear
not ...

In a back-alley garage from 1950 to his 1964 death, James Hampton quietly endeavored to exalt God in a monumental shrine of his creation, *The Throne of the Third Heaven of the Nations' Millennium General Assembly*. Preserved for posterity, the majestic assemblage resides at the Smithsonian.

Hampton left his native Elloree, SC during the Great Migration for his brother's Washington, DC home and work as a short-order cook. Just after his 23rd birthday, he noted a remarkable vision: *This is true that the great Moses the giver of the 10th commandment appeared in Washington, D.C., April 11, 1931.*

After three years of military service in the Pacific, the World War II veteran returned to DC, rooming in a boarding house and working for the General Services Administration (GSA). He soon experienced another vision: *It is true that, on October 2, 1946, the Great Virgin Mary and the Star of Bethlehem appeared over the nation's capital.*

Believing God instructed him to create *The Throne*, the devout Hampton toiled as a janitor at GSA until midnight then spent hours in his rented alley sanctum crafting the sublime display from scavenged refuse: cardboard, foil, jelly jars, discarded furniture and light bulbs. Though he hoped to find a "holy woman" with whom to share his divine fervor, he remained unmarried.

Only when rent went unpaid for the first time in fourteen years did the garage owner realize that his reclusive tenant had passed away, leaving behind the glinting marvel which included a fourteen-pointed star similar to that of the Nativity Grotto in Bethlehem. Topped by the words, "Fear Not" were more than 180 pieces of foil-wrapped praise. Handwritten "Archives for the State of Eternity" hint at the biblical inspiration for the homage. Penned by "St. James, Director for Special Projects for the State of Eternity," the texts include both English and an as-yet undeciphered language Hampton claimed to have received from God. And on the wall, Proverbs 29:18, "Where there is no vision, the people perish."

Though the garage contents were offered to Hampton's sister, she did not accept. Ultimately curator Harry Lowe acquired *The Throne* for the Smithsonian. Famed art critic Robert Hughes lauded it in *Time Magazine*, saying it "may well be the finest work of visionary religious art produced by an American."

LUNDER CONSERVATION CENTER ⓰

Smithsonian Donald W. Reynolds Center for American Art & Portraiture
Third Floor Mezzanine and Fourth Floor
8th and F Streets NW
• Open: Daily 11:30am—7pm. Closed December 25
Free entry
• Metro: Red, Green and Yellow Lines to Gallery Place/Chinatown

Go behind the curtain

The crucial work of the art conservator has been traditionally secreted away from view. But at the Smithsonian Donald W. Reynolds Center for American Art and Portraiture, the public now has the unprecedented opportunity to "go behind the curtain" and see the rooms where it happens.

Located in the historic U.S. Patent Office building shared by the Smithsonian American Art Museum (SAAM) and the National Portrait Gallery (NPG), the Lunder Conservation Center is the first art conservation facility in the U.S. to allow museum visitors permanent behind-the-scenes glimpses of all aspects

of vital preservation work. Publicly visible through floor-to-ceiling glass walls, conservators examine, treat and preserve paintings, prints, drawings, photographs, sculptures, folk art objects, decorative arts and frames from the SAAM and NPG collections. Even when the state-of-the art 10,200 square foot facility's studios and labs are unoccupied, educational kiosks and videos along the corridor elucidate the merger of art and science in conservation. Before and after images reveal the immaculate skills of the conservators. The innovative, Keck Award-winning center also offers tours, public and professional programs and outreach initiatives.

NEARBY:

The Luce Foundation Center houses over 3,000 artworks in glass cases for public study and visible storage. In the mid-19th century, as the Model Hall of the U.S. Patent Office, the very same space displayed glass-enclosed, working scale models of inventions submitted for patent. Open nearly a decade before the Smithsonian Institution, it became an oft-perused museum of the industrial age. During the Civil War, however, it temporarily became a place for soldiers to bunk between the display cases, tended to and written of by nurse/poet Walt Whitman.

NATIONAL ACADEMIES BUILDING FAUX FRONTS

⓱

500 blocks of 6th Street, NW
• Metro: Red Line to Judiciary Square

> *Preserving historic downtown row houses*

The 500 block of 6th Street NW, save for four Federal-style town houses on its east side which hearken to an earlier era, is contemporary and commercial, anchored on the F Street end by Engine Company Number Two's brutalist firehouse and at the E Street corner by the National Academies' state-of-the-art Marian Koshland Science Museum. On closer inspection, the houses, whose doors seem to invite neighborly visitation yet offer no egress aren't homes at all, but the preserved facades of historic row houses, cladding the office side of the National Academies (see pg. 69) complex. Although the properties were not landmarked at the time of early 21st-century development on-site, rather than demolish all evidence of the block's architectural history, the architects, with guidance from preservation organizations, incorporated them into the new building's construction. The street maintains some semblance of its original sightline, with the towering new National Academies building set back from the pedestrian path.

TRICKING THE EYE IN PENN QUARTER

Argentine Naval Attaché building mural

On Indiana Plaza, near the oft-maligned Temperance Fountain, stands the historic National Bank of Washington building designed by James G. Hill in 1889. Since the 1980's, when the Romanesque Revival building became home of the Office of the Argentine Naval Attaché, its flat eastern wall has featured a *trompe-l'œil* mural depicting the building facade. The artist faithfully replicated in paint, the rich texture of the rough-faced granite blocks used in the building's construction.

Pepco substation

In strolling distance of Ford's Theatre Center for Education & Leadership (see pg. 57) line drawings and architectural salvage from area buildings create in 2D - 3D interplay, a fanciful facade on the once nondescript substation of the Potomac Electric Power Company (Pepco) on the block of 8th Street between D and E Streets, NW. With detailing that endeavors to maintain the aesthetic of the surrounding area — commercial or residential Pepco individualizes its substations.

Nearest metro: Archives-Navy Memorial-Penn Quarter

CLARA BARTON MISSING SOLDIERS' OFFICE 🔟 MUSEUM

437 7th Street NW (historic address 488½ 7th Street)
• Open: Thur—Sat 11am—5pm (last admission); open Mon—Wed by appointment
• Entry fee: check website
• Tel: 301-695-1864 for appointments or to schedule a group tour
• www.clarabartonmuseum.org
• Metro: Red Line to Gallery Place; Green or Yellow Lines to National Archives or Gallery Place
70, 74, D3, D6, and 13Y Metrobuses stop directly outside the museum

> *An attic discovery reveals a hidden history*

On the day before Thanksgiving 1996, longtime General Service Administration carpenter Richard Lyons was led to discover a secret stash, hidden for over 100 years. While inspecting a disused Seventh Street building, which formerly housed a shoe store but was now slated for sale and likely demolition, he heard a strange noise and felt a tap on his shoulder . . . but he was the only person there. He'd entered a small room at the end of the third floor corridor. Looking about with a flashlight, he spied an envelope jutting out from above. Addressed simply to Edward Shaw, Washington City, it hearkened to a distant past. Intrigued, Lyons climbed into the crawl space above and found an unexpected bounty of over 1000 artifacts, including a handsome sign that read "Missing Soldiers Office 3rd Story, Room 9 Miss Clara Barton." He'd discovered the long-forgotten former DC home, supply storeroom and office of the woman most famously known as the founder of the American Red Cross in 1881. Clarissa "Clara" Barton had lived out her last fifteen years in a 38-room Glen Echo, Maryland home that functioned as an early Red Cross office. But prior to that, she'd been a teacher in her native Massachusetts and New Jersey, before coming to Washington as a clerk for the U.S. Patent Office. One of the first women to secure a position in the federal government, Barton was fired upon the arrival of the Buchanan administration in 1857 and rehired with the incoming Lincoln administration in 1861 in a lower-paying copyist position. She found lodging in the same boarding house as her colleague Edward Shaw at 488½ Seventh Street, just steps away from their jobs at the Patent Office. As the Civil War began and troops were in dire need of supplies, Barton rallied to obtain and distribute them to the front lines, earning the soubriquet, "angel of the battlefield."

At the war's end, she conceived of a way to continue her good work, helping families to locate and confirm the fate of missing soldiers. Word of her efforts spread quickly. So inundated was her home with queries from loved ones that she cut a mail slot into the door of room nine. From the 63,000 requests for help she received, Barton and a committed staff located over 22,000 men, some of whom were still alive. Remarkable artifacts — from a shirt believed to be worn by Barton while grazed by a bullet as she cared for a fallen soldier to published rolls of missing men — illuminate a chapter lost to history in the meticulously restored museum.

OLD POST OFFICE PAVILION CLOCK TOWER ⑲

1100 Pennsylvania Avenue NW
- Open: 9am—5pm (last entry at 4:30pm) daily, except Thanksgiving and Christmas
- Not accessible through the hotel. Entrance at back of building next to Starbucks; expect security check
- www.nps.gov/opot
- Metro: Blue and Orange Lines to Federal Triangle

> *Capital heights, home to the Bells of Congress*

Occupying an entire city block between 11th and 12th Streets NW, on that prestigious thoroughfare, Pennsylvania Avenue, stands the late 19th-century Old Post Office building. With a 315 foot-high clock tower, it is the third tallest structure in the nation's capital, after the Washington Monument at 555 feet and the Basilica of the National Shrine of the Immaculate Conception at 329 feet. Built between 1892 and 1899, the Richardsonian Romanesque structure was the first federal building to house its own electric plant. Its location, however, proved not to be the best for the postal service, which opened a new branch across from Union Station in 1914 (see pg. 179). By the late sixties, the building had fallen into disrepair and was slated for demolition. An advocacy group, "Don't Tear it Down," the predecessor to the DC Preservation League, rallied to save it. Nancy Hanks, then Chair of the National Endowment for the Arts (NEA), successfully lobbied Congress to revoke the demolition order in 1971.

After necessary renovations from 1977 to 1983, the landmark would reopen as The Pavilion at the Old Post Office, a mixed-use facility housing retail boutiques, eateries and such federal tenants as the NEA and the National Endowment for the Humanities. Ambitious plans to rival New York City's

New Year's Eve festivities in Times Square led to the Post Office Pavilion's annual lowering of a neon "Love Stamp" from the clock tower at the stroke of midnight to bring in the new year.

National Park Service rangers conducted tours of the clock tower until the building once again closed for renovation and conversion into a luxury hotel in 2014. Although the hotel is privately owned by the 45th U.S. President, the tower remains in the public interest, with NPS ranger-led tours offered daily. Offering a view of the vast building atrium, a glass-enclosed elevator whisks you to the tower, where incredible 360-degree vistas await on the observation deck.

BELLS OF CONGRESS

Cast by the same foundry as the Liberty Bell, the ten Bells of Congress, replicas of those at Westminster Abbey, were a Bicentennial gift to the U.S. from Great Britain's Ditchley Foundation. But where to put one of the largest sets of change-ringing bells in North America — all 13,000 pounds? Not at the Capitol building, as Ditchley intended. A perfect fit came with the Old Post Office clock tower, and the bells were installed in 1982. The all-volunteer Washington Ringing Society peals the bells on the opening of Congress, federal holidays, days of national mourning and regular Thursday evening practice sessions. The bells are not publicly accessible just yet, but if you are in the vicinity on a Thursday between 7—8:30 pm, just stand and listen to the mastery of a time-honored tradition.

TERRACOTTA ROOF ANTEFIXAE

20

Robert F. Kennedy Justice Department Building
950 Pennsylvania Avenue NW
• www.justice.gov
• Metro: Green or Yellow Line to Archives Station or Federal Triangle Station

Skyward delights

Amid all the neoclassical architecture of the Federal Triangle, and the pediments emblazoned with allegorical figures, take a moment to look even higher at the building commanding the city block bounded by Pennsylvania and Constitution Avenues and Ninth and Tenth Streets, Northwest. The Robert F. Kennedy Justice Department Building, like many of its neighbors, is topped with Ludowici red clay interlocking roof tiles. But what sets it apart are the 1,100 polychromatic terracotta antefixae adorning the roof hip. It is the only federal building in the city to feature these architectural elements.

Hand sculpted by Boston Valley Terra Cotta from a 3D-scanned classical antefix, the 17¼" by 10⅝" gilt-tipped ornaments get their magnificent glint from the 1,400-degree firing of gold on the outer edges. While serving a decorative purpose, they also function as guards to prevent the avalanching of snow from the stepped roof to the ground below.

The antefixae rim the entire perimeter, but the best view is in the afternoon light on the Constitution Avenue side of the building. From the grand interior staircase of the Museum of Natural History just across the street, the tiles can be seen at eye level. And blocks away, the Old Post Office Tower tour (see pg. 52) offers an aerial perspective.

NEARBY:

EARLEY MOSAICS

Although the Robert F. Kennedy Justice Building houses a splendid collection of art (the largest of any General Services Administration-designed facility), it is open only to Justice Department employees and their guests. The rest of us must be satisfied with the rooftop jewels, Deco-era aluminum torchieres flanking the entryway, and a glimpse of the Earley mosaics visible in the coffered ceiling above each entrance. Astonishingly vibrant, they incorporate white quartz, blue and yellow ceramics, black and red vitreous enamel and gold. They were, as noted in a 1944 concrete trade publication, the first ever made from American materials (see pg. 133).

LINCOLN BOOK TOWER **㉑**

The Ford's Theatre Center for Education & Leadership
514 10th Street NW
• fords.org
• 202-347-4833
• Open: hours vary; call or visit website for details
• Admission: $3 for Historic site visit which also includes the museum and theatre tour. Reserve in advance online
• A limited number of same-day tickets are available first come, first served starting at 8:30 am at the box office
• Metro: Red, Blue, Orange, or Silver Line to Metro Center

The last word on this great man will never be written

I n Washington, DC, the 16th US President is celebrated nearly as often as is the city's namesake. Abraham Lincoln's likeness appears at least once in every quadrant and in suburban Maryland but the most recent tribute to the slain leader and emancipator of America's enslaved is neither a faithful depiction of his image in marble, bronze nor paint, but a gravity-defying stack of Lincoln-related books—actually replicas of books. Just across the street from the famed Ford's Theater where President Lincoln was felled by an assassin's bullet in April 1865, the modern monument stands in the atrium of the Center for Education and Leadership. Soaring 34 feet in seemingly endless skyward reach, it symbolizes "that the last word on this great man will never be written."

With over 15,000 books published on him, it has been said that Abraham Lincoln is the most written-about man in history, second only to Jesus Christ. The Ford's organization secured publisher's clearances to reproduce the cover art for over 200 of these books, most of which are currently in print, to apply to 6,800 "books" created of fireproof bent aluminum. The realistically rendered sculpture was designed and installed by Split Rock Studios, a firm specializing in museum design. Each book was glued into place by hand over the course of two weeks, moving from ground level to varying ladder heights to ultimately utilizing a forklift to top off the tower.

Among the titles included are scholarly works such as Harold Holzer's *The Living Lincoln*; first-hand accounts like Elizabeth Keckley's (former slave and seamstress to First Lady, Mary Todd Lincoln) *Behind the Scenes;* examinations of Lincoln's political genius, such as Doris Kearns Goodwin's *Team of Rivals*; stories of the assassination and its aftermath like James Swanson's *Manhunt* and Anthony S. Pitch's *They Have Killed Papa Dead* and humanizing tales of the august figure for children, such as *Abe Lincoln's Hat*. The 205 titles repeat throughout the tower, with a few strategically placed untitled "leather-bound books" to balance the composition.

THE MOTHERSHIP

㉒

Smithsonian Institution
National Museum of African American History & Culture
1400 Constitution Avenue NW
• Open: Daily 10am—5:30pm. Reserve timed passes online; limited same-day passes also available
• www.nmaahc.si.edu
• Metro: Blue or Orange Lines to either Federal Triangle or Smithsonian stations

> **The "mother" of all stage props**

When bandleader George Clinton, as "Star Child," called forth from the stage during the P-Funk Earth Tour of 1976/77, "Put a glide in your stride and a dip in your hip; come on up to the Mothership," it was a prelude to stagecraft at its funkiest. Glen Goins' soulful tenor repeatedly intoned "Swing down, sweet chariot, stop and let me ride," whipping the crowd of funkateers — loyal fans of the band Parliament-Funkadelic — into a frenzy as a silvery spacecraft (the Mothership) descended in pyrotechnic spectacle from the rafters. Bedecked in head-to-toe white fur, Clinton emerged from below the stage in a cloud of smoke and strobing lights as "Dr. Funkenstein," as if he'd disembarked from the spaceship itself, cementing the group's Afrofuturist mythology.

Years later, Dr. Kevin Strait, museum curator and former museum specialist of Musical Crossroads, a permanent exhibition at the National Museum of African American History and Culture (opened September 2016), learned the iconic prop was reported to have languished in a DC-area junkyard, the P-Funk legacy sold off for parts. Having had the good fortune to meet Bernie Walden, a former roadie for the band, Dr. Strait learned that another, smaller version of the Mothership existed. This paved the way for the museum's acquisition. Created for the band's tours in the nineties, it was in Clinton's possession at his Tallahassee, Florida home studio. Dr. Strait spoke at length by telephone with the funk legend to assure him that the museum would be "the appropriate home for his crown jewel," he says. On traveling to Florida, he adds, "The first thing I noticed when they answered the door was the Mothership just sitting there, part of the ceiling carved out to accommodate it — this enormous stage prop."

He explains the significance of the 1,200 pound aluminum spaceship to the museum's collection: "The Mothership is a fascinating artifact to explore the multiple histories of African American music and the evolution of black stagecraft. George Clinton's P-Funk incorporated diverse sonic influences: loud and guitar-driven rock music and of course, James Brown's rhythmic emphasis on the one. And popular culture influences ranged from the civil rights movement to psychedelia to black power and of course, science fiction. The Mothership owes a nod to Sun Ra; to Jimi Hendrix and other avant-garde musicians who envision space as the cosmic terrain to imagine Black freedom, as this liberated infinite zone that freed one's mind from the bonds of racism and poverty and other earthly and societal constraints.

It was a symbolic mode of transporting one's mind to this ethereal plane of thought and existence. In the song *Mothership Connection*, we hear Glen Goins summoning the Mothership by using lines that reference one of the most well-known spirituals in music. And we're reminded how tropes of freedom and liberation as expressed through song are as old as African American music-making itself."

SMITHSONIAN SLEEPOVERS

㉓

National Museum of American History
14th Street and Constitution Avenue NW or
National Museum of Natural History
10th Street and Constitution Avenue NW
• smithsoniansleepovers.org
• 202-633-3030
• See website for scheduled dates; sleepovers begin at 7 pm, check-out
the following morning at 9:00 am • There must be at least one adult for
every three children in any group that registers. No siblings younger
than 8. Chaperones must be 21 years or older. No adults without
children. All participants must pre-register by phone or online
• Admission: $135 for general admission and $120 for Smithsonian
Associate members
• Metro: Blue, Orange, or Silver Line to Federal Triangle

Night at the museum

When's the last time you solved an after-hours crime caper in one of the world's most prestigious museums? How about sleeping under a 50-foot whale? Oh to be a child.

Each summer the Smithsonian Associates, the folks who handle an incredible array of engaging programming as the educational and cultural arm of the Smithsonian Institution, present an opportunity for tweens to enjoy an unusual overnight experience. Children aged 8 to 12 are welcomed to choose between two major Smithsonian history museums, Natural History and American History for a night of interactive exploration of the exhibit halls. Why it's a kids' slumber party at the museum, chaperoned, of course.

At the National Museum of American History, participants will unravel the mystery theft of six valuable objects from the museum's collection. While roaming the museum galleries, the junior detectives must discover what's gone missing before the stroke of midnight. Tapping into their sleuthing skills, they collect clues along the way, guiding them to the crime scene and solving the caper. All the while enjoying games, experiments, and craft projects, before hunkering down into a satisfied slumber in their sleeping bags. Bright and early the next morning, the kids and their chaperones breakfast in the Stars and Stripes cafe, shop in the family store—open just for them—before departing.

At the National Museum of Natural History, Phoenix is the draw. After a night of exhibit-based craft projects, puzzles and games, guests view a short IMAX film before unrolling their sleeping bags beneath a giant North American right whale. Hanging in the Ocean Hall, it's a remarkable, full-scale model of a living female, Phoenix. Tracked since she was a calf, her specific physical attributes are well documented, down to her callosities, the uniquely patterned skin patches on a whale's head that serve as a "thumbprint." Like those at American History, participants in the Natural History sleepover enjoy breakfast in the morning at the Atrium cafe and last-minute shopping before saying goodbye.

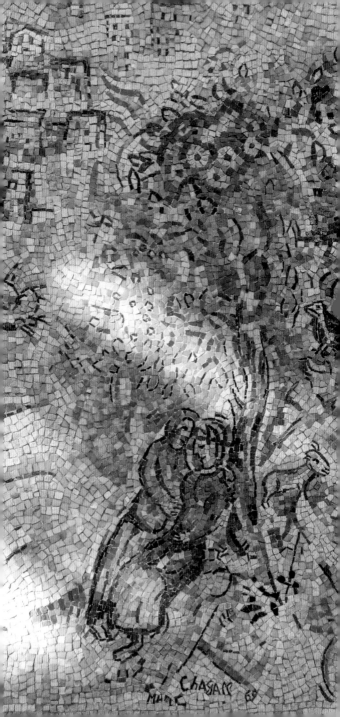

ORPHÉE BY MARC CHAGALL ㉔

National Gallery of Art Sculpture Garden
Constitution Avenue at Ninth Street, NW
- nga.gov
- Open Monday - Saturday 10:00 am - 5:00 pm; Sunday 11:00 am - 6:00 pm
- Metro: Green or Yellow Lines to Archives–Navy Memorial–Penn Quarter

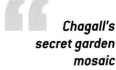

*Chagall's
secret garden
mosaic*

Beyond the Bunyanesque sculpture of a typewriter eraser and brush in the Northwest corner of the National Gallery of Art Sculpture Garden is a secluded magnolia grove evoking the Georgetown garden of arts patrons John and Evelyn Nef, its centerpiece the mosaic, *Orphée*. Marc Chagall conceived of the idea during a 1968 visit he and wife Vava made with their friends the Nefs. Wanting to gift them with artwork he remarked, "The house is perfect as is. But I will do something for the garden: a mosaic."

Mrs. Nef anticipated, perhaps, a small plaque, but when she and her husband viewed the maquette, a "wonderfully colored gouache painting" in a visit to Chagall's Cap d'Antibes atelier the following year, they were surprised to learn that the finished *Orphée* would stand 10 feet by 17 feet. As Italian mosaicist Lino Melano executed the work in Murano glass, Carrara marble, and colored stones, the Nefs built a 30-foot brick wall for their 28th and N Street garden to anchor the forthcoming masterpiece. With the Chagalls in attendance, the Nefs celebrated the installation of the work—the only privately installed outdoor mosaic by the artist in the United States— on November 1, 1971.

Of the principals involved only "Evvie" Nef lived to see the 21st century. Upon her 2009 passing, she bequeathed some 100 works of art, including the monumental mosaic to the National Gallery of Art. An exacting, nearly four-year conservation process brought *Orphée* which takes its name from the myth of Orpheus (depicted in a portion of the mosaic) from the Nef's private garden into full public view in a quiet setting that emulates the intimacy of its original home.

NEARBY

KNIFE EDGE

Architect I.M. Pei, confronting the trapezoidal shape of the plot selected for the NGA East Building, found a design solution and unifying motif in the isosceles triangle (two sides of equal length). The "Knife Edge" at 4th Street and Madison Drive is precisely 19.47 degrees, forming the corner of one of the two triangles which comprise the structure of the building. Repeated throughout the interior, find the base to side proportion of 1:1.5 in the skylights, marble paving tiles, and more.

ROTUNDA OF THE PROVINCES ECHO CHAMBER ㉕

Embassy of Canada
501 Pennsylvania Avenue NW
• canadianembassy.org
• 202-682-1740
• Metro: Green or Yellow Line to Archives

*Reverberating
rotunda*

Sited prominently on a prime corner of Pennsylvania Avenue in full view of the Capitol building is the diplomatic home of Canada in the United States. Designed by acclaimed Canadian architect Arthur Erickson, the new chancery opened in 1989, after the mission outgrew its original Embassy Row facility. Anchoring the east-facing courtyard is the Rotunda of the Provinces, its twelve pillars symbolizing the ten Canadian provinces and two territories at the time of the building's construction; and its dome holding an acoustic secret—it echoes any sound emanating from directly below it.

Although the rotunda base is a lovely circular waterfall representing the great Niagara Falls shared by the United States and Canada, the sound of cascading water is not magnified by the echo chamber. No, the aural sweet spot is much more subtle. To experience the sonic bounce-back, you must stand beneath the very center of the dome; those on the periphery won't hear a thing. Unlike the metaphorical echo chambers of Washington which reverb far and wide.

Other hidden auditory delights in the city include a similar dome echo in the Philip Johnson Pavilion at Dumbarton Oaks (see page 87) and the beloved statue of Einstein at the National Academy of Sciences. If you stand directly center to speak, your voice will amplify and it'll seem Al is making eye contact as he listens.

NEARBY

THE SPIRIT OF HAIDA GWAII SCULPTURE

For the embassy courtyard, Erickson commissioned First Nations artist Bill Reid of the Haida Gwaii archipelago (Queen Charlotte Islands) to create a sculpture. The resulting 20-foot bronze is considered the late artist's masterwork. Gathered in a small canoe, mythic creatures, animals, women, and men evoke the Haida belief in oneness of living beings. Of his piece,

Reid wrote a Gatsbyesque statement: "There is certainly no lack of activity in our little boat, but is there any purpose? Is the tall figure who may or may not be the Spirit of Haida Gwaii leading us, for we are all in the same boat, to a sheltered beach beyond the rim of the world as he seems to be or is he lost in a dream of his own dreaming? The boat moves on, forever anchored in the same place."

DEMOCRACY IN ACTION EXTERIOR CERAMIC FRIEZE ㉖

West Courtyard of the Henry J. Daly Municipal Building
300 Indiana Avenue NW
• mpdc.dc.gov/page/police-headquarters
• 202-727-4218
• Open Monday to Friday 9 am – 5 pm
• Metro: Red Line to Judiciary Square

Heroism and brutality documented in clay

Secreted away from common view in the courtyard of the Municipal Building, a 1941 frieze depicts the activities of Washington's Police and Fire departments. The last of the WPA projects by eminent ceramicist Waylande Gregory, the marvelously-executed sculptural relief created quite a stir upon its installation. It portrays the firemen heroically, whereas the police, helpful in most vignettes, give a drubbing to what is thought to be two black men in another.

Ceramics scholar Dr. Tom Folk explains: "The title of the work is of course, sarcastic, as Gregory felt that as far as African-Americans were concerned, democracy had yet a long way to go. He was publicly trying to show in a mural for the exterior of Washington's Metropolitan Police Department, the real hardships that black people were experiencing at that time."

The Police Department took umbrage, requesting its removal. Sculptor Paul Manship of the US Commission of Fine Arts and First Lady Eleanor Roosevelt interceded on behalf of the work, at 81 by 8 feet high, then the largest ceramic sculpture in the world.

Though the panel was saved, the door to the courtyard remained locked for years. In fact, it still is to everyone except the occasional municipal employee on a smoke break. However, anyone can see the frieze through the window; visibility is great. With a zoom of your camera, admire up-close the hundreds of subtly glazed, fired terracotta tiles. Though Gregory may have created a

stinging indictment of racial bias, closer inspection calls into question by whom. The redhead standing in conflict with police in the controversial panel doesn't appear to be black yet does appear to be kicking the black man on the ground. So who's brutalizing who? Excessive police force, or does the cudgeling cop protect the man on the ground from the knife-wielding guy? You decide.

HEALTH AND WELFARE MURAL

In the East Courtyard, Art Deco muralist Hildreth Meière's less controversial WPA frieze *Health and Welfare* depicts ten scenes illustrating public health and welfare benefits available to Washington residents.

NEARBY

MOSAIC MAP OF WASHINGTON

Need to pay a parking ticket, register a firearm or see your parole officer? Glinting underfoot in the C Street lobby, Eric Menke's 1940 terrazzo floor map of the city (partially obscured by metal detectors) welcomes you.

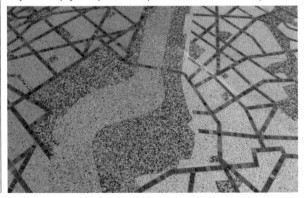

KECK CENTER LOBBY

②⑦

The National Academies Building
500 5th Street NW
• national-academies.org
• Open: Monday to Friday 9 am – 5 pm; photo ID required
• Metro: Red Line to Judiciary Square

*A visual
encyclopedia*

Slow Rondo, the kinetic sculpture above the cluster of buildings at Fifth and F Streets NW draws the eye to the block-long complex dedicated to the sciences. One building, The Keck Center, appears like many post-modern structures downtown; an office building you might walk past unless heading into work. And it is.

But before the thousand employees of the National Academies head to their offices there, they pass through a remarkable visual encyclopedia created by artist Larry Kirkland. This large-scale, multidimensional public artwork encompasses the three walls of the lobby. The walls of Absolute black granite and Crema Marfil marble are according to the artist's website, "engraved and etched with images," (such as Leonardo da Vinci's 1489 drawing of the human spine) "that represent the sciences and man's relationship with the environment." Cast bronze objects such as the human heart and mounted natural specimens including a 40-million-year-old petrified tree ring create dimension in the installation. Fourteen seminal scientific equations appear on the walls and floor from Albert Einstein's renowned $E=mc^2$ to Stephen Hawking's 1974 Equation for Black Hole Temperature.

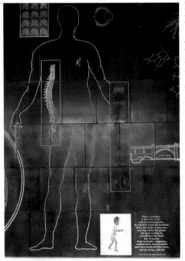

Moving the viewer through humankind's efforts of invention, innovation and understanding of the universe on the left marble wall; biology, medicine and our relationship to the environment on the central granite wall; and the human drive to shape the environment both to its benefit and destruction on the right marble wall, each wall bears more than a dozen elements. Cataloguing the didactic texts for each element of the installation is a comprehensive pamphlet available at the lobby desk.

GERMAN-AMERICAN HERITAGE MUSEUM   (28)

719 6th Street NW
- gahmusa.org
- 202-467-5000
- Open: Tuesday to Friday 11 am – 5 pm
- Admission: free; donations accepted however
- Metro: Red, Green, or Yellow Line to Gallery Place/Chinatown

The only national museum of German-American heritage and culture

On the gray townhouse at 719 6th Street, built for Civil War vet and merchant John Hockemeyer, a yellow banner reads "German-American Heritage Museum" in both Chinese characters and English. Though the neighborhood has since the 1930s waxed and waned as DC's Chinatown, it had been a 19th-century German community.

German presence on this continent goes back to 1608 Jamestown. As the District saw a late 1800s uptick in immigration, Carl Schurz became the first German-born US senator. Architect Adolf Cluss elegantly altered the cityscape. Emile Berliner went from clerking at a 7th Street haberdasher (now the Goethe Institute) to inventing the gramophone. Hockemeyer Hall with its bowling alley, one of the first in the city, was a hub of local activity.

The building, now a museum, celebrates the history of Germans in America—the largest ancestry group in the country after 400 years of immigration—and their enduring stamp on national life. A staircase, a who's who of German-Americans, leads up to the exhibition hall presided over by a giant bust of Handel.

Programming explores a vast spectrum from New World innovations to Old World traditions, such as Karneval. "Karneval is as big in Germany as in New Orleans," says Executive Director Petra Schürmann. With guilds similar to Mardi Gras krewes, "princes" and "princesses" in court costume mock the establishment in debauched mirth. In the Black Forest, they don frightful masks, make noise and burn things to "chase away the evil winter spirits," Schürmann says. And finally in Munich, the elegant masquerade ball reigns with Venetian-styled masks.

Once a month, the museum hosts a Bavarian brunch tradition, *Frühschoppen* or "early glass," with beer, pretzels, sausages, and an invited guest speaker. Ongoing oral history project Einsteinchen gathers and preserves the stories of German-Americans.

DECLARATION OF INDEPENDENCE: PUBLISHED IN GERMAN ONE DAY BEFORE IT WAS IN ENGLISH

In the museum, a framed broadside reveals a little-known fact; because the German language newspaper in Philadelphia had an early print run, the Declaration of Independence was published in German one day before it was in English.

No matter your heritage, you likely had a German-influenced childhood. For kindergarten, thank Margarethe Schurz; jelly beans, confectioners Schrafft's and Goelitz; blue jeans, Levi Strauss; Snoopy, Charles Schultz; and "Barbie," her German predecessor *Bild Lilli*.

SECRETS OF THE NATIONAL BUILDING MUSEUM

29

401 F Street NW
• nbm.org
• 202-272-2448
• Open: Monday to Saturday, 10 am – 5 pm; Sunday, 11 am – 5 pm; closed December 25
• Admission: docent-led tours of building, free; exhibit access: adults, $10; seniors, students, youth, $7
• Metro: Red Line to Judiciary Square; Yellow or Green Line to Gallery Place/Chinatown

> *Hidden legacy in Meigs' old red barn*

I f you've been near Judiciary Square, you've seen the imposing tripartite structure of red brick unlike anything around it. Erected in the mid-1880s to house the Pension Bureau, the National Building Museum remains unique in the civic architecture of the city.

Inspired by Michelangelo's Palazzo Farnese, civil engineer and Army Quartermaster General, Montgomery C. Meigs designed a grand pension building for war veterans. But his building had to be both fireproof and inexpensive, thus the red bricks in a granite and marble town. He mimicked the palace's cornices with lion heads (only one of which remains, hidden inside on the third floor) and egg-and-dart moldings. But if you look closely you'll see a direct martial reference in lieu of acanthus leaves and the like. Meigs boldly placed upturned cannons and bursting bombs as decorative flourishes.

For all its thoughtful details: easily-navigated stairs for the war-wounded, ventilation apertures in the brick facade and a magnificent exterior frieze honoring fellow veterans including "a plantation slave freed by war," it was mocked as "Meigs' old red barn."

Inside, the Great Hall holds a few secrets as well. Topped by gilded Ionic-Corinthian capitals, the massive faux-marble central columns—smoothed over by plaster—are made of 70,000 bricks each. On the second-floor arcade, seventy-two cast-iron Ionic columns border the perimeter. Forward-thinking Meigs stored pertinent documents of the day in their hollows as time capsules of the late 19th century. For as he stated, "historians or antiquarians of the age when ruins of this building…shall be opened to the curious."

Taking advantage of a finger-sized hole created in one of the columns by a vandal, the museum, in 1995 hired Pentax to do endoscopic imaging of the contents, which includes an 1883 newspaper.

Noted by the meticulous Meigs are nineteen other columns with hidden ephemera including maps, War Department records and a copper facsimile of the Declaration of Independence.

Check out the rotating exhibits on the built environment and be sure to stop in the museum shop, arguably the best in this city of museums.

DC FIRE & EMS MUSEUM

Engine Co. No. 3
439 New Jersey Avenue NW
• 202-673-1709
• Open: call for appointment
• Admission: free, but donations are appreciated

From hayloft to history

From outside, the Engine Company No. 3 firehouse looks true to what it is, an active station of the DC Fire Department. With no signage to indicate its current iteration, however, the third floor of the building is now home to the DC Fire & EMS Museum.

Conveniently located near Union Station, it offers a timeline of Washington history filtered through the growth and activities of its fire department. A hook outside the top floor attests to its original use as a hayloft; the station was built, after all, in 1916 during the days of horse-drawn engines.

The unit disbanded in 1993 and Walter Gold, the affable president of the Friendship Fire Association, envisioned the property as a museum. By 2001, the hayloft was rehabbed into just that and Engine No. 3 reinstalled. Under the auspices of the Smithsonian Affiliates, the heating system was replaced to meet the climate control standards of the esteemed institution.

The space flows from early fire history until the present, with fascinating artifacts of the brave endeavor. Marked "B. Key 1727," a leather fire bucket (those in leather signified wealth) owned by Francis Scott Key is the oldest item in the collection.

Gold describes the Fire Zouaves, who astonished with their feats of acrobatic firefighting in 1861 and the last run of the fire horses before the equine system gave way to motorized engines in 1925. Their 1905 steam engine sits below in the garage bay. He chuckles over an odd "forerunner to the fire extinguisher" that required mixing the chemicals of two glass globes into a third and throwing it into the fire. "That idea didn't last long." He points out the telegraph alarm system—one card for every major intersection in the city—corresponding to code from the city's fire call boxes (see page 107) prior to the 911 system.

In the Kids Korner, animated mascot "Safety Bear" gives talks on smoke detectors, "stop, drop, and roll," and designated outdoor family meeting places in the event of fire.

HAVE A DC FIREFIGHTING ANCESTOR?
Historically, every firefighter signed off on an activity log. The folks at the museum will look for your relative's signature in the fire records ledgers and make a copy for you.

NORTHWEST 1

THE SECRET STONEYARD

Rock Creek Park
Near Rock Creek Horse Center
5100 Glover Road NW
• Not officially open to the public
• Metro: E2/E3/E4 Military Road crosstown Metrobus Line

Capitol rubble

Nearly subsumed by nature just beyond the stables of the Rock Creek Horse Center are random stacks of architectural ruins. They are collectively an "active" stoneyard, but the major activity seems to be an encroachment of moss and lichen. Amid all the solid rectangular blocks, glimpses of embellishment—ornamental corbels and cornices hint of a grand structure. A cluster of rounded finials evokes a weathered cache of ancient amphora. Like the Corinthian columns rising from a gentle knoll at the Arboretum's Ellipse Meadow (see page 193), they are US Capitol remnants. Unlike the Arboretum columns, no patron stepped up to rally for their preservation and public display after a mid-century renovation by the Architect of the Capitol (AOC). So, since 1959 they've moldered in unheralded beauty along a Rock Creek horse trail near a crescent-shaped pond dubbed "The Smile."

By virtue of its pedigree and location, the unenclosed stoneyard is under the auspices of both the AOC and the National Park Service whose staffers will stridently shoo the curious away. But a respectful pass-by of the pleasantly mysterious discovery in the center of our great public park is worth a stroll.

BLACK SQUIRRELS

Melanistic creatures get a bad rap. Black woolly caterpillars as harbingers of harsh winters; black cats portend bad luck. But nothing is more beautiful than a sinewy panther (a melanistic jaguar) with a sleek black coat. In 1902 and 1906 Ontario's Rondeau Provincial Park sent eighteen melanistic squirrels of the ubiquitous Eastern gray species to the Smithsonian in exchange for a few of their grays. The Canadian cousins, released in the National Zoo, proliferated and migrated beyond zoo confines. Of their migratory patterns, Smithsonian curator of mammals, Richard "Thor" Thorington Jr., says "My impression is that the frequency of melanism changes over time. For a while we had a prolific female black squirrel in our neighborhood, which resulted in a high frequency of melanism." Now there are almost none in his nabe. At the time of writing, several scampered about eating downed Osage oranges in Montrose Park (see page 89). Still more intensely pigmented critters gathered acorns in Rock Creek Park.

FELIX E. GRANT JAZZ ARCHIVES

❷

University of the District of Columbia
4200 Connecticut Avenue NW
• lrdudc.wrlc.org/jazz/
• 202-274-5265
• Open: by appointment only—materials are non-circulating
• Metro: Red Line to Van Ness-UDC

A cornucopia of jazz treasures open to the public

Clark Terry's trumpet; a Birdland card signed by John Coltrane; 11,000 jazz albums including several 78 rpm. These treasures are but a few in the Felix E. Grant Jazz Archives at the University of the District of Columbia. Unlike many university archives, the Grant Archives are unique in their open policy of access, making available to the public a plethora of jazz materials for on-site as well as online viewing and listening. Archives curator, Professor Judith Korey of the UDC Jazz Studies Program and Rachel Elwell, media technician, musicians both, bring their passion for the music to the visitor experience.

Namesake broadcasting pioneer and jazz authority Felix E. Grant distinguished himself at several Washington radio stations for forty-five years. Credited with bringing the sound of Bossa Nova to the District and by extension the US, Grant introduced the genre to local guitarist Charlie Byrd. Subsequently Byrd recorded the seminal 1962 release *Jazz Samba* with Stan Getz at DC's All Souls Church. In 1964 Grant received the Order of the Southern Cross, Brazil's highest civilian honor bestowed on a non-Brazilian.

After Duke Ellington's 1974 death, Grant successfully petitioned civic honors for the legendary native son. Both Western High School, converted to a public arts school, and the Calvert Street Bridge were renamed for the Duke. The archives house ephemera of Grant's 1987 effort to discover Ellington's birth site at 2129 Ward Place NW and the Southern Cross medal. His extensive donated memorabilia formed the core of the archives which have since grown considerably with important acquisitions including a working Victrola, recording equipment, listening stations with music and digitized recordings of lectures and interviews, books, photos and other items highlighting the significance of the jazz canon. Prominently positioned, Calvin Jones' trombone honors the late trombonist and director of the UDC Jazz Studies Program.

With Grant as host of the 1960 Lorton Jazz Festival, a stellar lineup including Count Basie, Joe Williams, Louis Armstrong, Nancy Wilson, and the Charlie Byrd Trio performed before 2,000 inmates of Lorton Reformatory (see page 310).

DARTH VADER GROTESQUE

❸

Washington National Cathedral
3101 Wisconsin Avenue NW
• nationalcathedral.org
• 202-537-6200
• Open: daily, dawn to dusk
• Admission: guided gargoyle tours: May to September $22/adult, $18/youth, student, senior and military (with ID); self-guided tours, free
• Metro: Red Line to Tenleytown/AU then 31, 32, 36, or 37 bus; Dupont Circle then N2, N3, N4, or N6 bus; or Woodley Park then 96, 97, or X3 bus

> **Sith lording over the grounds**

Directing water away from its hallowed walls, the Cathedral Church of St. Peter and St. Paul has 112 gargoyles and over 1,000 of their non-spouted cousins, grotesques. Some are traditionally fearsome—taloned devil and coiling snake; some whimsical—a happy basenji and protesting hippie. One, in particular, is a fascinating combo of both. How, pray tell, did a likeness of the infamous *Star Wars* villain, Darth Vader come to grace a spire of the congressionally-delegated "National House of Prayer"?

During renovation of the west towers in 1985, the cathedral, in conjunction with *National Geographic* held a competition inviting children to design and submit ideas for the grotesques to top the gablets of the gothic structure. Of approximately 1,400 entries, four were chosen to be replicated including

Anakin Skywalker's alter-ego. Thirteen-year-old Christopher Rader of Kearney, Nebraska placed third in the contest with his impressive drawing of the treacherous character. Sculptor Jay Hall Carpenter created the original carver's model which master stonemason Patrick J. Plunkett then carved in limestone. Rader's Vader looms far above the northwest corner of the cathedral. Not surprisingly, the dark side.

NationalCathedral.org suggests: *First, bring binoculars! Darth Vader is very difficult to see by the naked eye. Leave the building through the ramp entrance which is through the wooden doors near the standing statue of Abraham Lincoln. Go down the ramp, and step onto the grass on your right. Then, turn around and look back up at the tower closest to you. Start at the top of the tower. There are two large pinnacles, or points, on the corners of the tower and a much smaller one in the center. Follow the center pinnacle down and find the first gablet, or tiny peaked roof. Darth Vader is the grotesque on the north, or right-hand side.*

Before you pack up the binoculars step inside the cathedral to glimpse a bit of the moon. Literally. Embedded in the "Space Window" for all earthly posterity is a piece of lunar rock, a memento from Apollo 11 and man's first steps on the moon.

THE SHRINE, GLASS FOREST
OF THE PALISADES

❹

Left of the entrance to Palisades Recreational Center
5200 Sherier Place NW
Follow the former trolley path; if you see something glinting, you've arrived
• Metro: serviced most directly by the D6 Metrobus which stops at Dupont Circle, Farragut North, Farragut West, Metro Center, Union Station, and Stadium Armory Stations

Art for art's sake

A woodland folk art fantasy, it's an ever-changing installation of mixed-media sculptures from the hearts and hands of economist James MacMahon with help from his sons Kazimir (Kaz) and Carl. Imagine forest fairies taking up the mantle of recycling, transforming the detritus of man and nature into enchantments of odd beauty, sound, and light. Strewn about a wooded area by Palisades Park, fallen tree limbs and artfully arrayed branches morph into inspired sculpture. Lassoed bike parts and random pieces of hardware chime in the wind as reflective bits of broken mirror dangle from the trees in a luminous dance. It's been called the "glass forest," but the MacMahon sons dubbed it *The Shrine*. To? "A shrine to life, to enjoyment and building," Kaz says. "This is pretty much my dad's version of a mid-life crisis." Crafting the free-form works of art in nature provides cathartic release from the day job.

Though their mother, gallerist Dale Johnson of Watergate Gallery is a painter, Kaz and Carl tended toward a different medium. "We've always done earth art, like stacking rocks." (British environmental sculptor Andy Goldsworthy is a favorite.) Working at a hardware store, Kaz has gotten scrap parts and random pieces of metal. "I'm like *Great we can use this, we can make wind chimes. Why not*?" he says. "Whenever I'm back home hanging with my folks, I'll just come out here for a little while and build something. If the wind takes it down, so be it."

They are pretty Zen about it all. Nature sculpts *The Shrine* as much the MacMahons do. When Hurricane Sandy slammed the area in fall 2012, it toppled the treeline that once enclosed it in its own little forest room and downed many of the assemblages. But from the debris, they created more work. They are respectful of the land, never harming living growth and clearing the trash, food wrappers and the like that others sometimes leave behind. Kaz likes to mill about and observe visitors' reactions to their creations. "It's art for art's sake," he says, "there's no profit, there's no gain there's only fun and anyone can appreciate it, they can just walk on back."

THE ROBERT WOODS BLISS COLLECTION OF PRE-COLUMBIAN ART   **⑤**

Dumbarton Oaks Research Library & Collection
1703 32nd Street, NW
• doaks.org
• 202-339-6400
• Open Tuesday - Sunday 11:30 am - 5:30 pm; closed on Federal holidays
• Admission: Free for the museum, check website for current fees for the garden • Fully accessible
• Metro: Red Line to Dupont Circle; Blue, Orange or Silver Line to Foggy Bottom/GWU or Rosslyn Stations; Circulator or 31, 32, 36, D1, D2, D3, D6 & G2 buses.

A collector's obsession

Forward-thinking philanthropists Mildred Barnes Bliss and Robert Woods Bliss conveyed their glorious estate to his alma mater, Harvard University in 1940. Tucked quietly away in Georgetown, Dumbarton Oaks, with its stunningly beautiful gardens, houses collections of rare books, works of art and grand furnishings. The Blisses conceived of their donation as a "home of the humanities, not a mere aggregation of books and objects of art," where scholarship thrives in the extensive research library and archives, as well as access to the magnificent art and artifacts.

Of Robert Bliss' first glimpse of an Olmec jadeite figure at a Paris antiquary, he said, "That day the collector's microbe took root in--it must be confessed--very fertile soil. Thus in 1912 were sown the seeds of an incurable malady!" Though his collecting interests were quite broad, his passion for the art and artifacts of the pre-contact Americas, would over the next fifty years until his death, compel Bliss to acquire objects from some thirty ancient American civilizations. His fervor would help shape the emergent study of the rich indigenous American culture prior to the arrival of Columbus.

Championing the artistic merits of Pre-Columbian objects, which had been relegated to museums of natural history, Bliss loaned items from his collection to many museums across the country and to exhibitions in Paris and Stockholm. The entire collection displayed on long-term loan at the National Gallery of Art from 1947 - 1960, with a catalog of the works published in 1957.

The Blisses commissioned modernist architect Philip Johnson, best known for the Glass House, to design a structure to house the Pre-Columbian collection permanently. He submitted the design and model of an eight-cylinder domed glass pavilion in 1959. In evoking the age-old, domed Turkish madrasas of the East to house the ancient American artifacts of the West, Johnson not only bridges hemispheres, he draws a parallel to another stellar Bliss collection, that of the artifacts of the Byzantine Empire.

The resulting series of curved glass walls undulate around an unroofed fountain, creating eight circular galleries punctuated by the central water spray--nine perfect circles in a perfect square amid a leafy glade. Johnson wanted the garden to "march right up to the museum displays and become part of them." Mr. Bliss passed away the year before The Robert Woods Bliss Collection of Pre-Columbian Art opened on December 10, 1963.

GAS LAMPS OF MONTROSE PARK ❻

3099 R Street NW
202-673-7647 Department of Parks
• Open: park open daily, dawn to dusk
• Metro: 30N or 30S Metrobus passes several stations: Friendship
Heights, Tenleytown-AU, Eastern Market, Potomac Ave, Naylor Road and
Southern Ave

> **The last functioning gas public lampposts in the District**

Relics of early 20th-century public works, the gas lampposts of Montrose Park, the first public park in Georgetown, hearken to an era before electricity powered all street lamps. Nineteenth-century industrialist Richard Parrott staked his claim on a sloping hillside tract for a residence and his rope-making enterprise in 1804, calling his estate Elderslie. Charitably, he allowed the public to take their leisure on his grounds (known locally as Parrott's Woods) to stroll, picnic, and celebrate Independence Day. After his 1822 death, the property passed through a succession of owners including Captain William and Mary McEwen Boyce, who, upon purchase renamed it in honor of the Scottish Earls of Montrose. With his accidental 1858 death and hers in 1880, the estate slipped into decline. Eventually, local resident Sarah Louisa "Miss Loulie" Rittenhouse, led a movement to successfully petition Congress to buy the $110,000 acreage for use as recreational parkland in 1911.

In transforming the private estate into a public park, cast-iron gaslight lampposts were installed along the length of what had been Parrott's ropewalk for twisting hemp yarns into hefty cordage. Built in 1912 by the American Streetlight Company, the black fluted posts are fitted with scalloped lanterns topped by decorative finials. With their evocative amber glow, they are the only functioning municipal gaslights extant in the District.

BOXWOOD HEDGE MAZE

Bordering a pergola erected by the ropewalk in 1913, a wee cluster of shrubbery now a bit overgrown has lost some of its manicured former glory. But what a treat for the kids! Think *The Shining* minus the height, eerie music and a creepy Jack Nicholson.

NEARBY

TREASURES OF TUDOR PLACE

Capt. Boyce's sister Jane married George Washington Parke Custis Peter, a great-grandson of America's first First Lady, Martha Washington. Six generations of the illustrious Custis-Peter family occupied nearby Tudor Place before Armistead Peter 3rd deeded the property to the public interest in 1983. His 1919 Pierce-Arrow 48-B5 Roadster with its Rolls Royce headlights is among exquisite family treasures open to public view at the mansion and gardens. 1644 31st Street.

THE PEABODY ROOM

7

Georgetown Neighborhood Library of the DC Public Library
3260 R Street, NW
• dclibrary.org/georgetown
• 202-727-0232
• Open Monday and Wednesday 11 am - 7 pm; Second and Fourth Saturdays 9:30 am - 5:30 pm; other times by appointment 202-727-0233
Metro: Red Line to Dupont Circle, transfer to D2/Glover Park Metrobus; or take Georgetown Circulator bus from Union Station (Red Line) or Rosslyn (Blue, Orange, Silver Line)

The spectrum of Georgetown life

The Peabody Library opened on O Street in 1875 at the bequest of financier George Peabody was precursor to a larger Georgetown branch library inaugurated in 1935 with transferred Peabody collections and a room dedicated in his name. Unique in its inclusion of artifacts and artworks beyond the expected books, maps, photos, and manuscripts, its first librarian was called a "curator."

Jerry A. McCoy, current Special Collections Librarian doesn't hesitate to salvage discarded bits of Georgetown material culture for the Peabody Room. The inveterate collector copped a 19th-century gate and some bricks from Yarrow Mamout's former property. Guinea-born, Arabic-speaking Yarrow remarkably retained his Fulani name (anglicized spelling) and Muslim faith through 45 years of slavery. Manumitted in 1796, he worked, saved and eventually bought stock in the Bank of Columbia and a lot on Dent Place where he lived, died in 1823 and is thought to be buried.

Though on loan to the National Portrait Gallery until July 2019, a portrait of the elderly Georgetowner, painted in 1822 by James Alexander Simpson, the first instructor of drawing and painting at Georgetown College, is the "crown jewel" of the Peabody Room.

Having had a premonition of fire, McCoy says it is one of the two things he'd grab, in his "rescue scenario." The other, a bound volume of the 1776 Maryland Gazette newspaper which published the Declaration of Independence. He kept a chain ladder at the ready for a window escape with a treasure under each arm.

On April 30, 2007, while at his other DC Public Library post, the Washingtoniana Room, he got word of the Georgetown blaze. Luckily, firefighters extinguished the flames before they could ravage the priceless collection. Their efforts, however caused extensive water damage.

A new Peabody Room designed by Martinez & Johnson opened in the original library's attic in October 2010. Delighted by the space, McCoy is grateful to reestablish the collection there. But the improvement came at tremendous cost as damaged materials languish in storage without funding to restore them. However, the collection, including house history files on nearly every home in Georgetown remains impressive and its greatest asset, Jerry's stewardship.

FRIENDSHIP HOUSE GARDEN STAIRWAY ❽

Alley at Wisconsin Avenue near R Street NW
• Metro: Red Line to Farragut North; transfer to Georgetown-bound DC Circulator bus

> **What is now an alley was once her swimming pool...**

Evalyn Walsh McLean. Had she lived in current times, she'd have been a social media maven, her bon-mots setting Twitter abuzz; her insouciant, ciggie-dragging selfie clips on Vine; and fabled pics wearing the Hope Diamond—both she and her Great Dane—all over Instagram.

A shared secret of nearby Peabody Room (see page 91) librarian Jerry McCoy, a hidden staircase across the avenue from the venerable neighborhood library is a remnant of the generous heiress and socialite's R Street final home. What is now an alley was once her swimming pool. Many prominent Georgetown citizens have lived in the 1818 house, including a mayor, but none so storied as Mrs. McLean who took up residence in a 1941 divorce downgrade.

Her memoir, *Father Struck It Rich*, tells of the Colorado gold-mining windfall that catapulted her family into the nouveau riche and to a grand four-story mansion in Washington (now the Indonesian Embassy, page 141). In this rarefied childhood, she met young *Washington Post* scion, her future husband, "Neddie" McLean. As a teen gravely injured in a car wreck which killed her younger brother Vinson, she became addicted to the morphine she took for pain.

Married in 1908, she and Ned, both prone to excess, lived indulgently, entertained lavishly and drank heavily at the sprawling 175-acre McLean family estate, Friendship. With endless generosity, Evalyn hosted both

the social elite and wounded soldiers. She held court, sporting the massive diamond and passing it around for her guests to try on. The 1911 purchase of the reputedly accursed gem led to public scrutiny of their every misfortune in an attempt to illustrate and quantify the "curse."

   While Evalyn and Ned were away at the Kentucky Derby, their 9-year-old son Vinson met an eerily similar fate as his namesake uncle when he was struck by a car. Ned's philandering ruined their marriage; his mental stability collapsed, and he died in a Baltimore sanitarium in July 1941. After trustees of Friendship sold the estate to the government, Evalyn bought a smaller home she christened Friendship House, continuing her high-society lifestyle. Here her daughter Evalyn married much-older former Senator R.R. Reynolds that October. Five years later Evalyn Jr. would die at her mother's home from a sleeping pill overdose. Grieving Evalyn Sr. succumbed to pneumonia the following year at age 60.

LEGEND OF THREE SISTERS ROCKY ISLETS 9

Mid-Potomac River, 38.9039°N, 77.0806°W
The islets can be viewed clearly from the Key Bridge connecting Georgetown to Rosslyn, VA, or up close by kayaking, canoeing or paddleboarding up to them from Fletcher's Boathouse
• Metro: Blue, Orange or Silver Line to Rosslyn, walk across Key Bridge; or Circulator bus travels to Georgetown and Rosslyn

A cautionary tale of curse and creation myth

Older than the city of Washington and America itself is the legend of the Three Sisters. This trio of rocky islets upriver from Georgetown figuring in the creation stories of the great Powhatan Confederacy, were noted by John Smith in 1607 and appeared on L'Enfant's early plans for the federal city. Over time and retelling, the details of the tragic saga vary. Some with a curse of the river passage, some not, but all with the mighty Potomac claiming three souls and offering them up again in granite. In the lyrical, contemporary prose of DC author Breena Clarke, the "sisters" represent three drowned Catholic nuns.

Algonquin legend tells of rival tribes on either side of the Potomac and holds that the three sisters were the brave daughters of a *kwiocos* (shaman). In one version of the story, they are avenging angels, seeking retribution for the slaughter of their betrothed by rival Susquehannock on the opposite shore. In another, they are devoted sisters, determined to rescue their kidnapped brothers from their cross-river captors. In both, their plans are dashed. But in one, as the young women are overtaken by fierce winds and strong currents, they join hands and exclaim that if they cannot cross the river there, no one ever will. And with a bolt of lightning, they were gone. By daybreak, three rocks had emerged from the deep where the girls succumbed.

According to lore, a death knell tolls across the waters of the accursed crossing before they claim the next life. There doesn't appear to be a high incidence of drownings in this part of the river, yet it's interesting to note that the numerous plans to erect a bridge there have all failed each time they arise, from L'Enfant in 1789 to Hurricane Agnes sweeping away early construction in 1972.

As an agricultural appellation, "Three Sisters" refers to the trinity of the main Native American crops in North America: squash, corn, and beans. Their companion planting is depicted on the 2009 Sacajawea US dollar coin, known as the "golden dollar."

THE LOST THREE SISTERS OF THE CHESAPEAKE

In the West River, a Chesapeake Bay tributary, a triad of small islands once stood off Horseshoe Point, hunting grounds of the Conoy Indians. Via colonial

headright, a 50-acre tract, Edward Parrish settled the swampy parcel in 1663. By 1678, he'd acquired about 1,100 acres that he leased as farmland. A century later, the *Totness*, a huge brigantine with a cargo of contraband tea from Britain ran aground on the islands in July 1775. Outraged locals set the brig aflame, reprising 1773's Boston Tea Party. By the mid-1800s, engulfed by the bay waters, the low-lying islands were lost completely.

POTOMAC AQUEDUCT ABUTMENT ⑩

Above Water Street/Whitehurst Freeway near the end of M Street NW
• Metro: Red Line to Farragut North; Blue, Orange, or Silver Line to
Rosslyn; transfer from either to Georgetown-bound DC Circulator bus
• No safety rail cordons off Georgetown abutment, so it's best not to go
after dark

*Ledge
on the river's edge*

High above the Georgetown shore of the Potomac River stands a graffitied relic of 19th-century mercantilism, the stone abutment of the former Alexandria Aqueduct, also known as Potomac Aqueduct for the body of water it traversed. A craggy perch dipped in color, it's a palimpsest of time-worn mementos of visits from lovelorn teens to skilled graffiti writers. It's a magnificent vista of river activity, the northern Virginia skyline and just to the east, the familiar concrete arches of Key Bridge, which upon its 1923 opening eclipsed the storied, but modest aqueduct.

In 1830, the merchants of Alexandria (part of the federal district prior to the 1847 retrocession back to Virginia) aspired to reap the benefits of trade from the forthcoming Chesapeake and Ohio (C&O) Canal in Georgetown. With a Congressional charter, the Alexandria Canal Company formed, its efforts culminating in the 1843 opening of a river-spanning canal crossing to transport commercial cargo directly from the C&O to the Alexandria Canal.

During the Civil War, the trough was drained, and the bridge was appropriated for use as a military roadway. In 1866, the army relinquished control and the span was restored as a canal aqueduct. The owners built arching wooden trusses to support, much to public consternation, a toll road above. Eventually, engineering studies would condemn the bridge's safety, and it was closed in October 1886.

Army engineer Lt. Col. Peter Hains led the repurposing of the aqueduct to a free bridge, replacing the wooden structure with iron trussing on the original stone piers. It opened to great fanfare on April 11, 1888. In the early 1900s an electric trolley service shuttled commuters over the bridge from Georgetown to Rosslyn. Citizens enjoyed boating this stretch of the Potomac, navigating its stone piers for years until safety concerns cropped up once again, and construction began on Francis Scott Key Bridge. Though it formally closed on July 9, 1918, the structure stood in the shadow of the taller Key Bridge until razing began in 1933. The stone piers, however, were retained to help

protect the newer bridge from ice floes. Today one pier remains as a historical marker, the other seven were dismantled in 1962.

The two arches of the Georgetown abutment also remain. One shelters the boats of the Potomac Rowing Club.

THE EXORCIST STEPS ⓫

Prospect and 36th Streets NW (top of stairs); M Street at Canal Road
(bottom)
• Metro: no station is immediately close, so grab a cab, do a subway/bus
combo or don your walking shoes
The following stations have nearby DC Circulator stops to Georgetown:
Red Line to Farragut North or Union Station; Blue, Orange, or Silver Line
to Foggy Bottom; Orange Line to Rosslyn (in Virginia, so if it's a good day,
enjoy the stroll across Key Bridge over the Potomac)

> *Take*
> *the plunge*

In Georgetown, just beyond the intersection of Prospect and 36th Streets a narrow flight of stairs leads steeply down to the end of M Street. Made famous in the chilling 1973 film, *The Exorcist*, the stone staircase called the "Hitchcock Steps" by film crew members provided the backdrop of character Father Karras' climactic plunge from the demonically possessed Regan MacNeil's bedroom to his death approximately five stories below.

Used as the exterior of the MacNeil home, the house at 3600 Prospect Street doesn't actually abut the stairway, as movie magic makes it seem. A replica facade placed at the stairs was fabricated with "candy glass" allowing the Father Karras stunt double, Charlie Walters to crash through the window and plummet down the seventy-five stairs, a stunt he performed twice. If you look very closely at the scene, you can see the half-inch-thick rubber padding placed on each step to cushion the fall.

The stone arch above the vertiginous passage has become an ill-advised perch for daredevil teens while the stairs below are a fitness challenge for local runners. But don't stop there, visit some of the other sites from the Academy Award-winning film. Glimpse the magnificent Key Bridge and the C&O canal; stop at Holy Trinity Church, site of the sermon scene (3513 N Street NW); visit the campus of Georgetown University (37th and O Streets) for Dahlgren Chapel, site of the desecration scene and Healy Hall, site of the student protest film shoot; cap off the *Exorcist* exploration with a drink at The Tombs Bar (1226 36th Street NW).

BESOS ROBADOS

FILM FRANCES EN COLORES · DIRECCION: FRANCOIS TRUFFAUT · CON: JEAN-PIERRE LEAUD

CUBAN POSTER GALLERY

12

3319 O Street NW
• facebook.com/CubanPosterGallery
• Open: by appointment only except the twice-yearly open house in spring and fall
• cubanpostergallery@msn.com
• Metro: Circulator bus from either Rosslyn (Blue, Orange or Silver Line) or Dupont Circle (Red Line) Stations

Rarities of Cuban graphic arts

Just as cobblestones pave the way to the treasures of *La Habana Vieja* in Cuba, one of the few remaining cobblestone streets in Washington leads to a superlative trove of Cuban theatrical and political posters. Bill Brubaker, by dint of his Miami upbringing, developed "an affinity for Latin American culture." The widely traveled journalist first purchased a silkscreened Cuban movie poster in the 1990s after "informational materials" including posters were exempted from the US embargo on importing goods from Cuba. For over twenty years, he and his wife Freddi have amassed an impressive collection of about 2,000 different posters, dating from the 1960s to the present, that they hope to eventually sell or donate to a museum.

Brubaker followed a 2008 *Washington Post* buyout with a second act as a gallerist, sourcing additional copies—about 1,000—of the posters in their collection to offer for sale. In 2010, the Brubakers repurposed the garden level of their Georgetown home for the appointment-only Cuban Poster Gallery, highlighting limited edition posters by ICAIC, the Cuban Film Institute and offset-printed political and propaganda posters from OSPAAAL, the Organization for Solidarity with the People of Africa, Asia, and Latin America.

Since 1959, ICAIC has produced limited edition posters for every film shown on the island, Cuban or foreign. They enlist Cuban graphic artists to view the films and design original poster art for silkscreening by hand. "It was an aesthetic decision, but it was also a very nationalistic decision, a *We're going to make our own posters,*" Brubaker says of ICAIC. The remarkable graphics make these posters more than ads to fill cinema seats, they truly are works of art. Guayabera shirt collar flipped, smoking perhaps a Partagás cigar, the "benevolent-looking" vampire on the poster for the animated film, *Vampiros en La Habana* is the one that makes Brubaker "smile the most." He says: "We might be the only place in the world outside of Cuba where you can come in and browse hundreds of Cuban graphics."

Along the stretch of O Street between 35th Street and Wisconsin Avenue, exposed tracks embedded in the cobblestones are remnants of the underground conduit system that powered the DC Transit Route 20 electric streetcar through Georgetown.

NEARBY

GREAT WAVE MURAL

Just blocks away, an enormous, cresting wave graces the side wall of a townhome at 35th and O Streets. Tastefully executed in subtle shades of blue, it's J. McConnell's reproduction of the famed 19th-century Hokusai woodblock print, *The Great Wave off Kanagawa.*

DAW'S MUSKET BARREL FENCE ⑬

28th and P Streets NW
• Metro: Red Line to Dupont Circle; transfer to G2 Westbound bus toward Georgetown University

Guns into ploughshares

In a stroke of waste-not ingenuity, 19th-century gun and locksmith Reuben Daw repurposed a passel of surplus war muskets as pickets for the fences on some of his many Georgetown properties. England-born (in 1808) and Georgetown-raised, he at age 25 married his brother's widow Elizabeth. They had six children, all of whom he was able to grant property as they came of age; such were his real estate holdings and earnings from his Bridge Street (now M Street) business.

His address is listed in an 1834 local directory as South side of Bridge, possibly referring to the Old Stone House, today one of the oldest extant buildings in DC, and a known Daw domicile. For most of his life, Georgetown was an independent municipality until it was absorbed into the federal district in 1871; his 1891 death preceded the street name changes of his beloved burg in accordance with northwest quadrant naming conventions in 1895. Along with his Bridge Street holdings, he held property on Water, West, Green and Montgomery Streets (now K, P, 29th and 28th Streets). A May 23, 1853, *Evening Star* article mentions construction of a Daw property at "Green Street near West;" it is here that he placed the ingenious fencing.

Mining historical news articles yields conflicting stories of the guns provenance. Some say old "Rube" Daw grabbed the battery booty as recompense for funding the defense of the capital in the War of 1812; not likely at age 6. A more plausible story is that he bought at public auction a lot of breech-loading rifles from the Mexican War as the government had moved on to muzzle-loading musketoons as the *gun du jour*. The savvy merchant was then able to sell a few of the still-serviceable weapons and utilize the rest to fortify his home. Stripping the barrels of stocks and triggers, he crafted by hand the foundation of the fence, farming out only the work of the finials that top the muzzles.

MORE RECYCLED ARTILLERY

In addition to the sentinels lining the corner of 28th and P, remnants of the recycled artillery can be found yards away, cordoning off two other Daw properties—homes for his daughters Marion and Nannie—at today's 1516 and 1518 28th Street.

MOUNT ZION CEMETERY ⓮

27th and Q Street NW
- 202-234-0148 (call church to arrange tour, or go on your own)
- Open: during daylight hours
- Metro: Red Line to Dupont Circle, walk approximately six blocks

A forgotten necropolis

Just beyond the meticulously maintained grounds of Dumbarton House, the National Society of the Colonial Dames of America headquarters; just across the fence from Oak Hill Cemetery, grand eternal home to prominent citizens, a humble burial ground sits dilapidated in stark contrast. Barely acknowledged behind two Q Street apartment buildings, neglected graves of lives nearly lost to oblivion are a palpable reminder of a historic African-American presence in Georgetown.

Land for the Old Methodist Burying Ground was purchased in 1808 by the Montgomery Street Church (later known as Dumbarton United Methodist). The congregation included both free and enslaved blacks as well as whites. Despite the diversity, blacks remained relegated to balcony seating and the only known record of the initial cemetery survey indicates that 75 percent of the plot was reserved for white burials and the rest primarily for slaves. By 1814, a group of black members displeased by the inequity established a separate congregation under the auspices of the parent church. They purchased a lot in 1816 and built the Meeting House which would become Mt. Zion Methodist Episcopal Church.

A mutual aid association of free black women, The Female Union Band Society, formed in 1842 and bought the west end of the graveyard for proper burial of its members. Adjacent to the modest plot, white-only cemetery Oak Hill opened in 1849 followed by disinterments of buried whites from the Old Methodist Burying Ground and years of diminished usage. The last documented white burial was an unnamed child in 1869.

"For a sum of one dollar in hand," Mt. Zion Church in 1879 secured a ninety-nine-year lease of the vacant east end of the "Burying Ground" from Dumbarton Church. The conjoined cemeteries now known as Mt. Zion Cemetery are said to have been immaculately kept during the late 19th and early 20th centuries and were a hub of respectful community activity, particularly on Memorial Day when youths sold flowers, water, and lemonade at the entrance.

But all was not golden: there are reports of grave-robbing vandals and "night doctors" who sold corpses to medical schools. Wooden grave markers of the poor and enslaved rotted into nothingness. Soil erosion in some spots, overgrowth in others, compromised the safety of the grounds. The last burial on-site was that of the Female Union Band Society's Mary Logan Jennings in 1950: the city would prohibit further interments for non-compliance with Health Department regulations. The small memorial park languished amid the gentrification around it and convoluted claims to ownership.

In 1975, Vincent DeForest and the Afro-American Bicentennial Corporation conducted a comprehensive historical study of the cemetery, resulting in Historical Landmark of the National Capital status as well as placement on the National Register of Historic Places. In the years since, the site has once again fallen into disrepair, a ramshackle shell of its intended glory; headstones cracked, toppled and tossed aside; hallowed ground a mass tomb of the unknown.

The Society for the Preservation of Historic Georgetown has joined Dumbarton and Mt. Zion Churches in the restoration effort currently underway.

A STOP ON THE UNDERGROUND RAILROAD

It is widely speculated that the small brick retaining vault that housed corpses during inclement weather prior to burial also sheltered the living. Those fleeing the bondage of slavery are said to have awaited under morbid cover the signal of safe passage down the hill at Rock Creek. There, they'd follow the fall line north to the Mason-Dixon Line and across to freedom. Though there is no proof of this assertion, it is known through personal slave narratives that escapees did in fact pass through Georgetown.

SHERIDAN-KALORAMA *FIRE CALL BOX*   ⓯

Decatur Place at 22nd Street NW
• sheridankaloramacallbox.org
• Metro: Red Line to Dupont Circle

Art on call

During the aughts, Cultural Tourism DC led a wonderful initiative to repurpose the disused 1860s fire and police call boxes dotting the city, ghosts of an era before the implementation of the 911 emergency system. The project, *Art on Call*, enlists artists in various communities to restore the beauty of the time-weathered, oft-vandalized relics.

Neighbors of Sheridan-Kalorama embraced the mandate and began the Sheridan-Kalorama Call Box Restoration Project in 2003 to restore the sixteen call boxes within their community, creating a "mini-museum in each, combining local history and public art into a thematic journey through the history of the neighborhood." One such box is tucked away in a quiet corner not far from the whir of Dupont Circle. Transformed by artist Michael K. Ross, it is a perfect homage to the original intention of the fire call box.

Though we now take for granted that if there is a fire, we can dial 911 for immediate assistance, that system is not yet fifty years old. Prior to its advent, the fire and police departments were summoned to emergencies from these illuminated sentinels (triangular pediments for fire; rounded corners for police) scattered throughout the city.

Ross' *Fire Call Box* depicts an early 1900s horse-drawn fire wagon racing to answer a call for help. A lever pulled on the call box would transmit an alarm signal to central headquarters where a paper-tape register punched out the box number to dispatch aid to that location. Ross also contributed all nine bronze sculptures created for the Mount Pleasant area call boxes.

Art on Call is now managed by the DC Commission on the Arts and Humanities and the District Department of Transportation.

GODEY LIME KILNS

(16)

Junction of Rock Creek and Potomac Parkway and Whitehurst Freeway
at 27th and L Street NW
- nps.gov
- Metro: Red Line to Foggy Bottom

> ### *Reminders of an industrial past*

A t the edge of Foggy Bottom, engulfed by a tangle of motorways from Rock Creek Parkway to Whitehurst Freeway, are the forlorn ruins of the Godey Lime Kilns. Nearly 20 feet high, covered by years of encroaching foliage and the residue of half a century of lime-making, they are vestiges of 19th-century commerce in the city.

With 1864 came the only Civil War battle waged on Washington soil at Fort Stevens; the establishment of Arlington National Cemetery; and the relocation of William H. Godey and John A. Rheim's lime works to 27th and L Streets. Godey and Rheim moved their kilns to meet the growing demand for quicklime, a derivative of limestone used as an industrial glue. A prime spot on the east bank of Rock Creek and the canal's end, it was an ideal location to receive shipments of quarried limestone. The haul was a matter of yards from canal boat to kiln where fires blazed to burn off the carbon dioxide from limestone, leaving calcium oxide (lime) valued for architectural construction.

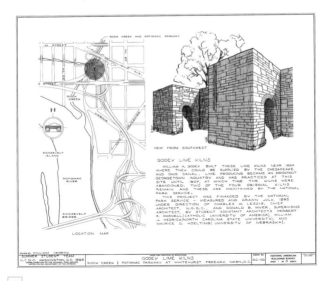

VIEW FROM SOUTHWEST

GODEY LIME KILNS

WILLIAM H. GODEY BUILT THESE LIME KILNS NEAR 1864 WHERE THEY COULD BE SUPPLIED BY THE CHESAPEAKE AND OHIO CANAL. LIME PRODUCING BECAME AN IMPORTANT GEORGETOWN INDUSTRY AND WAS PRACTICED AT THIS SITE UNTIL 1907, AT WHICH TIME THE KILNS WERE ABANDONED. TWO OF THE FOUR ORIGINAL KILNS REMAIN AND THESE ARE MAINTAINED BY THE NATIONAL PARK SERVICE.

THIS PROJECT WAS FINANCED BY THE NATIONAL PARK SERVICE — MEASURED AND DRAWN JULY, 1985 UNDER DIRECTION OF CHARLES W. LESSIG, CHIEF ARCHITECT, N.C.D.O., AND DONALD B. MYER, SUPERVISING ARCHITECT, BY STUDENT ASSISTANT ARCHITECTS HERBERT E. DARNELL(CATHOLIC UNIVERSITY OF AMERICA), WILLIAM J. HEDRICK(NORTH CAROLINA STATE UNIVERSITY), AND MAURICE D. HOELTING(UNIVERSITY OF NEBRASKA).

ROCK CREEK AND POTOMAC PARKWAY

M STREET

L STREET

ROCK CREEK

VIRGINIA

ROOSEVELT ISLAND

POTOMAC RIVER

ROOSEVELT BRIDGE

LOCATION MAP

DRAWN BY: WILLIAM HEDRICK
SUMMER STUDENT TEAM
N.C.D.O., WASHINGTON, D.C. 1985

GODEY LIME KILNS
ROCK CREEK { POTOMAC PARKWAY AT WHITEHURST FREEWAY, WASH.,D.C.

HISTORIC AMERICAN BUILDINGS SURVEY

Upon the elder Godey's passing in 1873, his son Edward, while still a teen, assumed control of the business operating under the name "Washington Lime Kilns." Twenty-five workers labored to maintain the wood-burning ovens which required three days of firing per load of limestone, a fact of which he was proud.

Substantial flooding on the C&O wreaked havoc in May 1889 and by December Edward died at Matley Hill Sanitarium in Baltimore. As stated on his death certificate, the "lime merchant" was 33. The kilns remained functional until 1908, when John Dodson, owner since 1897 abandoned them.

After years of blight, only two of the original ovens remained in 1965. Badly deteriorated, they were excavated, stabilized and now sit as a curiosity to passersby, a covert reminder of the area's industrial past.

FOGGY BOTTOM

The neighborhood gets its evocative name from its early days as a low-lying, swampy community inundated by a mix of nature's fog and the smog of local industry. Close to Godey's kilns, Washington's gasworks, the Heurich brewery and other manufacturers, the area drew an immigrant population of German, Irish, and Italian workers as well as newly-emancipated African-Americans.

DIPLOMATIC RECEPTION ROOMS

17

US Department of State
2201 C Street NW
• receptiontours.state.gov
• 202-647-3241
• Open: Monday to Friday; 45-minute tours at 9:30 am, 10:30 am and 2:45 pm; must be scheduled in advance by phone or online
• Not recommended for children under 12
• Wheelchairs and sign-language interpreters available with advance notice
• Admission: free; the rooms are entirely contributor-supported—those interested in making a tax-deductible financial or object donation can contact the State Department
• Metro: Blue, Orange, or Silver Line to Foggy Bottom

Stately appointments of diplomacy

Of the forty-two elegantly-appointed rooms reserved at the US State Department for diplomatic reception, eight are now open for thrice-daily docent-led tours. That is unless they are pre-empted by visiting dignitaries. The business of diplomacy does trump the public gaze.

The rooms, decorated almost entirely in American-made furnishings are a testament to the tenacity and genteel tastes of Clement E. Conger. As Department of State Deputy Chief of Protocol during the Eisenhower administration, he suggested that a suite of rooms be devoted exclusively to serve diplomatic functions in the new State Department building. Aghast upon seeing the rooms allotted with floor-to-ceiling plate glass, exposed steel beams, wall-to-wall carpeting and acoustical tile ceilings, he likened them to a 1950s motel and began a thirty-year quest to transform them. He doggedly solicited donations of pristine furniture and objects relevant to the early years of the country, and funds to renovate the rooms. No tax revenue is ever used to furnish the suite. By 1989, the architectural upgrades complete, the rooms befit their lofty purpose of international diplomacy. Of the John Quincy Adams Drawing Room, former Secretary of State Madeline Albright, said "How better to urge intractable parties toward peace than to point out the desk where Benjamin Franklin signed the Treaty of Paris?"

An incredibly knowledgeable docent will guide you through many rooms before culminating in the grandeur of the Benjamin Franklin State Dining Room. Named for the "Father of American Foreign Service," it is the largest room in the suite, its lectern irresistibly beckons a photo op.

Named for the first Secretary of State, the Thomas Jefferson State Reception Room with its pedimented doors, American Chippendale furniture and his portable writing desk, is a favorite of former Secretary of State Hillary Clinton.

"AM I NOT A MAN AND A BROTHER?"

Jefferson in life, owned hundreds of slaves and three Wedgwood cameos of Cupid and Psyche. Recently added to the room that honors him are three Wedgwood anti-slavery Jasperware medallions inscribed "Am I not a Man and a Brother?" and featuring a shackled black man in bas-relief, cuffed hands reaching up. Oh, the irony.

For information on the Great Seal, see following double page.

INITIATORY AND ESOTERIC SYMBOLISM OF THE GREAT SEAL OF THE UNITED STATES

The symbols of the Great Seal of the United States of America (approved in 1782 and adopted as coat of arms in 1790) have their roots in Freemasonry, thanks to some eminent Masons (Benjamin Franklin, Thomas Jefferson, William Churchill Houston, and William Barton) who contributed to the design.

On the seal, a golden halo breaks through a cloud round a constellation of thirteen silver stars on an azure background, above a bald eagle with wings outstretched, holding an olive branch in its right talon and a bundle of thirteen arrows in its left. A ribbon fluttering from its beak bears the Latin motto *E pluribus unum* ("Out of many, one"), an evocation of national unity represented by the thirteen stars symbolizing the thirteen original states of the Union.

This halo ("Sun in his Glory" in heraldry) stands for the Grand Architect of the Universe blessing and protecting the United States, which is why a perfect six-pointed star (hexagram) can be drawn round the arrangement of the thirteen stars, the geometric shape symbolizing the Supreme Deity of all peoples and all religions. Borne on the breast of the eagle is a shield with thirteen alternating stripes in white and red, surmounted by a blue horizontal band or chief. This is an allegory of the original thirteen states that came into being on earth after falling from the stars, a veiled allusion to the biblical theme of the "heavenly Jerusalem and earthly Jerusalem." This sense of heavenly Paradise and earthly Paradise was based on earlier beliefs that considered North America to be the Promised Land, the New Jerusalem of charismatic, but also Masonic, movements. So the imperial eagle evokes not only the ancient Roman Empire, but particularly the eagle *Kadosh* (derived from the Hebrew word for "holy" or "consecrated"), the "perfect initiates," the true Spiritually Enlightened (Illuminati) which the ancient Kabbalistic traditions represented by an eagle—symbol of the Sun whose rays are also gripped by an eagle's left talon, while the right talon with its olive branch expresses the Peace of the Just.

The colors of the shield on the eagle's breast evoke the cardinal virtues that every Mason must possess and transmit to humanity: the red of Mars expresses *valor*, the white of the Moon *purity*, and the blue of Venus *justice*. According to the practice of gematria (substitution of numbers for the letters of the Hebrew alphabet), the value of these colors is 103, which corresponds to the phrase *Ehben ha-Adam* ("Stone of Adam"), suggesting the perfect ashlar, that is to say, the Cubic Stone of the Master Mason, a symbol of spiritual perfection. The number 103 is also the value of the noun *Bonain*, a rabbinical term meaning "Builder," the Master Mason.

On the reverse of the Great Seal is an unfinished pyramid surmounted by a triangle with the Eye of Divine Providence at its center, surrounded by a golden halo. Above is the Latin phrase *Annuit cœptis*, "He (God) favors us," and below, another motto: *Novus ordo seclorum*, "New order of the ages." The pyramid, an allegory of *strength* and *durability*, evokes the Initiatory Tradition of the West as well as the Mountain of Initiation that every initiate must climb, with regularity, until the confrontation with God at the summit, this encounter aiming at being united with Him (represented by the resplendent eye). The use of this symbol, passed down from the early Christians of Alexandria and derived from ancient Egypt's Eye of Horus, can be explained by the fact that North American Masons were primarily Christians (Catholics, Lutherans, or Calvinists).

The first appearance of the Eye of Divine Providence in Masonic iconography dates back to 1797, with the publication of Thomas Smith Webb's *The Freemason's Monitor*, as a way to remind all Masons that their thoughts, feelings, and actions are constantly observed by God, the Grand Architect of the Universe. This symbol persisted in Masonic circles as the expression of Absolute Divinity, the purpose of the motto *Annuit cœptis*, which attributes to God the honor of founding the United States of America according to the national myth. This phrase is taken from Book IX of Virgil's *Aeneid*, when Ascanius, son of Aeneas, prays to the Father of the Gods, Jupiter Almighty, to favor his bold undertakings.

The expression *Novus ordo seclorum*, from Virgil's Fourth *Eclogue*, was interpreted by medieval Christians as a prophecy of the coming of Christ to usher in a new Golden Age of the world. It was Charles Thomson who in 1782 suggested using the term to mark "the beginning of the New American Era" from the date of the Declaration of Independence (1776).

From 1935, the initiatory allegory on the reverse of the Great Seal also featured on the back of dollar bills, at the instigation of President Franklin Delano Roosevelt, a leading Freemason.

In the Kabbalistic tradition, the allegorical group of all these figures carries the value 273, as does the Hebrew phrase *Ehben mosu habonim* ("Stone which the builders refused"), referring to the lost key of the Initiatory Mysteries. This phrase is well known to all Masons following the York Rite or Royal Arch, commonly known as the American Rite. The value 273 is also that of Hiram Abiff, architect of Solomon's Temple, the main character of the legend after the ritual of the 3rd degree of Freemasonry.

The number thirteen features on both sides of the Great Seal, reflecting the sense of secular and social death that allows spiritual resurrection and the consequent resurgence of a new human society, just and perfect, that would be unique among the many existing societies (*E pluribus unum*). This is a reference to Synarchy (Universal Harmony), an occult principle now largely forgotten despite being one of the main reasons behind the foundation of the United States.

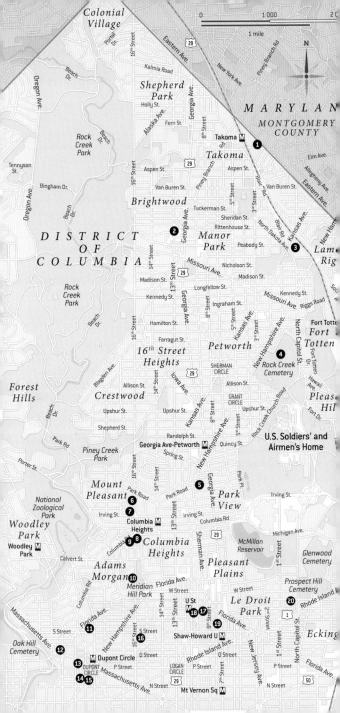

NORTHWEST 2

BOUNDARY STONE NE 2

❶

Maple and Carroll in Takoma Park
• Metro: Red Line to Takoma

*One
of the first federal
monuments*

Now this one is a bit tricky. On the Maryland side of the stone, the address is 7100 Maple Avenue. On the DC side of the stone, the address is 6980 Maple Street NW, which is also confusing since this is the second northeast boundary stone of the original federal city, before North Capitol Street became the line of demarcation between east and west. The through-streets of Takoma DC become avenues in neighboring Takoma Park MD, thus DC's Maple and Carroll Streets are Maple and Carroll Avenues across the "state" line.

What is clear, however, is the residual engraving on the stone, one of the still-legible of the forty stones marking the city's original boundaries. Like all the stones, its District-facing side is inscribed "Jurisdiction of the United States." On the opposite side is inscribed "Maryland" (Virginia stones are inscribed accordingly). Engraved on the third and fourth sides of every stone are the year of its placement and its magnetic compass variance.

In 1791, President George Washington issued a proclamation revealing the boundaries of the "district for the permanent seat of government." On April 15, 1791, the south cornerstone was laid with great ceremony at Jones Point (see page 307). All Virginia stones were placed in 1791; all Maryland stones in 1792. Placed at 1-mile intervals around the perimeter of the 10-mile square (with larger stones at the north, south, east, and west corners) they constitute the first federal monuments.

An 1846 retrocession returned to pro-slavery Virginia the 33 square miles that the commonwealth had ceded for the establishment of the anti-slavery federal district. Fourteen markers of the northwest and southwest boundaries stand in what are now the Northern Virginia cities of Alexandria, Arlington, and Falls Church.

The Daughters of the American Revolution set up protective fences around each stone in 1915, but fences cannot stop the ravages of time and weather on the the soft Aquia Creek sandstone from which they are made. Though some fare well, others have eroded to stumps.

Equidistant between Takoma Metro and the area's reigning rooster in bronze (see page 279), the marker is a "stone's" throw away from the shops and restaurants of quaint Old Takoma.

VESTIGES OF FORT STEVENS ❷

6001 13th Street NW
- Tel: 202-673-7647
- www.nps.gov/places/fort-stevens.htm
- Metro: 53 bus to 14th Street and Fort Stevens Drive

> **The only Civil War battleground within the District borders**

In 1860, the Union-sympathetic capital city was surrounded by Maryland and Virginia, slave-holding states sympathetic to the Confederate cause. As the certainty of civil war became apparent, the Lincoln Administration seized land conducive to strategic placement of fortifications and built earthworks encircling the Union capital.

Today's Brightwood was known in the 1820s as Vinegar Hill, a free black settlement, the first of its kind in the city, before much of it was claimed to create Fort Massachusetts, expressly to defend the major thoroughfare, Seventh Street Turnpike (now Georgia Avenue).

By 1862, the fort was expanded and renamed in honor of slain Brigadier General Issac Stevens. On July 11, 1864, after a Confederate tactical win 35 miles away at the Battle of Monocacy, Lt. General Jubal Early gave his troops rest before launching a full-on assault to capture the capital city at Fort Stevens the following day. By then, Union reinforcements had arrived to bolster the defenses and after a day-long battle — observed from the ramparts by the sitting President — Early and his troops retreated.

There were an estimated 500 Confederate casualties and 374 on the Union side. President Lincoln might have made 375 as he stood upon the parapet at

Fort Stevens; he was the second of two U.S. Presidents to come under enemy fire while in office (the other being James Madison while in command of an artillery battery in Battle of Bladensburg/War of 1812.) An apocryphal tale has it that Colonel Oliver Wendell Holmes (future Chief Justice of the Supreme Court) bellowed "get down, you damn fool!" as the Rebels fired upon the Commander-in-Chief. Early is said to have bragged, "We didn't take Washington, but scared Abe Lincoln like Hell."

Today, some of the earthworks remain: a four-acre section of the decommissioned fort preserved as a public park and memorial to the only Civil War battle waged within the boundaries of DC; a stone and plaque mark the spot where Lincoln came under fire; a bronze relief model of the fort mounted on a John Earley mosaic concrete base shows its original layout; and reproduction civil war cannons point out toward the residential area abutting the commercial district of Georgia Avenue, where lie the remains of 41 Union veterans in the hidden Battleground National Cemetery.

Each July there's a commemoration of the Battle of Fort Stevens with an artillery demonstration and re-enactors portraying the principal characters of the historic event.

AUNT BETTY

One hilltop property, 11 acres of farmland belonging to free black woman Elizabeth Proctor Thomas and her husband James, was seized by Union soldiers to create Fort Massachusetts. As she sat crying under a Sycamore tree with her infant as her home was demolished, President Lincoln is said to have walked up to her and said, "It's hard, but you shall reap a great reward." After the war, her land was returned, but no recompense for her lost home was offered; the President had been slain and no one in power authorized his verbal promissory note.

DON CICCIO E FIGLI

3

6031 Kansas Avenue NW
- Open: Saturday 1pm—6pm for tours and tastings
- Tel: 202-957-7792
- www.doncicioefigli.com
- Metro: F1 bus from Takoma (Red Line) or Cheverly (Orange Line) to the intersection of Kansas and Eastern Avenues; 7-minute walk from there

> *Amalfitani recipes, American made; that's amari!*

In Lamond, a quiet neighborhood where a 19th-century terracotta clay works once stood, an unassuming mid-century building houses large terracotta amphorae. The amphorae are vessels for Don Ciccio e Figli's alchemical magic — crafting traditional liqueurs of the Amalfi Coast.

Each Saturday from 1pm—6pm, owner Francesco Amodeo II and Jonathan Fasano, a knowledgeable and engaging ambassador for the brand, conduct complimentary tasting flights and tours of the distillery, offering samples of their artisan spirits and sharing the story of each. Afterward, visitors are welcome to purchase Don Ciccio e Figli cocktails, and passionate mixologist Amodeo mixes a mean one.

Creating spirits since 2012 in small batches, amari (bitters) chiefly among them, from recipes that date back as far as the 17th century, Amodeo continues a legacy begun by his great-grandfather Vincenzo Amodeo in 1883. His grandfathers, namesake Francesco "Don Ciccio" Amodeo and Giovanni Porpora, revived the family business in 1951 by building a small distillery in the Furore hills near Positano and Capri. A devastating earthquake in 1980 destroyed both the distillery and the lemon trees from which they made their popular limoncello, shuttering the business.

Born two years later, Francesco II recalls the aroma that first captured his imagination, "My dad was a Concerto drinker; he drank it after meals. He had a beard and mustache, so when he kissed me, the smell of the coffee and all the botanicals would come out."

In adulthood, Francesco II traveled by donkey to the remote mountain town of Tramonti to get permission to reproduce the espresso/barley digestif from the convent where it originated in 1696. In lieu of a recipe, he was given a bottle to figure it out. But after a year-long futile attempt to recreate what he'd tasted, he returned to Italy and appealed to the former convent housekeeper, who showed him how to create it.

"That's how our Concerto came to light," he says, "We just modernized it a little bit. We use less sugar so the fresh ingredients will shine." Fresh is their hallmark: fennel in their Finochietto, artichokes in the Carciofo, prickly pears for their once-a-year Fico d'India. Following tradition, the walnuts used in their Nocino are harvested green on June 24, the feast day of San Giovanni.

PORPORA'S AMPHORAS

Riffing on Grandpa Porpora's 1967 Ferrochina (an age-old anemia tonic) Don Ciccio e Figli developed the award-winning Ferro-Kina, the first American-made iron amaro, macerating the botanicals in the giant amphoras.

THE ADAMS MEMORIAL ❹

Rock Creek Cemetery
Section E, Lot 202
201 Allison Street NW
• stpaulrockcreek.org
• 202-726-2080
• Open: daily, including holidays 8 am – 7 pm; office Monday to Friday 9 am – 5 pm, excluding holidays
• Metro: Red, Green or Yellow Line to Fort Totten; then taxi or 60 Metrobus to cemetery

> *The Mystery of the Hereafter*

In the gently sloping hills of the city's oldest cemetery (open since 1719) a dense cluster of yew trees encircle the unmarked yet monumental Adams gravesite. Mrs. Marian "Clover" Adams, a gifted photographer, took her life on December 6, 1884, with a vial of the potassium cyanide she used in processing her photos. "Five of Hearts," a spirited coterie including Clover, her husband, Henry, scion of the celebrated Adams family, John and Clara Hay and bachelor Clarence King, was the hit of Washington society. Her suicide shocked the city.

Mr. Adams had her interred with a simple headstone while he pondered for a few years an appropriate memorial. Noted sculptor and friend Augustus Saint-Gaudens rendered not her likeness, but an allegorical figure inspired by the beauty and equipoise of the statuary the widowed Henry saw during travels in Japan. The seated bronze figure, shrouded, of indeterminate sex and peaceful countenance has been called Saint-Gaudens' masterpiece. Architect Stanford White designed the hexagonal plot with an elegant exedra bench opposite the sculpture for contemplation. No epitaph breaks the fluid lines.

Though Saint-Gaudens called the tragic mondaine's memorial *The Mystery of the Hereafter,* it became known in popular culture as "Grief," much to Henry's dismay. He groused in a 1908 letter "Do not allow the world to tag my figure with a name! Every magazine writer wants to label it as some American patent medicine for popular consumption—Grief, Despair, Pear's Soap, or Macy's Men's Suits Made to Measure."

In 1918, Henry too, was buried there. Contemporary landscaping quite nearly encloses the memorial in meticulously sculpted yew, adding another element of mystery to the enigmatic figure.

Said to be haunted by the spirit of Mrs. Adams, with soft crying, gentle footfalls and the faint whiff of almonds, the Hay-Adams Hotel stands on the site of the former Hay and Adams homes at Lafayette Square.

It wasn't until a deathbed letter in 1901 to his black common-law wife, Ava Copeland, did Clarence King 'fess up to his astonishing double life. "Passing for black" under the guise of Pullman porter James Todd, the blue-eyed blond, raised five children with Ava. By dint of his "work" on the rails, he was often away, returning to his true identity as an eminent white geologist. John Hay honored his fellow "Heart" by providing for his family.

HISTORIC TENTH PRECINCT POLICE STATION ❺

MPD Fourth District Substation
750 Park Road NW
• 202-576-8222
• Metro: Green Line to Georgia Avenue/Petworth

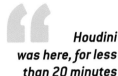

Houdini was here, for less than 20 minutes

As Washington greeted a new year on January 1, 1906, master escape artist Harry Houdini successfully freed himself from what was at the time the most secure jail in the city. In town for a performance at the Chase Theater, he was granted the opportunity to free himself from the station house of the Tenth Precinct. Police Chief, Major Richard Sylvester, boasting of the new station's infallibility invited Houdini to have a go at it.

As was his custom, the self-described "Expert Handcuff Manipulator," asked to see the cell and the locks to be used prior to his attempt. In a bit of bait and switch Sylvester agreed then changed the locks at the last minute. Houdini removed his garments before he was secured by five locks in Cell No. 3 and his clothing in another. Undaunted, he successfully unshackled himself, recovered his clothes, dressed and presented himself to the incredulous wardens and Major Sylvester within 18 minutes.

In a news post later that week, the chagrined Houdini spoke of the undeserved animus he received from police personnel. After having escaped jails from London's Scotland Yard to Moscow's

Siberian transportation cell, he said, "It remained for Washington to treat me like a common malefactor."

In keeping with the ideals of the City Beautiful movement, the handsome building with its rufous facade of brick and terracotta created an authoritative presence while integrating seamlessly into the block of rowhouses. Diamond diaperwork rests below a decorative cornice. An ornate cartouche holds an oculus window. Below, bold letters carved in high relief proudly proclaim "10th Street Police Precinct."

Now home to the Metropolitan Police Department Fourth District substation, the red-brick edifice stands in pristine condition. But put your camera away, photos are frowned upon.

The manacled "Handcuff King" struck again on January 6 escaping from "Murderer's Row," in the DC Jail on 19th Street SE. He was out in 2 minutes. Further shaming the police force, he performed "musical chairs" on the prisoners, breaking into and switching their cells. The Seneca sandstone building no longer exists.

AURELIUS BATTAGLIA MURALS AT MOUNT PLEASANT LIBRARY ❻

3160 16th Street NW (entrance is on Lamont Street)
• Open: Mon—Thur 9:30am—9pm; Fri—Sat 9:30am—5:30pm; Sunday 1pm—5pm
• Tel: 202-671-3121
• www.dclibrary.org/mtpleasant
• Metro: Green or Yellow Lines to Columbia Heights

Destined for Disney

For generations, visitors to the children's section of the Mount Pleasant branch of the DC Public Library have been enchanted by two cozy reading alcoves adorned by whimsical anthropomorphic animals painted by native Washingtonian, Aurelius Battaglia in 1933. However, few realize the extent to which he sparked the imaginations of children well beyond the DC area. Commissioned by the Public Works of Art Program — designed to help unemployed artists during the Great Depression — the murals *Animal Circus* and *Animal Orchestra* were just the beginning of a long, impressive career trajectory.

Born in the District to Sicilian immigrants Giuseppe "Joseph" and Concetta "Mary" Battaglia, young Aurelius showed prodigious artistry by the age of six, despite a vision impairment. He would attend and eventually teach at the Corcoran School of Art before beginning a career as a caricaturist for several publications, from *The Washington Tribune* to *Vanity Fair*.

For the library commission, Battaglia rendered a delightful menagerie most children have only seen live in a zoo: a lion, a gorilla, an owl, a hippo, penguins, giraffes and, perhaps presciently, elephants, all dressed in clothing and interacting animatedly in a distinctly human way. He created several additional works for the government including the watercolor painting *Utopia* in the mid-1930s to envision the New Deal planned community of Greenbelt, MD. In 1937 he would join the animation team at Walt Disney Studios, contributing to many beloved Disney classics — notably *Dumbo*, *Pinocchio* and *Fantasia* — until 1941, when a Disney animators strike inspired the launch of the animation studio United Productions of America (UPA). At UPA he would direct the BAFTA-nominated 1955 animated short *The Invisible Moustache of Raoul Dufy,* a charming take on the life of the French painter, narrated by Hans Conried of *Rocky & Bullwinkle* fame.

All the while, Battaglia continued to create illustrations — some decidedly adult, like those for *Esquire* magazine — but primarily he became a well regarded and highly prolific illustrator of children's classics, such as the Little Golden Books series and the visual encyclopedia for young kids, *Childcraft,* until his death in 1984. After water damage to the Depression-era canvases from a roof leak, conservator David Olin of Great Falls, VA meticulously restored the treasured artwork to its original vibrancy as part of an overall library renovation. At the ribbon cutting ceremony in 2012, Battaglia's daughter Nicola presented the library with her father's watercolor study for the murals.

SUNS CINEMA

3107 Mount Pleasant Street NW
- Open: Bar opens Tue—Sat 7pm—close; Sunday 6pm—close
- Check website for film schedule
- www.sunscinema.com
- Metro: Green or Yellow Line to Columbia Heights

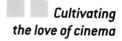

*Cultivating
the love of cinema*

An idea born of the themed movie nights sociable cineastes David Cabrera and Ryan Hunter Mitchell once hosted in their Mount Pleasant apartment, Suns Cinema opened in May 2016 with support garnered from a clever crowdfunding campaign.

The film buffs wanted to expand "Uncle David's Movie Nights" to "cultivate the love of cinema through daily screenings" in an independent, neighborhood venue. They thought they'd struck gold after landing a location in the former Suns Discount Store, complete with the cool signage that gave their burgeoning theater its name. Though they subsequently lost that space, they found another — a storefront across the street from Saint Martin's (Mitchell's hair salon). And no small consolation, they were able to snag the Suns sign that now fronts the community theater/bar.

Stop by to get your repertory cinema fix with other cinephilic kindred spirits — the place seats forty — in quirky comfort reminiscent of an eccentric auntie's parlor. Have a cocktail or two at the bar with Flora Scalamandré's zebras trotting across the wall in a field of "Masai red" and imagine Margot Tenenbaum, single barrette, kohl-rimmed eyes, wearing Lacoste and unbearable ennui, talking on a Princess phone. Cabrera and Mitchell chose the iconic wallcovering as a wink to the character's bedroom in the Wes Anderson film *The Royal Tenenbaums*. In addition to documentary and narrative film screenings, varied programming includes Saturday morning cartoons, movie trivia nights, and the satirical Fale University comedic lecture series. Among the many films shown at Suns have been Truffaut's *The 400 Blows*, Goddard's *Breathless*, Kubrick's *Dr. Strangelove*, Mel Brooks' *Young Frankenstein*, Jarmusch's *Stranger than Paradise*, Julian Schnabel's *Basquiat*, Jean-Pierre Jeunet's *Amelie*, and the Hal Ashby-helmed *Being There*, shot in late seventies Washington.

While shooting the 1962 film *Advise & Consent*, director Otto Preminger and his crew had unprecedented access to the Capitol building, except for the Senate Chamber. *The Washington Star* newspaper sent artist and Dupont Circle resident Lily Spandorf to sketch the Hollywood on the Hill action in pen and ink. Her assignment finished, she continued to access the set with her press pass and would ultimately complete a total of 70 images, including the exterior of the Sewall-Belmont House (now Belmont-Paul, see p. 182) and two gouache illustrations of the grand Tregaron mansion. So impressed was Preminger with her work that he presented selections at the film's premiere. Part of the U.S. Senate art collection, the beautiful illustrations are now available for viewing online at www.senate.gov.

MEXICAN CULTURAL INSTITUTE ❽

2829 16th Street NW
• instituteofmexicodc.org
• 202-728-1628
• Open: Monday to Friday 10 am – 6 pm; Saturday (during exhibitions) noon – 4 pm. Check website for holidays
• Admission: free
• Metro: Green Line (and Yellow Line during off-peak times) to Columbia Heights

Culture cache

Not only does the Mexican Cultural Institute host fascinating programs on Mexican art, artifacts and history including an exceptional *Dia de los Muertos* altar, its capacious, Beaux-Arts mansion integrates a panoply of aesthetic influences. Lining the walls of the grand, elaborately carved oak staircase, a vibrant mural chronicles ancient, colonial and modern Mexico. A lavish music room inspired by France's Château de Fontainebleau features a pipe organ. Blue and white Puebla ceramics dominate the sun-drenched conservatory, and an intact 1909 library stretches the width of the third floor.

Upon his wife Emily's passing in 1916, former Secretary of the Treasury Franklin MacVeagh moved out of the luxurious Nathan Wyeth-designed home she'd commissioned as a surprise for him. In 1921, the widower sold the property to the Mexican government for use as its embassy in the US with the proviso that its interior remain unchanged during his lifetime. Notably before MacVeagh's 1934 death, Diego Rivera protégé, Roberto Cueva Del Río was commissioned to paint staircase frescoes reflecting pre- and post-contact Mexican history and culture. A looming figure of Christopher Columbus, originally planned as a portrait of Spanish Conquistador, Hernán Cortés poignantly abuts the depiction of the founding of the Aztec capital at Tenochtitlán.

Painted tile work injects Mexican ambience into the formerly unornamented, exposed brick conservatory. Legendary volcanoes, *Popocatépetl* and *Iztaccíhuatl*, adorn a fountained wall, and the coats of arms for each state in the Republic of Mexico border the room brightened by quatrefoil clerestory windows.

The MacVeagh presence remains in the library with its leather-bound volumes, coffered ceilings, dark woods and sumptuous tapestries. The music salon retains its former glory with barrel vaulted ceilings, an ornate elliptical fireplace, a stained glass oculus window and a hand-painted Aeolian organ. Built for Emily MacVeagh at the cost of $15,000 in 1910, it is one of few extant residential pipe organs in the region.

Operating as a cultural arm since 1990, the Institute, far from the city's museum core is an unexpected public delight.

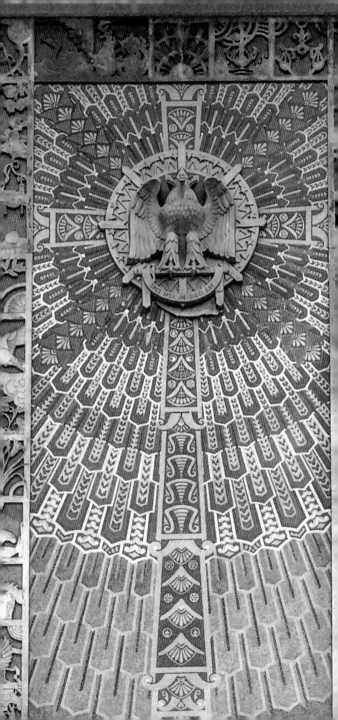

THE "EARLEY PROCESS" POLYCHROME CONCRETE IN THE DISTRICT ⑨
(DC Scottish Rite of Freemasonry, 2800 16th Street, NW)

The son of a fourth generation stonemason, John Joseph Earley was born in 1881 in New York City and raised in Washington, DC, where his father James, an ecclesiastic artist, sought work — among his creations is an obscure exterior relief sculpture of a monk at Georgetown University's Dahlgren Chapel.

John apprenticed with his father, upon whose passing in 1906 he would assume the helm of the workshop, steering it in a new direction. His early focus was on decorative stucco, which was popular at the time. One of his earliest commissions, in 1915, was to clad the concrete walls and balustrades of the developing Meridian Hill Park. But his model samples met with a disappointing reception. He and his associate Basil Taylor experimented with different approaches, eventually devising the material he dubbed "architectural concrete," expanding the possibilities of exposed aggregate concrete in architecture.

Earley further explored the aesthetic implication of utilizing colored stones in the aggregate mixture to create polychrome mosaic concrete. With unabated passion he reworked and refined the "Earley Process" — the considered selection of colored stones, the precise ratios of water to sand/cement, and the exacting removal of the surface layer of the mixture with wire brushes before hardening to expose the stones in relief.

Though aware of the value of strength and durability in the material, Earley's enthusiasm was greatest in exalting the aesthetic potential, utilizing it as an artist's medium. His 1920 patent application for step-gradation states, "Broadly, the object of this invention is to reproduce in concrete a surface colored after the impressionistic school." Indeed his works are imbued with a pointillist quality.

The Earley Studio produced prolifically for projects across the country

and their polychrome mosaic Great Seals adorn U.S. Embassies around the globe. Shortly before his death in 1945, John Earley sold the business to Basil Taylor. In 1955 Taylor passed it on to his son Vernon, who kept the studio running until 1973. In and around Washington, the Earley Studio's considerable contribution to the built environment is evident from homes and houses of worship to the DC Scottish Rite of Freemasonry, government buildings and even ◀ Reagan National Airport. Despite exposure to the elements and the passage of time, the vibrancy of the colors remains.

BOUNDARY CASTLE CURTAIN WALL 🔟

16th Street at Florida Avenue NW
• www.nps.gov/mehi
• Metro: Green Line (and Yellow Line during off-peak times) to Columbia Heights

> *A palimpsest of Hendersonian opulence*

A cross 16th Street from the lovely cascading fountain of Meridian Hill Park, an imposing stone wall surrounds a gated community of 1970s townhomes, a palimpsest of Gilded Age splendor. Steps from the corner of Florida Avenue, two castellated towers, conjoined by a retrofitted wall, once served as the gateway to Boundary Castle. The hilltop home of former Senator John Brooks Henderson and his suffragist wife, Mary (nee Foote), the residence took its name from Boundary Road (Florida Avenue) the bygone boundary of Washington City.

The Hendersons saw the potential in the land just north of the city's edge. Buying up multiple tracts, they developed them into palatial mansions starting in 1887 with their opulent "castle" of Seneca sandstone. Envisioning a new Embassy Row, they rented their properties mostly to foreign legations. An invitation to the elegant Boundary Castle was among the most coveted in the city.

The grand dame's vision grew ever loftier: in 1898 she submitted architectural renderings by Paul Pelz for an imposing new Executive Mansion to be sited directly across from her manse on Meridian Hill. That idea and the next for the site, the Lincoln Memorial were dashed. A proponent of the City Beautiful movement, she continued her quest to transform 16th Street into *the* grand boulevard of the city, successfully petitioning to rename it "Avenue of the Presidents." So unpopular was the name with citizens it was restored to 16th Street within a year.

She secured her legacy when she lobbied Congress to purchase her Meridian Hill property for use as a public park. Though the Federal Government bought the land in 1910, the park would not be completed until

five years after Mrs. Henderson's 1931 death.

Then known as Henderson Castle, it exchanged hands a bit before its razing in 1949. Nature would reforest a small wood before a new exclusive enclave, Beekman Place, opened on the site in 1977, retaining the historic perimeter wall.

Go on a Sunday afternoon then follow your ears across the street to the decades-old *Malcolm X Park Drum Circle*. And look for Joan of Arc, the only equestrienne statue of a woman in a city filled with monuments to men on horseback.

L. RON HUBBARD HOUSE

11

1812 19th Street NW
- lronhubbard.org/heritage-sites/dc.html
- 202-234-7490
- Open: 10:30 am – 6:30 pm; call for appointment
- Admission: free
- Metro: Red Line to Dupont Circle

The Scientologist's mecca

A contributing property to the Dupont Circle Historic District, the L. Ron Hubbard House, is an unexpected repository of microhistory. In 1955, the charismatic, flame-haired pulp writer, L. Ron Hubbard, on the heels of the success of his non-fiction tome *Dianetics* moved his base of operations from Phoenix to Washington, DC. On a quiet, residential side street off the main drag, the handsome, Flemish-gabled townhouse became home to Scientology, his new religious ideology. Sixty years and millions of adherents later, the historic house museum is known as the "Original Founding Church of Scientology," as distinguished from its much larger successor—the Founding Church of Scientology, an active church blocks away on 16th Street.

A mecca for Scientologists, the house, restored to its 1950s appearance in 2005, welcomes people of all faiths (or none at all) to tour the facility by appointment. The tour begins with the back story of Lafayette Ronald Hubbard (LRH) and a chronology of his larger-than-life professed exploits; from learning psychoanalytic theory at age 12 to barnstorming as "Flash" Hubbard to founding a 20th-century religion. Photographs and ephemera give a glimpse into the life of the adherents' revered leader and the development of his philosophies.

A back parlor, with chairs arrayed toward a podium, is the site of the first Scientology wedding and LRH's lectures. On the second floor, his 1957 office, just as he kept it over a half-century ago, with his Remington typewriter, Ampex tape recorders, Roneo mimeograph machine, Grundig radio, and artifacts of his world travels. Another room holds several iterations of the electropsychometer or e-meter, the device used in Scientology auditing "for measuring and indicating changes in the resistance of a human body." Finally, the tour ends in the massive library of Hubbard-penned books and recorded lectures.

L. RON HUBBARD IN WASHINGTON

Long before creating the Founding Church in the District, LRH attended DC's Woodward School for Boys, then George Washington University from 1930-1932. He was reputedly a balladeer for radio station, WOL, and reporter for the *Washington Herald*.

THE SHIP'S CAT OF ARGYLE HOUSE ⑫

2201 Massachusetts Avenue NW
• Metro: Red Line to Dupont Circle

> *Diplocat of Embassy Row*

Standing at feline sentry perched on an Embassy Row cornice ledge, the statue of an alert kitty surveying his catdom hints at the maritime history of the original owner, US Naval officer Frederick Augustus Miller.

Cats, with their heightened sensitivity and exceptional mousing skills have historically been kept on ships to predict weather fluctuations and of course, deter rodents. The châteauesque Miller mansion, constructed at the top of the 20th century, sits on a corner bluff at Massachusetts Avenue and 22nd Street. Honoring Civil War veteran Miller's retirement from Naval service, the Paul J. Pelz-designed home featured many nautical references, including the stone ship's cat that prompts a double-take from unsuspecting passersby.

Having served on several boards and enjoyed membership in the nearby elite club for men, Cosmos Club, Miller and his family were respected members of Washington society. After his 1909 passing, his widow Alice sold the house in 1913. It has been bought and sold many times over since then. During the Great Depression, it was subdivided into a boarding house, and today it boasts condominium units. An early 1980s fire destroyed many of the interior features original to the house, however.

The property's former garage, constructed expressly to store an automobile rather than a horse carriage, was one of the first of its kind. From 1986 - 2009, it was used to display a portion of the art collection of Olga Hirshhorn, widow of Hirshhorn Museum namesake, Joseph Hirshhorn. In a wink to the cat lording over the "big" house, Olga dubbed her 500-square-foot pied-à-terre triplex the "Mouse House." Displayed at a Connecticut museum in 2009, the "Mouse House Collection" now resides in the permanent collection of the Patty & Jay Baker Museum of Art in Naples, Florida.

GODDESS SARASWATI STATUE ⓭

Embassy of the Republic of Indonesia
2020 Massachusetts Avenue NW
• embassyofindonesia.org
• 202-775-5200
• Metro: Red Line to Dupont Circle

> *A Hindu statue offered by a Muslim country to a largely Christian nation*

In a city with more than its fair share of monumental bronzes honoring men, the towering vision of divine femininity fronting the Indonesian Embassy is a breathtakingly welcome spectacle. Rising 16 feet in pristine white concrete with touches of gilding, *Dewi Saraswati*, the Hindu goddess of knowledge and wisdom stands above a multiracial trio of studious children. A mere 3 percent of the populace in the Republic of Indonesia practice Hinduism, yet this most populous Muslim country in the world (88 percent of its citizens follow Islam) gifted the statue to the United States, a predominately Christian nation.

The gift commands both countries to strive for the ideal of religious freedom and affirms the resonant power of knowledge. With the diversity of the youngsters studying at the goddess' feet, it celebrates and encourages education and tolerance.

Bali, the smallest province in the Southeast Asian archipelago is home to the majority of Indonesia's Hindu population. A team of Balinese sculptors led by I Nyoman Sudarwa created the statue in three parts—upper body, lower body, and the base—and was flown to the US to construct it on site. Saraswati is depicted very traditionally with a serene countenance. Her four arms symbolize her presence in the physical (front arms) and spiritual (back arms) worlds. Her four hands denote the elements of the human personality in learning: *manas* (mind), *buddhi* (intellect), *chitta* (alertness), and *ahankara* (ego). Her rear hands hold a book and a mala (prayer beads) while her front hands are for holding and playing the *veena*, a sitar-like instrument. The goose at her feet, with its outstretched wings, represents her *vahana* (vehicle) and the unfolding white lotus on which they all emerge signifies Supreme Knowledge.

On a meditative park triangle, just blocks away, another revered Hindu figure stands, that of Mohandas K. Gandhi. The larger-than-life statue of the beloved Mahatma in full stride fronts the Embassy of India at 2107 Massachusetts Avenue.

MANSION ON O STREET

⓮

2020 O Street NW
• omansion.com
• 202-496-2020
• Open: visit the website for hours
• Admission: varies; visit the website
• Metro: Red Line to Dupont Circle

A hotel-event space-museum with thirty-two concealed doorways

Crossing the threshold of the adjoining properties which comprise the Mansion on O Street, you enter a mercantile fever dream, a zany romp through a multihyphenate dreamscape from the mind of an eccentric auntie. Here, the founder and inveterate dreamer H.H. Leonards Spero has merged the industries of hospitality, dining, art, and music into a hotel-event space-museum of stylistic diversity. With its mix of brows high and low, secret passages to discover, quirky bequests and everything-that's-not-nailed-down-is-for-sale shopping makes for an intergenerational good time.

Since purchasing in 1980 the first of four interconnected Dupont Circle townhouses and building a fifth, Spero has expanded a small bed-and-breakfast into a private social club, corporate and private event space, museum and non-profit foundation. With the exception of the Gibson guitar collection signed and donated by various guitar greats, just about everything contained within the five conjoined buildings can be purchased; from antique treasures to almost every tchotchke and trinket in between. The sacred and the silly mingle without irony, ecclesiastical art alongside long-forgotten vinyl recordings of the 1980s. A random neon bright 12-inch from one-hit wonder Nolan Thomas drew this explorer's eye to a secret door (one of seven discovered that day). On the other side, presiding unexpectedly and somewhat ominously over a hidden staircase, a looming Madonna and Child *santos* figure, pictured here.

One visitor, Chris Halliday loves the active engagement: "Unlike so many museums in DC that want you to keep your distance, O Street encourages you to explore, interact with, and even acquire their unique artifacts." Guests in search of secret doors are welcome to roam the buildings and open any doors they come across unless signage or security staff commands otherwise.

With the myriad twists, turns and passages both lateral and vertical, it is easy to lose track of what floor and even which building you are in as you seek out the venue's thirty-two concealed doorways. But what fun to go deeper into the rabbit hole; perhaps have high tea with a mad hatter while you're there.

HEURICH HOUSE MUSEUM ⑮

1307 New Hampshire Avenue NW
• heurichhouse.org
• 202-429-1894
• Open: guided tours only; public tours Thursday to Saturday; reserve online; private tours for ten or more by appointment only; email reservations@heurichhouse.com
• Admission: $5.00 per person ($3.00 for National Trust members)
• Metro: Red Line to Dupont Circle or Circulator bus Dupont Circle-Georgetown route to 19th Street and N Street NW

> *The pyrophobe's palace*

Southwest of Dupont Circle, visionary entrepreneur Christian Heurich's Gilded Age mansion stands today largely intact as it was when the German-born brewing magnate lived there over a century ago. Known as the "Brewmaster's Castle," the stately thirty-one-room residence was a model of 1892 innovation with an array of features from full indoor plumbing and circulating hot water heat to a pneumatic intercom system and combination gas and electric lighting fixtures.

Erected in reinforced steel and poured concrete, it was the first fireproof residence in the city. Though it has seventeen fully functional fireplaces, none were ever lit, as Herr Heurich had an intense but justifiable fear of fire. Two of his breweries and a prior home had burned down. A salamander, known in the folklore of various cultures as impervious to flame, rendered in copper tops the tower. Fireproofing measures were taken throughout the house from the grand staircase to the pocket doors. Even the wall treatment, which appears like flocked velvet, is actually sand-dipped (thus fire-resistant) painted embossed paper.

The home is filled with intricately hand carved woodwork by German craftsmen, most notably in the dining room and the beer baron's wonderful *bierstube,* or "beer hall," where he'd play a round of cards and hoist his stein until his teetotaling wife repurposed it as a breakfast room. Though the forward-thinking Heurich installed an elevator shaft in the four-story building, he vowed not to add an elevator as long as he could still climb the stairs. He climbed those stairs and ran his super successful brewery until his death in 1945 at age 102.

Preserved today as the Heurich House Museum, the house offers a fascinating glimpse of late-Victorian luxury. Not bad for an immigrant who arrived on these shores with $200 and became Washington's largest private employer and second largest landowner after the government.

MRS. HEURICH'S FATE-TRICKING DINNER GUEST

The superstitious Mrs. Heurich kept Michael, a porcelain-faced doll at the ready on the credenza. Should the number of guests in attendance at dinner ever be the unlucky number thirteen, Michael could restore a favorable balance as a seat filler.

HOUSE OF THE TEMPLE OF THE SCOTTISH RITE ⑯

Headquarters of the Supreme Council, 33°
Scottish Rite of Freemasonry, Southern Jurisdiction, USA
1733 16th Street NW
• scottishrite.org • 202-232-3579
• Open: Monday to Friday; June to August 9 am – 4 pm; September to May
10 am – 4 pm; closed federal holidays • Admission: free
• Metro: Green or Yellow Line to U Street; Red Line to Dupont Circle;
a 10- to 15-minute walk from either station

> **The jewel in the crown of Washington's many Masonic buildings**

Crafted solely from stone in the sacred way of the ancient stonemason, the House of the Temple of the Scottish Rite is home to the grandiloquent "Supreme Council (Mother Council of the World) of the Inspectors General Knights Commander of the House of the Temple of Solomon of the Thirty-third degree of the Ancient and Accepted Scottish Rite of Freemasonry of the Southern Jurisdiction of the United States of America." Solid and majestic, this is the jewel in the crown of Washington's many Masonic buildings.

Arousing awe in some and suspicion in others, it beguiles with its magnificence and confounds with its curiosities. Masonic symbols abound, imbued with cryptic meaning. The granite stairs to the elevated edifice rise in groups of three, five, seven, and nine. Monumental sphinxes of power and wisdom carved in situ flank the entrance. The number thirty-three, the highest degree of the Scottish Rite, features prominently. Thirty-three Ionic columns each of 33 feet encircle the building while as many bulbs ring each chandelier. Prevalent throughout is the double-headed eagle, emblem of the Rite. A marble table at the entry bearing the eagle motif is inscribed with the Latin, *Salve Frater*, "Welcome, Brother." And welcoming they are, with a friendly transparency not only to the brotherhood, but the general public. Opened to great ado in 1915, the John Russell Pope-designed building is inspired by one of the Seven Wonders of the Ancient World, the Tomb of Mausolus at Halicarnassus, from which we derive the word "mausoleum." Turns out, this monument to Freemasonry also serves as one. Circumventing city burial law by special Acts of Congress, Sovereign Grand Commanders Albert Pike, and later John Henry Cowles, are entombed "upright," as the tour guide tells us, "6-feet-deep" behind the walls.

A grand circular staircase leads to a lone chair for the Tyler, a ceremonial sword-bearing sentinel who guards the Temple Room during biennial sessions of the Supreme Council. Upon entering the room whose view is obscured by the back of an immense organ console, the first thing you see is a surprisingly mundane water cooler. But the grandeur is soon revealed. A domed skylight soars 100 feet above sacred books of several religions atop a marble altar (a central tenet of Freemasonry is a belief in a supreme being). Looming thirty-three-paned windows ombre upward from grilles of coiling snakes and darkened glass to clarity, evoking the Masonic motto *Ordo ab Chao*, "Order out of Chaos."

Find more on Masonic Washington and the icons of North American Freemasonry on the following double pages.

WASHINGTON: A CITY DESIGNED ON THE MASONIC PRINCIPLES OF THE CITY OF LISBON

The eponymous city founded by George Washington in 1791, from his neighborhood of Georgetown, was designed largely by French-born American Pierre Charles L'Enfant (Anet, France, August 9, 1754—Prince George's County, Maryland, June 14, 1825), a reputable architect and civil engineer initiated into Freemasonry at New York City's Holland Lodge No. 8. L'Enfant's plan was original in that it emulated the Pombaline Baixa district of Lisbon, rebuilt after the 1755 earthquake. Just as the lower town of the Portuguese capital is formed by a grid of streets laid out on either side of the main thoroughfare of Rua Augusta, in Washington the Capitol is the center of the city. Diagonal avenues intersect streets that, unlike the avenues, were designed to meet at right angles, and the intersections are marked by circles. In the same way that Lisbon's Baixa ends at the Praça do Comercio, Washington has a huge National Mall designed by the French architect. As in downtown Lisbon, the plan of Washington obeys the Masonic canons of sacred geometry, where the relationship between its main buildings and monuments suggests geometric shapes such as the set square (allegory of the Sacred Space), compass (allegory of Sacred Time), ruler (Rectitude), and the Masonic triangle (Perfect Delta). The hexagram and the pentagram are also found in the urban plan (see above). A closer look at the city map also reveals that the Capitol is round, symbolizing the upper part of the compass, which was originally circular. Pennsylvania Avenue, which connects the Capitol to the White House, represents one leg of the compass. Maryland Avenue, between the Capitol and the Thomas Jefferson Memorial, forms the second leg, even if in this case a ruler is needed to draw a line to get the effect because Maryland

Avenue is not perfectly straight, though it heads in the general direction of the Jefferson Memorial. The ensemble forms the Masonic compass.

The Masonic set square begins on Union Square, with Louisiana Avenue representing the first arm and Washington Avenue the second. A ruler is again needed to join up Louisiana and Washington Avenues to see the square emerge, as Louisiana Avenue ends on Pennsylvania, and Washington Avenue on Maryland, so the 90 degree angle is not complete. But by plotting the natural line of these avenues past their end points, the angle of the square is perfect.

The ruler is clearly visible when you draw a straight line from north to south (the city's cardo) from the center of the White House to the base of the Washington Monument, then to the east, toward the Capitol. In this way, the layout of the streets of Washington represents the three sacred symbols of Initiatory Freemasonry.

The Masonic Triangle is formed by the imaginary lines that connect the Capitol, the White House, and the Jefferson Memorial. The Eye of Divine Providence is represented by the Washington Monument, an obelisk lit up at the top; it is the city's tallest structure, rising to over 555 feet.

The lines of the initiation Pentagram are drawn on the map from Logan Circle, from which Rhode Island and Vermont Avenues branch off. They connect with Dupont Circle, where Massachusetts and Connecticut Avenues begin. This is the horizontal line along K Street (the decumanus or east—west road), the peak of the pentagram (five-pointed star) being represented by the White House.

The lines of the Hexagram of Enlightenment (six-pointed star) are traced from Dupont Circle, from which Massachusetts Avenue and 19th Street branch off. Together with Pennsylvania and New York Avenues, these form two interlaced triangles, i.e. a hexagram; the White House is located precisely at the lowest point where the triangles join.

All these are lines of force drawn up to make the city of Washington

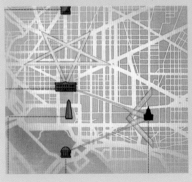

a great Domus Libero Muratori Illuminati, the Headquarters of Enlightened Master Masons, by Knowledge and Morality. Thus the metropolis is dedicated to the greater glory of the Supreme Architect of the Universe, the Divinity presiding over everything and everyone.

ICONS OF NORTH AMERICAN FREEMASONRY

George Washington, "Father of the Country," and Freemason

George Washington (February 22, 1732—December 14, 1799), first president of the United States of America selected the mid-Atlantic region astride Northern and Southern boundaries as the locale for the new Federal District. On the day that George Washington acceded to the presidency, the Bible used for his oath was that of St. John's Masonic Lodge, New York, at the time when he was a worshipful member of the Alexandria Lodge in Virginia. It can legitimately be claimed that the York Rite of Scottish Masonry played an active role in the founding of the nation and the development of its magna carta, the guarantor of national independence which is the Constitution. Thus the main role of "Father of the Nation" ended up in the hands of a high-ranking Master Mason.

George Washington was initiated into Freemasonry on November 4, 1752 for the fee of two pounds and three shillings. He then received the Elevation on March 3, 1753 at the Fredericksburg Lodge before attaining the rank of Master on August 4, 1753. It is assumed that he was the first Worshipful Master of the Alexandria Lodge No. 22 because his name heads the list of members of the Commission who were recipients of the letter ratifying the US Constitution in 1788. In addition to having made his presidential oath on a Masonic Bible before Minister Robert Livingston, Grand Master of the Grand Lodge of New York, he promoted the building of the Capitol. At the foundation stone ceremony on September 18, 1793, he even wore the insignia of Worshipful Master of Honor.

Albert Pike, game changer of American Freemasonry

Albert Pike (Boston, December 29, 1809—Washington, April 2, 1891) showed his intellectual and especially his spiritual brilliance from an early age. He was a poet and essayist who spoke sixteen languages, so his biographers say, and joined the Freemasons around 1840. In 1859 he was elected Sovereign Grand Commander of the Scottish Rite (Southern Jurisdiction), a charge of the 33rd degree, where he remained for the rest of his life, devoting much of his time to the study and development of the degrees and rituals of the Masonic Order.

In 1871, he created a sensation by publishing the book *Morals and Dogma of the Ancient and Accepted Scottish Rite of Freemasonry*, in which he built up the philosophical, historical, political, symbolic, and religious foundations of the Ancient and Accepted Scottish Rite. He developed the teachings of the 33 degrees, explaining the symbolism and allegory in light of his own understanding. This is a monumental work both in length and the extent of its teachings: 861 pages of morals and dogma, plus a reference section of 218 pages, in total thirty-two chapters discussing in detail the philosophical symbolism of each Masonic degree.

ALBERT GALLATIN MACKEY, CHRONICLER OF MASONIC SYMBOLISM

Albert Gallatin Mackey (1807—1881), a celebrated North American Masonic writer, confirmed that Washington was initiated during the war with France, at Military Lodge No. 227 of the 46th regiment. But for some reason Mackey does not cite the most important of George Washington's Masonic elevations: that of having as sponsor and occult advisor a Spiritual Master from the mysterious "Supreme Fountain of the World," such as the hidden Eastern kingdoms of Shamballah or Agharta, with many similarities to the Kingdom of Prester John of the Templars and medieval Hermetists.

According to Robert Allen Campbell's treatise *Our Flag* (Chicago, 1890), in 1755, when the founders of the nascent Republic were studying the proposed designs for the new flag, a strange man appeared, a kind of Count of St. Germain, a courtier banished from France to America where he traveled between what is now the city of Washington and the state of New Mexico. The stranger was said to be the owner of the Hacienda Del Destierro, at El Moro near Cimarron, and immediately won the respect and friendship of Benjamin Franklin and George Washington. This mysterious character, who in contemporary memoirs is simply known as the "Professor," was apparently over 70 years old but as vigorous as a young man. Tall and very dignified in appearance, he spoke with a tone combining authority and great courtesy. Like the Count of St. Germain, the Professor frequently talked of historical events as if he had been there himself. Then one day he suddenly disappeared.

Without a doubt the enigmatic Professor, along with Masonic morality, positively and irreversibly influenced George Washington's qualities and behavior, both spiritually and politically. In his farewell to the presidency speech in 1797, Washington called for a civic spirit and warned against party rule and involvement in external conflicts, reaffirming the separation of powers between Church and State. As one of the first to speak of religious tolerance and freedom of worship, he is noted for forbidding his troops to demonstrate anti-Catholic feelings when burning the effigy of the Pope on Guy Fawkes night 1775. When hiring laborers for his home at Mount Vernon, he wrote to his agent: "If they are good workers, they can come from Asia, Africa or Europe, they can be Muslim, Jewish, Christian or of any sect; they can even be atheists." In 1770, in reply to a letter from the Touro Synagogue, he insisted that as long as people behaved like good citizens, they wouldn't be persecuted for their beliefs or religion. This was a huge relief to the US Jewish community, as Jews had suffered discrimination and exile from many European countries.

PRINCE HALL, "FATHER OF BLACK FREEMASONRY"

Alluring to a group of fifteen 18th-century free black men in Boston were Freemasonry's ideals of liberty, equality, and peace. Among them, Revolutionary War veteran Prince Hall led their petition to initiation into Boston's all-white St. John's Lodge. Rejected they appealed to and were accepted by Irish Constitution Military Lodge No. 441 at Boston Harbor. Initiated on March 6, 1775, they would be granted authority to meet as African Lodge #1 in 1776. Warranted for Charter from the Grand Lodge of England in 1784, they formed African Lodge #459.

Prince Hall was appointed a Provincial Grand Master by H.R.H., the Prince of Wales in 1791, the year the first boundary stones were laid to mark the bounds of the new Federal City.

Upon Prince Hall's 1807 death, the Masonic organization was renamed in his honor. By 1923, Prince Hall Masons of the Washington DC area had raised funds to erect a temple at 1000 U Street; the first black Masonic order organized south of the Mason-Dixon line. Designed by African-American architect Albert Cassell, The Most Worshipful Prince Hall Grand Lodge remains today just above the U Street Metro. Prince Hall affiliated Freemasons have included WEB DuBois, Garrett A. Morgan, Sr., traffic signal inventor, Alexander Pushkin, Duke Ellington, Thurgood Marshall, A. Philip Randolph, DC "Mayor for Life," Marion Barry, and even Richard Pryor..

EGYPT ON THE POTOMAC

Cultural historian Anthony Browder conducts a study tour of the District, decoding the symbols that proliferate in the Masonic influence on the Nation's Capital. The 3-hour field trip explores how the American founding fathers interwove aspects of Nile Valley symbolism and philosophy into the burgeoning young nation. It uncovers "secrets hidden in plain sight," such as the Egyptian symbol Heru Bedhet, ("Know Thyself") which appears in the Washington Monument and once topped the entrance of every Egyptian temple in antiquity.

GRIFFITH STADIUM SINKS

Nellie's Sports Bar
900 U Street NW
• nelliessportsbar.com
• 202-332-NELL
• Open: Monday to Thursday 5 pm – 1 am; Friday 3 pm – 3 am; Saturday 10:30 am – 3 am; Sunday 10:30 am – 1 am
• Metro: Green or Yellow Line to U Street/African-American Civil War Memorial/Cardozo

Storied locale

A t the intersection of Ninth and U Streets, Northwest, a confluence of histories emerges at Nellie's Sports Bar. Just blocks away is Howard University Hospital, site of historic Griffith Stadium. Home to Washington baseball from 1911 to 1965, both the Major League team, the Senators and the Negro League team, the Homestead Grays played in the ballpark. It served also as the home stadium to the Washington Redskins for twenty-four seasons of NFL football. In homage to local sports history and in keeping with the bar's athletics theme, basins salvaged from the 1966 demolition of the beloved stadium are installed in the bathroom. Before kicking back a cold brew and a frankfurter, Nellie's patrons can wash their hands from the same faucets as legions of Griffith spectators before them.

Welcoming to all while catering to a gay clientele, Nellie's hosts sports-related events daily and a weekly drag brunch. The multilevel watering hole is punctuated throughout with memorabilia from retro sports equipment to college pennants. Fringed below one of the many wall-mounted flatscreen televisions is a collection of vintage fraternity paddles. Looming above the stately bar in Victorian glory are larger-than-life photographs of the two Nellies for whom the venue is named—the socialite great and great-great grandmothers of owner Douglas Schantz.

A LOCALE ON THE AFRICAN-AMERICAN HERITAGE TRAIL

It is fitting that photographic portraits would be a focal point of the space. 900 U Street was from 1911 to 1983 the home of Scurlock Studio and the gateway to historic "Black Broadway." Addison Scurlock was the preeminent photographer (along with his sons Robert and George) of African-American life in the District for the greater part of the 20th century. His photographs chronicle the aspirations of the black elite. To be photographed by Scurlock was a mark of status. To have one's portrait featured in the studio window was an honor. The site is marked with an informative plaque from Cultural Tourism DC.

The Scurlock Studio signage is housed in the collection of the Smithsonian National Museum of African American History and Culture.

AFRICAN AMERICAN CIVIL WAR MUSEUM ⓲

1925 Vermont Avenue NW
- Open: Mon—Fri 10am—6:30pm; Saturday 10am—4pm;
Sunday noon—4pm
- Free entry; donation appreciated
- Tel: 202-667-2667
- www.afroamcivilwar.org
- Metro: Green or Yellow Line to U Street/Afr Am Civil War Memorial/
Cardozo

Sic Semper Tyrannis

Making the ascent from the Vermont Avenue exit of the U Street Metro station, the eyes fall upon *The Spirit of Freedom*, a bronze sculpture by Ed Hamilton commemorating the 209,145 African American soldiers and sailors — their names inscribed on the surrounding wall of honor — who served the Union cause in the Civil War.

Directly across the street, tucked behind the historic Grimke School, stands the African American Civil War Museum with the mission to interpret the little-known history of the U.S. Colored Troops — motto, *Sic Semper Tyrannis*

— their decisive role in the war and the legacy of these valorous servicemen.

Comprising only one per cent of the Northern population when Congress passed the Militia Act of 1862, allowing free men of color into the armed forces, men of African descent became 10 per cent of the Union Army and an astonishing 25 per cent of its Navy after emancipation allowed the formerly enslaved also to join.

Having fought in every major campaign and battle during the last two years of the war, USCT regiments earned 25 Medals of Honor. In 1865, President Abraham Lincoln declared that, "Without the military help of the black freedmen, the war against the South could not have been won."

Fittingly, the museum resides away from the city's museum hub, in the U Street corridor — an area with a historic African American presence since the establishment of "contraband" camps there just after the war's end, where communities grew and flourished through Reconstruction and beyond.

The USCT were the precursors to the famed Buffalo Soldiers, the 25th U.S. Infantry Regiment that served from 1866—1946. Each Memorial Day, members from chapters of the Buffalo Soldiers Motorcycle Club nationwide make the Buffalo Thunder Memorial Ride en masse to pay tribute at the memorial statue. Civil War re-enactors conduct a commemorative presentation and lay a wreath on site.

CAPITAL POOL CHECKERS CLUB ⓳

813 S Street NW
- Open: Hours vary, call
- Entry fee: $3 donation is appreciated
- Tel: 202-234-5328
- Metro: Green or Yellow Line to Shaw/Howard U

For the love of the game, a bastion of old Shaw

A city-sanctioned mural of a gentleman playing checkers draws the eye to the otherwise nondescript Capital Pool Checkers Club. Like the celebrated Russian game *shashki*, pool checkers is a variation on standard checkers that allows movement in all directions for more dynamic play. The club, just blocks from the barbershop where it all started, is the members' one-room storefront sanctum. A stilled-in-time glimpse of pre-revitalization Shaw.

For over thirty years they have convened to an R&B soundtrack, punctuated by the staccato clatter of marbled resin game pieces against handmade wooden checkerboards and considerable trash talking. Charles "King of Hams" Johnson laughs that a *ham* is slang for a checkers novice, "Like everybody you see in here except me." Genial ribbing aside, the men also give each other proper credit for their unique abilities, evidenced in their checker handles.

Members include the lead singer of legendary gospel group The Highway Q.C.'s, Spencer "Chicago" Taylor; mathematician Oliver "The Stealer" Griffin; former stockbroker Tal "The Razor" Roberts, the club's president; and Freddie "The Hawk" Owens, a janitor from Baltimore who ranks in the top ten of the Top Master division of the American Pool Checker Association — its highest division. All sing his praises.

Club president Roberts shares that a "Freddie Owens move" is synonymous with brilliant play. Without a hint of braggadocio, the humble Owens quietly wins a round against the much younger Mike "Boy Wonder" Weaver. "If you ask me, Freddie's the best teacher in the country," Weaver says. "He was a ham too, 'til he learned his ABCs," chimes in Taylor, the wry, eldest member, who says the game "keeps the mind strong." Each touts the cerebral nature of checkers, deceptive in its simplicity. "It's a game of thought," Griffin says. "And it's all on you. You get all the blame if you lose, but all the accolades if you win."

Having done outreach with the kids of Perry Street Prep, Donald "Pressure Man" Cunningham hopes to empower even more of the city's children, seniors and the autistic with this underrated game of logic.

Frederick Douglass is reputed to have made the checkers set that still sits in the parlor of his home, Cedar Hill. (pg. 248)

CRISPUS ATTUCKS PARK

⑳

Bounded by the unit blocks of U and V Streets and the
2000 blocks of First and North Capitol Streets NW
• Open: 5 am—10 pm
• Tel: 202-546-8412
• www.crispusattucksparkdc.org
• Metro: 80 Bus to North Capitol Street and Rhode Island Avenue (80 bus
services Red Line Metro stations Fort Totten, Brookland, Union Station,
Gallery Place (also Yellow and Green) and McPherson Square (Blue,
Orange and Silver)

A community vision realized in Bloomingdale

A vision of landscaped loveliness, the humble Crispus Attucks Park isn't one you stumble upon, unless happenstance has you wandering the alleyways of Bloomingdale just west of bustling North Capitol Street. But what a delightful discovery it is, both for its oasis of green and the grassroots activism that willed it into existence.

Named for the first person killed in the Boston Massacre (a contributing factor to the Revolutionary War), its decades-long metamorphosis, from a disused telephone switching station to a 1970s—80s community center and museum to today's community owned, managed and lovingly tended secret garden, attests to the power of the everyday citizen in community organizing.

In the late 1960s, Chesapeake & Potomac Telephone Company (C&P) ceased operations at the 8,275 square foot building they'd occupied since 1910 and abandoned the site. Nearly a decade later, neighbors successfully lobbied C&P to convey the neglected 1.06 acre property for use as a community center. With a pro-bono building renovation and programming targeted largely at local youth, the center, under the auspices of the nonprofit Crispus Attucks Development Corporation (CADC), began operation in 1978 and eventually became the Crispus Attucks Museum and Park of the Arts (CAMPA).

Stripped of needed funding by citywide budget cuts in 1987, the once vibrant center languished until a fire in July 1990 gutted the building. The alley complex became a dumping ground for illegal construction debris and abandoned cars, a squat for the homeless and an incubator for illicit activity.

Once again the community rallied to improve the lot. In July 1995, DC Police cleared it of trespassers and unauthorized vehicles. The following September, the Embassy of Australia, in their "Clean Up the World" initiative, sent fifty employees to help CAMPA neighbors seal the blighted building, clean the park and plant trees. This reclamation of the park led homeowners to re-envision the space as an urban respite and they labored to break up the asphalt, only to learn that the DC Government had foreclosed on the property in 1998. With help from the American University Center of Law, CADC had the foreclosure dismissed and has since endeavored — in the spirit of cooperation — to maintain a publicly accessible private park.

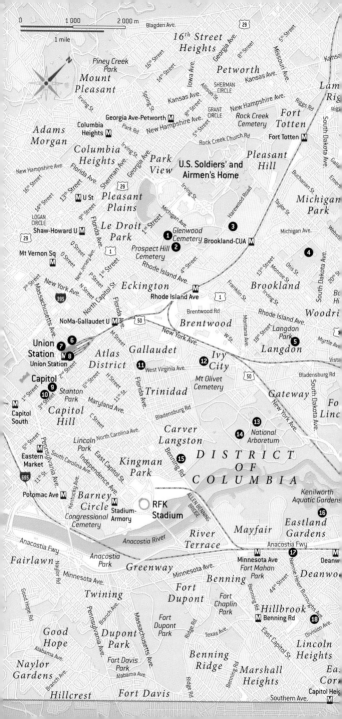

NORTHEAST

MICROSHOWCASE

❶

21 Evarts Place NE
- microshowcase.com
- Open: visit the website for tour dates
- Metro: 80 Metrobus stops at North Capitol and Evarts Streets

Tiny structures, big possibilities

I n the Northeast neighborhood of Stronghold wedged between the alleys of Evarts Street and Glenwood Cemetery, a slim, triangular plot signaled possibility to Brian Levy, who purchased it in March 2012. He set about transforming the 1/12th-acre lot of broken concrete and overgrown grass into a model of affordable, minimal, green living. An early incarnation of the space with four micro houses was called Boneyard Studios after its proximity to the graveyard. Now MicroShowcase, the evolving community features a tiny house built by the students of DC Academy of Construction and Design, a fruit orchard, flower, herb and veggie gardens, a studio shed and Levy's own Minim House to demonstrate the feasibility of small living in the urban environment. An apiary is in the works as well as a storage Quonset hut.

Current DC zoning prohibits habitable foundation-built dwellings in alleys under 30 feet wide, so Minim rests on a trailer. MicroShowcase proves that scaling back need not feel like deprivation, but rather liberation from excess. It squashes the notion that mobile homes and great design are mutually exclusive. *Minim House* brilliantly epitomizes this point. With 210 square feet of interior space, it is a beautiful powerhouse of multifunctional efficiency. When unbolted from its trailer *Minim* can be installed as a foundation home. The galley kitchen stovetop, when covered doubles as counter space. Foot pedals control and conserve sink water. With nesting stools and a sofa, the house seats ten comfortably. A wall window with the shade drawn is the perfect aspect ratio for projecting movies, 16:9. The queen bed rolls out from beneath the office platform. A closet provides ample storage. Shelving holds 150 books. A self-sustaining rainwater treatment system provides water. Solar power provides air conditioning and hot showers. A wet bath has an incinerator toilet. Propane heat and LED lights keep things warm and bright.

NEARBY

BRUMIDI GRAVESITE

Just across the cemetery wall are the modest graves of the Constantino Brumidi family. The "Michelangelo of Washington" is celebrated for his grand 19th-century frescoes, most notably *The Apotheosis of Washington* in the US Capitol dome.

BENJAMIN GRENUP MONUMENT

❷

Glenwood Cemetery, Section D
2219 Lincoln Road NE
- www.theglenwoodcemetery.com
- 202-667-1016
- Open: 6 am – 8 pm, 365 days a year
- Metro: Red Line to Brookland - CUA; transfer to G8 bus

Tribute to a fallen firefighter

O n the night of May 6, 1856, the all-volunteer Columbia Engine Company No. 1 in Capitol Hill responded to an alarm from the Shreeves Stables. As the brothers of Columbia No. 1 ran with their fine rosewood hand engine to douse the flames on 7th Street, 24-year-old firefighter Benjamin C. Grenup, was tragically crushed beneath the wheels of the engine in a collision with a lamppost on Pennsylvania Avenue.

The fraternal order of which he was a proud member honored his sacrifice in grand gesture. No modest headstone would mark their fallen brother's Glenwood Cemetery grave. In 1858, stone carver Charles Rousseau erected a monumental marble obelisk with memorial reliefs on each side of the square base, the most poignant (as well as morbid) of which depicts Grenup's demise. The inscription reads in part: "To perpetuate the memory and noble deeds of a gallant fireman, a truer, nobler, trustier heart, more loving or more loyal never beat within a human breast." Cordoned off by iron fencing transferred from the firehouse, the triangular plot is punctuated by red fireplugs at each corner.

In a time-honored tradition, rookies from DCFD Engine Company #3 (formerly Columbia Engine No. 1) make an annual memorial pilgrimage by fire truck to Grenup's grave, as he was believed for many years to be the first DC firefighter to die in the line of duty. That is until the story of an earlier fatality surfaced in 2010. John G. Anderson, of the Western Hose Company in Georgetown was killed on March 11, 1856, two months before Grenup. His remains now rest in an unmarked grave in Oak Hill Cemetery; its tombstone lost to the ages.

James Embrey of the DC Fire and EMS Museum (see page 75) speculates in a January 15, 2011 *Washington Post* article that in history's annals Grenup's grand obelisk for service to affluent Capitol Hill trumped the less-than-monumental grave of Anderson, who served then-impoverished Georgetown. Yet a quote unearthed from the 1856 *Washington Evening Star* article on his funeral suggests that Anderson's was not the first line-of-duty death either: "as such a casualty has not occurred for a long time, there will doubtless be a general turnout of the Fire Department."

SAINT
KATERI TEKAKWITHA

SAINT KATERI STATUE ❸

Basilica of the National Shrine of the Immaculate Conception
400 Michigan Avenue NE
- www.nationalshrine.com
- 202.526.8300
- Open: daily, year-round; April 1 to October 31, 7 am – 7 pm; November 1 to March 31, 7 am – 6 pm; check website for guided tour schedule
- Metro: Red Line to Brookland - CUA

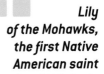

Lily of the Mohawks, the first Native American saint

In 1946, naturalized US citizen Francis Xavier Cabrini became the first American canonized as a Roman Catholic saint (see *Secret New York: An Unusual Guide* in this series). In 1975, Elizabeth Ann Seton's canonization made her the first US-born saint. It wasn't until 2012 that the 17th-century indigenous woman Kateri became the first Native American saint. Together the three are enshrined in the statuary of the Basilica of the National Shrine. Crafted in Vermont marble by Dale Lamphere, the St. Kateri sculpture is a gift of the Bureau of Catholic Indian Missions.

Kateri Tekawitha's epic path to sainthood began with her 1656 birth to a Mohawk father and an Algonquin Christian mother in what is now upstate New York. She alone survived the scourge of smallpox that killed her parents and younger brother in 1660. Her pockmarked face bore the ravages of the disease; her eyesight was greatly impaired. What she lacked in visual acuity she gained in spiritual clarity. She learned and honored the traditions of her Mohawk roots, yet felt an early call to the life of the devout. Some believe that there was a syncretic union in her practice of Catholicism and the belief systems of her Iroquois heritage.

Her family, suspect of the colonizers who introduced smallpox to the region and burned down their village when she was 10, dissuaded Tekawitha from interaction with Jesuit missionaries spreading the Christian gospel. Steadfast in her faith, she was baptized on Easter Sunday 1676, accorded the name Catherine and called "Kateri," the Iroquois pronunciation. Scorned and threatened by villagers opposed to Christianity, she eventually exiled to the nearby Mission of St. Francis Xavier, a settlement of Christian "Indians" in Canada. She served the sick and elderly, taught prayers to the children and performed harsh acts of penance believed to be responsible for her early demise on April 17, 1680. Claude Chauchetière, the priest at her deathbed, claimed that her last words were "Jesus, Mary, I love you," and that, upon her passing, the disfiguring smallpox scars vanished from her face, leaving her unblemished and radiant, "the Lily of the Mohawks."

Fr. Chauchetière began praying over the ill with her relics, healing them, he believed. Kateri was venerated by Pope Pius XII on January 3, 1943, beatified by Pope John Paul II on June 22, 1980, and finally canonized by Pope Benedict XVI on October 21, 2012. After thorough investigation of the 2006 spontaneous healing of young Jake Finkbonner from necrotizing *Streptococcus A*, the Vatican declared it a miracle of Kateri's intercession.

THE FRANCISCAN MONASTERY OF THE HOLY ❹ LAND IN AMERICA

Mount Saint Sepulchre
1400 Quincy Street NE
• myfranciscan.org
• 202-526-6800
• Tour hours: Monday to Saturday 10 am, 11 am, 1 pm, 2 pm, 3 pm; Sunday 1 pm, 2 pm, 3 pm
• Admission: free, donations appreciated
• Metro: Red Line to Brookland-CUA, then 15-minute walk or H6 bus toward Fort Lincoln

Holy theme park of the Catholic faith

Anchored by the Basilica of the National Shrine of the Immaculate Conception and the Catholic University of America, the Northeast neighborhood of Brookland boasts the largest concentration of Catholic institutions in the world, second only to the Vatican. Cloistered on a hilltop east of the university sits Mount St. Sepulchre, the monastic home of the guardians of the Holy Land.

Established in 1897, this DC monastery of the ancient order of Franciscans once housed six pioneering friars in a rat-infested, abandoned residence. Founding friar, Fr. Godfrey sold 2½ by 5 inch "building bricks" of paper containing a medal of St. Anthony of Padua for 10 cents each to fund the year-long construction of a new building. Today it is endowed with faithful replicas of the Lourdes grotto; of Holy Land shrines, making the devotional experience possible in Washington for those unable to make a pilgrimage to Palestine; and the early Christian catacombs of Rome with exacting reproductions of the original frescoes lining the narrow passages.

Entombed in crypts below the main church are the remains of two saints originally interred in Rome: St. Benignus, and the child whose Latin burial inscription translates as "innocent resting in peace." Martyred by the Romans in the early 2nd century and canonized as St. Innocentius, he lies in repose encased in a glass reliquary; his skull covered by a wax mask of tranquil expression, his mummified hands wrapped in gold mesh.

Our tour was led by a jovial Friar who referring to his monastic vows of poverty, chastity and obedience quipped, "No money, no honey and no say!" As we made the catacomb descent, a young woman declared in all sincerity, "This is great! A holy theme park for Catholics."

FOR A SPIRITUAL RETREAT

In stark contrast to the Byzantine Revival architecture of the monastery sits a simple retreat space, the Hermitage. The modernist structure is designed by students from the School of Architecture at the Catholic University and oriented east toward Jerusalem. Secluded in a wooded glade, it invites quiet and solitary contemplation. Featuring a bed, bath, kitchenette, and washer/dryer, it is available for 1-7 days of single occupancy.

CHUCK BROWN MEMORIAL ⑤

Langdon Park
2901 20th Street NE at Franklin Street

"Wind me up, Chuck!"

An icon of DC culture, Charles Louis "Chuck" Brown was celebrated as a "legend of Washington music" — along with the late "March King" John Philip Sousa and jazz maestro Duke Ellington — by the National Symphony Orchestra (NSO) at their annual Labor Day concert on the Capitol lawn in 2011.

Go-Go, with its distinctive funk-derived percussive sound, call-and-response interactivity, and reliance on live instrumentation, is a homegrown music genre and Brown one of its pioneers. After joining the orchestra on the evening's bill for symphonic arrangements of some of his hits, Brown and his band, The Soul Searchers, closed the show. Eight months later, the "Godfather of Go-Go" passed away. On August 22, 2014 — what would have been Brown's 78th birthday — friends, family, and fans gathered despite rain for the dedication of the Chuck Brown Memorial at the 20th and Franklin Street section of Northeast's Langdon Park.

"Wind Me Up, Chuck!" — a catchphrase chanted at Brown's concerts, gives Jackie Braitman's interactive memorial its title. At the entrance of the park, the abstract sculpture features a 16 foot louvered representation of

the performer, guitar in hand, extending the mic to his audience. Motion sensors trigger multicolored flashing lights when a visitor enters the sculpture platform. Synchronized to the rhythm of "Chuck Baby," a popular Brown line-dance track, four large lights at the back of the "stage" represent four descending notes played by a trombone eight seconds into the song.

Nestled in a crape myrtle grove, the guitar pick-shaped plaza by Marshall Moya Design features a curved wall inscribed with a timeline of Brown's life and legacy, complete with photo highlights throughout, including legendary Globe promotional posters.

Around town, Brown's visage appears on a few murals, including an exterior wall of Ben's Chili Bowl. The 1900 block of 7th Street NW, where he once shined shoes in front of the Howard Theatre, is christened Chuck Brown Way in tribute. His 1973 ES-335 Gibson guitar (dubbed "Blondie" for its light wood body) and its fuchsia velvet-lined case are in the collection of the Anacostia Museum (see pg. 245)

NEARBY:

Overlooking the opposite end of Langdon Park is the Bing Thom-designed Woodridge branch of the DC Public Library, the first DCPL facility with a roof terrace. And a splendid one it is, with outdoor seating, sedum plantings for stormwater runoff, and even DC Punk Archive-sponsored summer concerts, along with the magnificent view. 1801 Hamlin Street NE.

APA GREEN ROOF & LABYRINTH ⑥

10 G Street NE
- apa.org
- 202-336-5519
- Open: Monday to Friday 7 am – 7 pm
- Admission: free
- Metro: Red Line to Union Station

DC's only rooftop labyrinth

Though the word "labyrinth" can evoke terrifying visions of the creepy hedge maze in the film *The Shining*, a true labyrinth, as in the beautiful medieval path at Chartres Cathedral in France, is unicursal—only one path into the center and out again. The ancient, contemplative practice of labyrinth walking is in the midst of a millennial revival in churches, parks, and gardens across the metropolitan area. High above the hubbub of Union Station, though, is the only rooftop labyrinth in the region. With the Capitol dome in full view, the 3,000-square-foot green roof of the American Psychological Association building welcomes the public to enjoy an alfresco oasis.

Fully accessible, the trellised terrace offers ample seating, a few cafe tables and three labyrinths: a paved 42-inch that invites a meditative stroll and two others, of the fingertip variety, which allow for a labyrinth journey without the need to walk.

A project of TKF Foundation, which is committed to funding public green spaces to provide places of sanctuary, the roofscape is true to the TKF creed: open spaces heal mind, body, and spirit. Along with their aesthetic beauty, the wisteria-draped trellises add a functional cooling effect. The neighboring sedum plants mitigate stormwater runoff into local waterways by retaining approximately 45,000 gallons of water on the roof during a typical year of average rainfalls.

The seven-circuit Santa Rosa Labyrinth features a "heart-space on the fourth path which is approached from all directions," says its designer Dr. Lea Goode-Harris. "This gives another dimension of meaning to this meditative labyrinth walk, attention to what matters to the heart. I can't think of a better place to contemplate what really matters in the city that symbolizes what it means to be American."

APA employees are treated to frequent meditation classes on the rooftop, but self-guided labyrinthine journeys are available to all. Access the roof via the center elevator on the right side of the lobby to the penthouse level. Breathe deeply and find your center above the fray.

LABYRINTHS AND THEIR SYMBOLISM

In Greek mythology, one of the first labyrinths was built by Dædalus to enclose the Minotaur, a creature born of the love between Queen Pasiphæ, the wife of King Minos of Crete, and a bull. According to some archæologists, the origin of this myth may lie in the complex plans of the Palace of Minos in Knossos, Crete. Only three people were able to find their way out of the maze: the first was Theseus, who had gone to Crete to kill the beast. Ariadne, daughter of Minos, fell in love with Theseus and gave him a ball of thread so that he could find his way out. Dædalus was also able to escape along with his son Icarus after he was imprisoned in his own labyrinth by Minos. (Some versions say that Minos wanted to prevent Dædalus revealing the plans to this labyrinth, others that Minos wanted to punish him for giving Ariadne the idea of the thread.) It turned out that Dædalus' own design for the labyrinth was so cunning that the only way for him to escape was to fly out using the wings he had made for himself and Icarus from feathers and wax.

Although the Mesopotamian, Egyptian, Hopi, and Navaho civilizations all designed and built labyrinths, there are also examples located in Europe dating from prehistory. Other notable labyrinths built in the Christian era

are to be found in the catacombs of Rome and in the churches of San Michele Maggiore in Pavia, San Savino in Plasencia, and in Lucca (Italy), as well as at Chartres and Reims (France).

These labyrinths tend to face westwards, the direction that evil spirits are said to come from (the west, where the sun sets, represents death). As these evil spirits are believed to advance in a straight line, the labyrinths are designed to trap them before they reach the churches' choir.

The relatively complex symbolism of labyrinths is also linked to the meaning of life, signifying man wandering through the universe, ignorant of where he is coming from or where he is going. At the same time, the centre of the labyrinth represents the safe haven of divine salvation and the heavenly Jerusalem – reached only after a necessary rite of passage that may be painful and tortuous at times. The attainment of this goal is symbolized by the flight of Dædalus and Icarus, which denotes both the elevation of the spirit towards knowledge and of the soul towards God. Ariadne's love for Theseus symbolizes love for another being, the two halves that permit an escape from the absurd human condition.

OWNEY THE POSTAL DOG

❼

National Postal Museum
2 Massachusetts Avenue NE
• postalmuseum.si.edu
• 202-633-5555
• Open: daily 10 am – 5:30 pm; closed December 25
• Admission: free
• Metro: Red Line to Union Station

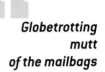

I n the twilight of the 19th century, a postal clerk abandoned a scrappy pup at the Albany, New York Post Office. That employee's identity is lost to history, but the dog went on to international acclaim as

Globetrotting mutt of the mailbags

Owney the Postal Dog, the much-beloved unofficial mascot of the United States Postal Service, in whose memory a stamp was issued in 2011.

He appeared in 1888, milling about the mailbags, sometimes napping on them. Where the bags went, so too went the terrier-mix mutt, first on mail wagons then Railway Post Office trains across the state and ultimately the country. Railway mail clerks welcomed his appearance on their cars as his presence was thought to bestow safe passage; in an era of frequent train wrecks, never did an Owney-toting train crash.

Ensuring his return should he wander; his collar tag read "Owney, Post Office, Albany, New York." Soon others affixed tags to his collar, marking his travels like luggage stickers. The jingling medals marked his movements as he trotted along. Over time, the copious souvenirs weighed down the poor pooch. The Postmaster General gave him a body harness to redistribute the load. As the medallions mounted in ever greater numbers, they'd be removed for safekeeping in Albany.

In an 1895 celebrity-heightening publicity stunt, he was shipped as a "registered dog package" on an "Around-the-World" goodwill voyage. In mid-August he departed Tacoma, Washington aboard the Northern Pacific mail steamer, *Victoria*, en route to China and Japan, traveling with his blanket, comb and brush in a mini-suitcase. On the British steamship, *Port Phillip,* he journeyed to Shanghai and Singapore, through the Suez Canal on to Algiers and finally New York City where he boarded a Tacoma-bound train for his return in late December.

By June 11, 1897, aging and unwell, he'd become Owney the ornery. He bit a Toledo, Ohio mail clerk and was "put down" by a US Marshal's bullet. Postal

employees funded taxidermy of their fallen canine comrade and sent his remains to Post Office Headquarters in Washington, DC. Transferred to the Smithsonian in 1911, Preserved Owney now sits in the atrium of the National Postal Museum, harness and several tags intact.

UNION STATION ROMAN SENTINELS ❽

50 Massachusetts Avenue NE
- Shops open Mon—Sat 10am—9pm; Sunday noon—6pm
- Metro: Red Line to Union Station

> **Modestly standing sentry**

Designed by Daniel H. Burnham to unify the city's various railroads in one central terminal, Washington's grand Union Station opened to great expectation on October 27, 1907. Burnham drew inspiration from the ancient Baths of Diocletian in Rome, so it's no wonder that Roman sentinels commissioned from the sculptor Louis Saint Gaudens (younger brother of Augustus, sculptor of Grief, pg. 123) keep watch over the building. Outside, six statues stand guard over the portico doors. Along the stone coping rimming the barrel-vaulted main hall, 40 more loom above — a striking counterpoint. To much public consternation, the installation of the soldiers was delayed until February 1913.

When Saint Gaudens submitted maquettes of his vision for the sculptures, identical men with variations on the uniform of 2nd-century Roman Gaul soldiers, he was asked to provide "modesty shields" for the pantless figures designed to be historically accurate. Classical nudity be damned, a sense of turn-of-the-century propriety prevailed and Saint-Gaudens created a *scutum* (shield) bearing an eagle sigil and the United States motto *E Pluribus Unum,* "out of many, one." A glimpse behind the shields, however, shows little more than a vague anatomical reference.

Athlete Helmus W. Andrews, a 5'9", 168-pound fullback from Pomona College in California, served as artist's model for the soldiers, variously referred to as centurions and legionaries. Oddly enough, the statuary widely regarded as Saint-Gaudens' masterwork left its muse unimpressed. When Andrews visited the station in 1957, he described them as "pretty crummy."

THE PROGRESS OF RAILROADING

Even more impressive than the Roman legionaries are Saint-Gaudens' six allegorical figures high atop the façade of Union Station. Carved in granite by Italian stonecutter Andrew Bernasconi, the 18 foot statues are worth a lingering upward gaze. Most notably, representing electricity, is Thales, crowned by a diadem of electrostatic charge, holding massive lightning bolts within his strong grip.

NEARBY:

MARCO POLO RAIL CAR

When traveling to or from Washington via Amtrak, look for the Marco Polo on track seven. The deep green 1927 Pullman car was for many years the preferred mode of travel of President Franklin D. Roosevelt, himself the son of a railroad executive. Nine feet wide and 74 feet long, it held a stateroom, a large dining room that seats eight, a kitchen, a sitting room, and four bedrooms and lavatories. Roosevelt used it for his whistle-stop tour, as well as hosting dignitaries such as Madame Chiang Kai-Shek, Queen Wilhelmina of the Netherlands, and the industrialists Firestone, Mellon, Studebaker, and Woolworth. Owned by Norfolk Southern Corporation, it is today privately utilized for corporate business.

BELMONT-PAUL WOMEN'S EQUALITY NATIONAL MONUMENT ❾

144 Constitution Avenue NE
• Open: Wed—Sun 9am—5pm. Ask about guided tours
• Free entry
• Tel: (202) 546-1210
• www.nationalwomansparty.org
• Metro: Red Line to Union Station; Blue, Orange or Silver Line to Capitol South; then 15-min walk

> **Bastion of women's rights**

In 1799, Robert Sewall began home construction on lots purchased from Daniel Carroll, one of the framers of the U.S. Constitution and one of two commissioners to the lay the first boundary stone (see p. 117) of the new federal capital. The mansion extant at the corner of Constitution Avenue and Second Street, Northeast is one of the oldest buildings in the city. It has served as home to both Secretary of State Albert Gallatin and later Senator Porter Dole of Vermont. As the site of armed resistance to the British invasion of 1814, the Redcoats retaliated by setting the property aflame. In 2016, by proclamation of President Obama, it became a national monument.

Through its many iterations (Georgian, Early American, Federal, Classic Revival, Victorian and French Mansard periods), the property stood as an architectural timeline of Washington. It was bought in 1929 by suffragist Alva Vanderbilt Belmont to serve as the headquarters of the National Woman's Party (NWP). Founded by suffragist leader and author of the Equal Rights Amendment, Alice Paul, the NWP's strategic location near the Capitol puts the organization squarely in proximity to the legislature.

Formerly known as the Sewall-Belmont House for its illustrious former owners, the newly christened Belmont-Paul Women's Equality National Monument honors Belmont and Paul's ardent feminist activism. The museum welcomes guests with its signature stained glass fanlight and busts of the sheroes of the movement. Exhibition artifacts of the women's equality journey include exceptionally preserved suffrage banners and sashes; news

weeklies *The Suffragist* and *Equal Rights*; Congressional voting cards including Senator John F. Kennedy's (MA) 1953-54 abstention from voting on the ERA; and cartoonist Nina Allender's political art.

Located in the former Sewall stable, the Florence Bayard Hilles Feminist Library is the first such library in the United States. It was opened with Belmont's book collection in 1941 and rededicated in honor of former NWP president Florence Hilles in 1943.

BETSEY GRAVES REYNEAU'S JAIL DOOR PIN

An accomplished painter held in the National Portrait Gallery, Reyneau's portraits of NWP leaders are in the Belmont-Paul collection. Reyneau was among 16 women arrested for picketing the White House on July 14, 1917. All were given a draconian 60-day sentence at Occoquan Workhouse (see p. 310) then pardoned by President Wilson three days later. The pin commemorates her resistance.

FLORIDA HOUSE

10

1 2nd Street NE
- floridaembassy.com
- 202-546-1555
- Open: Monday to Friday 9 am – 5 pm
- Metro: Blue, Orange, or Silver Line to Capitol South

The only state embassy in the nation

The restored Victorian rowhouse at the northeast corner of Second and East Capitol Streets predates its distinguished neighbors. Southwest is the Jefferson Building of the Library of Congress, completed in 1897; southeast, the Folger Shakespeare Library in 1932 and northwest the US Supreme Court Building in 1935. Built in 1891 as a residence for Edwin Manning of the Library of Congress architectural team, it is now home to Florida House, the only state embassy in the United States. Who knew?

Vacationing in DC in the late 1960s, Floridian Rhea Chiles and her family found themselves lost on Embassy Row. One of her young children said, "Let's go to Florida's embassy, and they will tell us where we are." When her husband, Lawton Chiles won a Senate seat in 1972, they decamped for the District, where Mrs. Chiles spied a "for sale" sign at a boarded-up house at 200 East Capitol Street. Remembering her child's innocent suggestion, Mrs. Chiles conceived of the idea for an embassy representing her home state. Putting up $5,000 and securing $120,000 from friends in Florida, she bought the derelict property and supervised its restoration. Changing the official address to 1 2nd Street, she founded Florida House to provide respite and cultural exchange to Floridians visiting the nation's capital.

Over forty years later the house still boasts a remarkable view of the Capitol dome from a second-floor window, stained glass transoms original to the house and a surprisingly intact gold-leaf mirror. A relic of Gilded Age heiress, Evalyn Walsh McLean (see page 92) whose son-in-law, Senator Robert Rice Reynolds owned the property from 1939 to 1950.

All are welcome to visit, enjoy the southern hospitality with a glass of cold Florida orange juice and peruse rooms filled with furnishings donated from Floridians and the works of Sunshine State artists.

THE HIGHWAYMEN

Florida House maintains a rotating exhibition of folk art paintings from "The Highwaymen," a prolific group of twenty-six self-taught African-American painters credited with creating over 200,000 *en plein air* works since the 1960s. The painted vistas document the changing Florida landscape surrounding US Highway 1.

GALLAUDET UNIVERSITY   ⑪

800 Florida Avenue NE
• Gallaudet.edu
• 202-651-5000
• Open: schedule daily guided campus tours in American Sign Language or with voice interpreters online ; or grab a map at the visitor center for a self-guided tour
• Metro: Red Line to NoMa-Gallaudet U

> ### *Genesis of the football huddle, by the deaf and hard of hearing*

In its illustrious history as the preeminent school for the deaf and hard of hearing in the world, Gallaudet University is credited with the genesis of the gridiron football huddle, a tradition in the American sport enjoyed by deaf and hearing communities alike.

First organized in September 1883, the Gallaudet college football program is one of the oldest in the country. The Gallaudet Kendalls (named for founder Amos Kendall) defeated every local collegiate football team until a Georgetown University win in 1890. By 1892, Kansan Paul Hubbard joined the Kendalls as quarterback. Realizing that his signed plays could be read by the opposition during practice, he gathered his offensive line into a tight circle to obscure his hand signals from view. Ultimately he carried the custom over into league games.

The now iconic circular formation had a practical application in the hearing world as well, isolating the team players from crowd noise as they listened to the quarterback's calls. The huddle caught on and integrated the gridirons of both collegiate and professional football throughout the country and ultimately incorporated into other team sports around the world such as cricket, soccer and Australian rules football.

After many team name changes over the years, Gallaudet adopted the powerful yet fleet-footed bison as a mascot. In the "Bison Zone" stands the Gallaudet Athletics Hall of Fame, a wall honoring the achievements of Gallaudet athletes from Paul Hubbard in the 19th century to Kathryn A. Baldridge, women's basketball coach in the 21st century.

BISON DRUM

Starting in 1970, from its sideline post the bass drum "spoke" for the quarterback, with a hearing impaired-friendly snap count. Wheeled on casters down to the line of scrimmage where a manager pounds out the timed count, the gigantic drum reverberates the cadence call to players who feel the vibrations. Though the team now employs a silent count system, the storied drum remains on the sidelines, an emblem of Gallaudet football.

NEW COLUMBIA DISTILLERS SATURDAY TASTING TOURS ⓬

1832 Fenwick Street NE
- greenhatgin.com
- 202-733-1710
- Open: free tastings, tours and sales Saturday 1 pm – 4 pm
- Metro: Red Line to NoMa - Gallaudet U

> **The first post-Prohibition distillery in Washington**

Inspired by the famed Prohibition-era bootlegger to Congress known as the "Man in the Green Hat," Michael Lowe and his son-in-law John Uselton dubbed the first product of their Northeast distillery Green Hat Gin. After an apprenticeship with a West Coast craft distiller, the entrepreneurs set out on their own in 2011, securing a 90-year-old warehouse in the transitioning industrial neighborhood of Ivy City, near the landmarked Art Deco Hecht Company warehouse. Though craft brewing abounds in DC, the family-owned business is the first distiller of spirits in the city in over a century. In addition to their signature gin, plans are afoot to introduce rye whiskey.

Each Saturday the distillery hosts public tours of the facility for a look at the small batch operation, its copper alembic still a gleaming focal point. One of the personable, enthusiastic distillers chronicles the artisanal process of creating their delightfully smooth and gently aromatic juniper-based spirit from mill to mash, fermentation to concentration, clarification to distillation, botanical infusion to chill filtering and finally, hand bottling. Inhaling the aromas of the botanicals used in the distinct gin blends precedes a tasting flight, completing the sensory experience.

THE MAN IN THE GREEN HAT

In a clandestine ten-year insider operation, green hat-wearing WWI vet George Cassiday supplied illicit inebriants to a staggering four out of five members of Congress—even those who supported Prohibition. He averaged a brisk twenty-five bottles a day from 1920 to 1925 out of the Cannon House Office Building basement until Capitol Police caught him. Brazenly, the Congressional hooch-slinger simply moved to the Senate side, delivering his banned booze in a leather briefcase for five more years. A teetaling Fed known as the "Dry Spy" snared him in a 1930 sting after a raid on his Southeast home uncovered 266 quarts of liquor. He served an 18-month jail sentence signing out at night and returning each morning. In "The Man in the Green Hat," a series for the *Washington Post*, he revealed his bootlegging exploits and the hypocrisy of Congress (though he never identified individuals) instigating eventual Repeal.

NATIONAL BONSAI & PENJING MUSEUM ⓭

US National Arboretum
3501 New York Avenue NE
• bonsai-nbf.org
• 202-245-2726
• Open: Daily 10 am – 4 pm; closed federal holidays
• Metro: Blue, Orange, or Silver Line to Stadium Armory; transfer to the B2 Metrobus; disembark the bus on Bladensburg Road at Rand Street, just past the Arboretum sign on the right; walk back to sign at R Street and then down R Street two blocks to Arboretum entrance

> **Wonders of longevity and artful cultivation**

A mid the many treasures of the overlooked gem, the National Arboretum, is a collection of trees cultivated in the Japanese art form *bonsai* (盆栽) "planted in a container," and its lesser-known Chinese antecedent *penjing* (盆景) "tray scenery" (which dates back to the Tsin dynasty AD 265—420). These miniaturized trees are not genetic dwarfs, but rather works of art in tandem with nature, skillfully cultivated to limit growth and manipulate shape; their cultivation a reverential practice. Some appear windswept, some stoically reaching toward the sky, still others mind-bogglingly contorted. The open-air museum encourages tranquility as one moves from one arboreal cluster to the next.

In 1972, China presented President Richard Nixon with eight penjing trees. Moved to the Arboretum upon his departure from office, they were the first of their kind in the national park. Come 1976, Japan gifted the US with fifty-three bonsai trees in celebration of America's bicentennial. These formed the core of what has become the National Bonsai & Penjing Museum. Its oldest specimen, a Japanese white pine has been in training since 1626, surviving both the bombing of Hiroshima on August 6, 1945, and the Trans-Pacific flight to the States over thirty years later. In the 1980s Hong Kong collector Dr. Yee Sun-Wu donated several penjing, balancing the collections in separate pavilions, of artfully-trained Japanese and Chinese trees. A third pavilion, the John Y. Naka North American Pavilion, features the late Japanese-American horticulturist's *Goshin*, a magnificent juniper forest planting as well as sixty-two other trees trained by North American cultivators. A gift of Jack B. Douthitt, the sinewy pasture juniper pictured has been in training since 1980.

Penjing, more so than bonsai, incorporates rocks amid the trees in its diminutive landscapes. Sometimes viewing stones are featured solely, suggesting mountain ranges and other natural rock formations. Interspersed throughout the collections, many are in the International Pavilion along with ikebana displays (the Japanese art of flower arrangement).

NATIONAL CAPITOL COLUMNS

US National Arboretum Ellipse Meadow
3501 New York Avenue NE
• usna.usda.gov
• 202-245-2726
• Open: Friday to Monday 8 am – 5 pm
• Metro: Blue, Orange or Silver Line to Stadium Armory; Transfer to the B2 Metrobus; disembark the bus on Bladensburg Road at Rand Street, just past the Arboretum sign on the right; walk back to sign at R Street then down R Street two blocks to Arboretum entrance

Acropolis now

Evoking the ancient ruins of the Temple of Poseidon in Greece, the stately National Capitol Columns soar above a knoll at the federal arboretum. Quarried of Aquia Creek sandstone by slave labor in 1828, the Corinthian columns once supported the East Portico of the United States Capitol, providing a grand inaugural setting for many an American president. They beg the question then, of how these 1880s architectural remnants became the focal point of a 20-acre meadowland in the middle of Northeast. By the time the Capitol underwent a 1958 east-front expansion to correct the appearance of a dome too large for the supports underneath, the porous sandstone pillars were replaced with more durable Italian marble.

Resurrected decades after their dismantling through the efforts of National Arboretum benefactor, Ethel Garrett, the columns were restored and erected on the grounds in 1984 at the Ellipse Meadow, a site chosen by renowned British landscape designer Russell Page. Etched into the stone terrace created of steps salvaged from the old site are names of contributors to the $2 million project. Below, a small rivulet of water gently cascades into the pool below,

reflecting the columns and providing a swimming pond for local Mallards.

Across the Ellipse, a lone Corinthian capital (decorative column topper) with its requisite curled acanthus leaves sits on a pedestal, inviting an up-close examination of the artistry of the 19th-century stone carvers who created the monumental pillars. Another broken Corinthian cap rests angled on the ground as if toppled from its post. Of the twenty-four original Capitol columns, twenty-two stand erect in the field. With only their fluted surfaces as a reminder of their lofty past, the other two, sans capital and base rest cracked on their sides at the summit of Mount Hamilton lording over the Azalea Collection.

LANGSTON TERRACE DWELLINGS **15**

21st and G Street NE near Benning Road
• Metro: DC Streetcar from Union Station to 19th and Benning Rd NE

> *The first federally-funded public housing development in Washington*

In 1934, a paucity of housing in Washington left limited options for those with limited means. The unemployed often lived in squalid, ramshackle alley residences. The working poor weren't much better off, renting what they could afford—less than stellar apartments or cramped rooms. The Alley Dwelling Authority established a "slum clearance" plan to eliminate alley communities within ten years and provide alternative housing to displaced residents. Under President Roosevelt's New Deal, the Public Works Administration created affordable housing for low-income "colored" families in Northeast's Kingman Park.

Called Kingman Terrace, the project was renamed the aspirational "Langston Terrace" to honor John Mercer Langston, the Reconstruction-era congressman from Virginia, founder and dean of the Howard University School of Law, and uncle to the poet Langston Hughes. Erected by mostly black laborers, the complex was designed with cultural sensitivity by African-American architect and native Washingtonian, Hilyard Robinson.

For the design, Robinson looked to the International Style he'd studied in Germany and symbolically into the future. An ornamental frieze over the courtyard passage, *The Progress of the Negro Race* by Daniel G. Olney echoes the sentiment with figurative terracotta panels depicting vignettes of the African-American experience.

On a knoll above Lake Kingman and the Anacostia River, it was a prime locale for this experiment in public housing, the first of its kind in the District. Accessibility to a main thoroughfare, mass transit, and "Negro" schools within walking distance were key.

The families of the 274 units created a close-knit community. They planted gardens, bought groceries collectively, formed a credit union, started a laundry-room library, built a photo darkroom and during an era of whites-only ice rinks in DC, created a makeshift rink on the courtyard in winter.

Of the twenty-five babies born to residents during the inaugural year of Langston Terrace, all were thriving upon the first anniversary. In light of infant mortality rates among black Washingtonians, the *Evening Star* newspaper documented the Langston success story in the May 7, 1939 issue.

In *Childtimes: A Three Generation Memoir*, prolific children's book author Eloise Greenfield fondly chronicles her Langston childhood during the Great Depression.

KENILWORTH PARK & AQUATIC GARDENS ⓰

1550 Anacostia Avenue NE
- nps.gov/keaq
- 202-426-6905
- Open: daily 7 am – 4 pm; closed Thanksgiving, Christmas, and New Year's Day
- Metro: Orange Line to Deanwood; take Polk Street exit, cross the Kenilworth Avenue pedestrian overpass, take immediate left on Douglas Street and walk down to Anacostia Avenue, make right and enter park at one of the gates (approximately 12-minute walk)

Off-the-radar oasis

Due to wickedly humid summers, DC is shadowed by an oft-repeated myth of swampland creation. Not so. True however, is a history of tidal wetlands in our riparian city. The sole remaining freshwater tidal marsh lies east of the Anacostia River at Kenilworth Park and Aquatic Gardens. The only park of its kind managed by the National Park Service, it's home to an impressive array of marsh-dwelling flora and fauna. Upwards of seventy-five bird species inhabit the area. A chart indicating the best season to spot each is available for download on the NPS website. Friendly, on-site rangers will give a heads up on what to look for.

Every season yields a new delight. Winter's bare trees give unobstructed views for birding and spotting otters, minks, even foxes. Springtime marks the return of the verdant landscape, dam-building beavers and trilling songbirds. Summer brings a breathtaking expanse of aquatic flowers: water lilies bloom in June and come July, lotus blossoms stretch heavenward. As the park grows ablaze in autumn color, deer and geese roam freely, the wild rice matures, lotus pods seed the ponds and velvety cattails release their pollen to begin the cycle again.

The park is the enduring legacy of one-armed Civil War veteran, W.B. Shaw and his widowed, visionary daughter, Helen Shaw Fowler. Making his home on a marshy parcel of land in the burgeoning DC suburbs, Shaw planted twelve water lilies from his native Maine. He became an avid water gardener and with his thriving floral bounty, opened Shaw's Lily Ponds.

A Corcoran-trained artist, Helen painted lovely watercolors of the flowers. The first woman in DC to obtain a truck drivers license, she made plant deliveries. The business flourished under her management. She added rare lilies Nile Blue and Amazon Victoria to their offerings and opened the gardens to paying visitors for Sunday picnics. It became a hotspot among the social elite, hosting three Presidents. Upon her father's 1921 passing, she fought to protect the gardens from encroaching river dredging. Though the Department of the Interior bought the property in 1938 for use as a public park, Helen remained in her home until her 1950s death.

The under-explored treasure with its pond paths and marsh observation boardwalk is worth the walk from the Metro. Remember these are wetlands; it gets muddy. Wear closed-toe shoes. To see summer blooms at their best, visit early before flowers close in the heat of the day.

MARVIN GAYE PARK

Minnesota and Nannie Helen Burroughs Avenues NE
• Metro: Orange Line to Deanwood

⑰

*Marvin
sang here*

On the banks of Watts Branch, the largest tributary of the Anacostia River, a teenaged Marvin Gay, Jr. found a place to sit, dream, and sing. One of his first performances was at Barnett's Crystal Lounge at the corner of Foote Street and Division Avenue, now the Riverside Center. He lived at the nearby East Capitol Dwellings and with fellow Cardozo High School students, formed a doo-wop group, DC Tones, which later became the Marquees. Bo Diddley, then living in Northeast, caught wind of the young group and escorted them to New York to produce the single "Wyatt Earp," the first recording on Marvin's way to R&B superstardom. And ending his name with "e."

Formerly under federal jurisdiction, Watts Branch Park was turned over to an underfunded city in the 1970s, ushering in an era of decline. The strains of Marvin Gaye's seminal song "Mercy, Mercy Me (The Ecology)" seemed an apt anthem for change. The park that provided the backdrop to the late singer's early a cappella stylings was renamed in his honor in 2006 following a major revitalization effort to restore the natural beauty of the long-neglected urban glade. Local volunteers led by the National Recreational Parks Association and Washington Parks & People cleared debris in the millions of pounds; seventy-eight abandoned cars to thousands of hypodermic needles from what was known as "Needle Park." Over 1,000 native trees have since been replanted, as this neighborhood in transition looks to a bright future.

A mosaic medallion installed by G. Byron Peck and six youth assistants in 2010 features a likeness of Gaye from the cover of his legendary, socially conscious album, *What's Going On?* Former First Lady "Ladybird" Johnson is also honored for the 8-acre wildflower meadow she dedicated in the park on May 18, 1966, as part of a city beautification initiative.

BO DIDDLEY'S DC HOME

Mr. Elias McDaniel loved being in DC near the Howard Theater so the singer known as Bo Diddley bought a house at 2614 Rhode Island Avenue NE. Living there from the late 1950s to the mid-1960s, he built a home studio in his basement where he recorded his *Bo Diddley is a Gunslinger* album and helped emerging talents like Gaye and others from local schools like Cardozo, Roosevelt, and Armstrong who sometimes backed him on his recordings.

HISTORIC DEANWOOD ⓲

Start at grounds of the former Nannie Helen Burroughs School
601 50th Street NE
• Metro: Blue or Silver Line to Benning Road

> ## We Specialize in the Wholly Impossible

The Nacotchtank tribe hunted, fished, and traded on the banks of the Anacostia before the Scot Ninian Beall came to America as an indentured servant. He eventually owned a wide swath of the Washington metro area, including northeast farmland (and slaves). Some of the major thoroughfares of Far Northeast carry the nomenclature of the white families who subdivided the area in the late 18th and early 19th centuries; Benning Road, Sherriff Road. Julian Dean named his parcel Deanwood.

One of the easternmost neighborhoods in the District, Deanwood, by virtue of geography and relative isolation from Northwest power brokers, became a magnet for African-Americans who moved from servitude to self-sufficiency. They were able to purchase property and build affordable homes in the semi-rural subdivision. Kia Chatmon, of the Deanwood History Committee, says of her long self-reliant community, "early residents were industrious craftspeople, entrepreneurs and civic leaders who ensured that their community's needs were met." Small business boomed.

When bigotry prevented her from getting a teaching post, Nannie Helen Burroughs, in 1909 at age 26, opened the National Training School for Women and Girls. Her motto, *We Specialize in the Wholly Impossible*. Atop a large hillside tract she purchased overlooking the city, her school was a source of inspiration. She believed that education, vocational training, and women's suffrage would empower women of color. Each student had to pass a class in African-American history in order to graduate.

In 1921, architect H.D. Woodson and John Paynter, whose ancestors included slaves who attempted to escape on the *Pearl* schooner (see page 298) opened Suburban Gardens at 50th and Hayes Streets NE (pictured left). The only amusement park ever opened within DC boundaries, it welcomed black people when African-Americans were banned from popular Glen Echo Park in suburban Maryland.

EMPOWERHOUSE: DC'S FIRST PASSIVE HOUSE
With a little sweat equity, two single-parent families helped build their modern, cost-effective, energy-efficient solar-powered home. The modern facade incorporates a front porch, a cultural touchstone. Ms. Burroughs would be proud. Gault Place NE at 46th Street.

SOUTHWEST

KILROY WAS HERE ENGRAVINGS ❶

National World War II Memorial
1750 Independence Ave SW
• nps.gov/wwii
• 202-619-7222
• Open: 24 hours a day; rangers are on duty to answer questions 9:30 am – 11:30 pm daily, and to provide interpretive programs every hour on the hour 10:00 am – 11:00 pm
• Metro: Blue, Orange, or Silver Line to Smithsonian

> *Viral sensation of World War II*

Somewhere in the vast granite and bronze expanse that is the National World War II Memorial, two identical engravings inconspicuously immortalize the ubiquitous graffiti tag of the Allies during the war, "KILROY WAS HERE." They punctuate the solemnity of memorializing the bloodiest war in US history, with a cultural icon that while light-hearted, came to symbolize Allied presence.

How "Kilroy" came to be the viral sensation of World War II is the subject of conjecture, but the generally accepted version of the story is found in a 1946 article in the *New York Times*. James J. Kilroy, a rivet inspector at the Fore River shipyard in Quincy, Massachusetts, diligently plied his trade, recording the days' numbers in chalk. When he discovered the small marks were easily rubbed away, he started writing "Kilroy was here," affirming his presence and completion of work. So busy was the shipbuilding production that Kilroy's seal of approval was left on the vessels that departed the yard. Kilroy's legend loomed large as GIs duplicated the inspector's scrawl at every port of call, a memento of Allied presence. By the height of the tagging frenzy, "Kilroy" had somehow alighted in Europe, Asia and Africa, thus a legend was born. The accompanying doodle of a man peering over a wall is a mashup of the "Kilroy" phrase and a popular drawing in Britain during that era, "Mr. Chad."

A 1946 radio search for the "real" Kilroy yielded forty men claiming the identity. James Kilroy, whose story was corroborated by other shipbuilding employees, won the grand prize, a 40-foot trolley car donated by the American Transit Association. The tram came in handy, as an extension of his residence, home to his large family with nine children.

> Spoiler alert: If you want to discover "Kilroy" on your own, look no further; otherwise head toward the memorial wall of stars and look for the Delaware and Pennsylvania pillars on either side. In the gated area behind each the peeping man appears.

AIR MAIL

THE WORLD'S FIRST AIRPLANE MAIL TO BE OPERATED
AS A CONTINUOUSLY SCHEDULED PUBLIC SERVICE
STARTED FROM THIS FIELD MAY 15, 1918.

THE ROUTE CONNECTED WASHINGTON, PHILADELPHIA
AND NEW YORK. CURTISS JN 4-H AIRPLANES WITH A
CAPACITY OF 150 POUNDS OF MAIL FLEW THE 230 MILES
IN ABOUT THREE HOURS.

THE SERVICE WAS INAUGURATED BY THE POST OFFICE
DEPARTMENT IN COOPERATION WITH THE AVIATION SECTION
OF THE SIGNAL CORPS OF THE U. S. ARMY. ON AUGUST 12, 1918,
THE SERVICE WAS TAKEN OVER IN ITS ENTIRETY BY THE
POST OFFICE DEPARTMENT.

THIS MARKER WAS ERECTED BY
THE AERO CLUB OF WASHINGTON.
ON THE FORTIETH ANNIVERSARY
MAY 15, 1958

US AIRMAIL SERVICE LAUNCH MARKER ❷

Ohio and West Basin Drives SW
• Metro: Blue, Orange, or Silver Line to Smithsonian: a 17-minute walk
from there

*Follow
the railroad tracks*

On an open stretch of West Potomac Park, a small boulder curiously overlooks the Boundary Channel. A plaque affixed to it commemorates the launch of the first continuously scheduled US Airmail Service from the site on May 15, 1918, seven years after Britain had inaugurated the world's first scheduled service.

Assembled for the milestone departure were sitting President Woodrow Wilson, US Postmaster General Albert Burleson and a host of federal officials including then-Assistant Secretary of the Navy, Franklin D. Roosevelt. Two pilots from the US Army Signal Corps were assigned to relay flights on Curtiss "Jenny" biplanes from the Polo Grounds in Washington, DC and Belmont Park in Long Island, NY respectively, to Philadelphia's Bustleton Field where they'd exchange mailbags, initiating Washington—Philadelphia—New York air mail service.

By virtue of his personal connections, rookie aviator Lt. George Boyle garnered the plum assignment of piloting the northbound flight from Washington. He was greeted by President Wilson; gifted a wristwatch by the Hamilton Watch Company; and given a map and advice, "Follow the railroad tracks," from Maj. Reuben Fleet, organizer of the mission.

Though loaded with well over 100 pounds of mail, the Jenny's takeoff was thwarted by an empty fuel tank. Mechanics fueled the plane and Boyle departed at 11:47 am. Disoriented, he followed the railroad tracks in the wrong direction. A mere 18 minutes later he made a hard landing on farmland south of Washington, breaking the propeller. Authorities dispatched a truck to retrieve the downed courier and the mail which would not be flown to Philadelphia and on to New York until the next day. His colleague on the southbound NY—Philadelphia leg, Lt. Torrey Webb, however, discharged his duty to complete the first successful US Airmail Service flight.

Three days later, Boyle once again attempted to make the DC—Philadelphia run. Once again he flew off course, and ultimately crashed on the golf course at the Philadelphia Country Club. Fortunately he was unharmed, and the mail put on a train to New York. He was summarily relieved of his duties.

CUBAN FRIENDSHIP URN   ❸

East Potomac Park
Ohio Drive SW by the Inlet Bridge
• Metro: Green, Yellow, Blue, Orange, or Silver Line to L'Enfant Plaza;
take the 9th and D Streets SW exit, it's a bit of a walk from there on the
Promenade to the footpath at Benjamin Banneker Circle; Blue, Orange, or
Silver Line to Smithsonian and the East Basin Drive Bridge.

> *Remembering the Maine, Cuban independence and lost amity*

An obscure monument on a road less traveled, the Cuban Friendship Urn holds not ashes, but a tale tinged with mystery, amity, enmity, and entangled intentions. Now situated south of the Tidal Basin near the inlet bridge in East Potomac Park, the pedestaled marble vessel has landed in a few spots in the District since its Havana creation.

In January 1898, as tensions flared over the struggle for Cuban liberation from Spanish rule, President McKinley sent the battleship USS *Maine* to Havana Harbor to protect Americans and American interests there. On February 15, the ship inexplicably exploded and sunk, claiming the lives of 266 men, more than half of the crew. Amid speculation that the explosion was Spain's retaliation for US support of Cuban independence, an inquest failed to determine the cause. Hyperbolic news reports stirred public outrage. "Remember the Maine, to Hell with Spain," was a rallying cry as the nation ventured into the Spanish-American War which ultimately freed Cuba from colonization.

An imposing bronze eagle at its apex, a columned monument erected in 1925 on the Malecón waterfront in Havana honored those lost on the sunken warship. A hurricane the next year toppled the memorial. A commemorative urn crafted from its wreckage bears carvings of an eagle, wings spread; two neoclassical figures on each side clasp hands above the sinking ship on the back. The Spanish inscription translates to: The memory of the Maine will hold in lasting duration, through the ages, the ties of friendship between the people of Cuba and the people of the United States of America.

In January 1928, President Coolidge gave the keynote address of the Pan American Congress in Havana, thirty years after the fateful arrival of the *Maine* on the same shores. Grateful for US support, the Cuban Republic gifted the country with the urn as a symbol of goodwill. Installed among the roses of West Potomac Park that May, it was dismantled in 1947 to make way for the northbound 14th Street Bridge.

It's thought to have fronted the Cuban Embassy until US-Cuba diplomatic relations soured in 1961. Though National Park Service (NPS) records indicate that it was placed in storage in 1963, an anonymous tipster sent photos of the discarded urn, leading to its discovery near the former NPS headquarters in 1996. Rededicated on the centennial of the USS *Maine* sinking, it sits in odd obscurity.

ONEG SHABBAT MILK CAN ❹

United States Holocaust Memorial Museum
100 Raoul Wallenberg Place SW
• ushmm.org
• 202-488-0400
• Open every day except Yom Kippur and Christmas Day
The Permanent Exhibition and special exhibitions are open 10 am – 5:20 pm, with extended hours in spring; March through August timed passes are required for the Permanent Exhibition
• Admission: free; reserve passes online
• Metro: Blue, Orange or Silver Line to Smithsonian

Secret archive of the Warsaw ghetto

Unearthed from beneath 58 Nowolipki Street in Warsaw, Poland on December 1, 1950, a corroded milk can brought to light the second cache of hidden archives of Polish Jewry under Nazi occupation in the Warsaw ghetto. Today that milk can and a casting of the ghetto wall are on permanent, poignant display on the third floor of the United States Holocaust Memorial Museum.

Historian Emanuel Ringelblum began a chronicle of ghetto life in October 1939. Fully believing that truth will out, his efforts expanded into an underground resistance movement organized to preserve an accurate picture of Jewish life in occupied Poland. Code-named *Oneg Shabbat*, "Sabbath delight" for the clandestine meetings organizers held on the Sabbath, the archive documents the rich culture and spiritual devotion which continued to thrive despite hunger, crowding, and constant threat. By 1942, the organizers had amassed copious materials for the 2,000-page book they called *Two-and-a-Half Years* (the period of German occupation to date). Newspapers and posters, photographs and correspondence, minutes of meetings all made it into the archive. Broadsides for symphonic concerts reveal the sublime continuity of culture and ration cards of 189 calories a day attest to the cruelty of all-too-common starvation.

The archives were stashed inside mundane vessels: tin boxes and milk cans, sealed and buried beneath bunkers under public buildings. The first was at a school on Nowolipki Street on August 3, 1942. The second, below the same building in February 1943, and the last, at 34 Swietojerska Street, on April 18, 1943, the day before the start of the Warsaw ghetto uprising.

Ringelblum escaped with his family in March 1943, but returned for Passover and was thrown into the Trawniki labor camp. He again escaped into hiding with his family, only to be captured like so many others and killed among the ghetto ruins a year later.

Two surviving Oneg Shabbat staffers identified the location of the first part of the archives and ten metal boxes were recovered on September 18, 1946; the second section of the archives on December 1, 1950. The final installment beneath Swietojerska Street has never been found.

Also known as the Ringelblum Archive, the important collection goes down in the annals of history for its sweeping veracity. As its namesake once wrote "We aspired to reveal the whole truth, as bitter as it may be. Our documentation is authentic, not touched-up."

THIRD THURSDAYS AT THE PEACOCK ROOM ❺

Freer Gallery of Art
1200 Independence Avenue SW
• asia.si.edu
• 202-633-1000
• Open: daily 10 am – 5:30 pm; closed December 25; third Thursdays from noon – 5:30 pm
• Admission: free
• Metro: Blue, Orange, or Silver Line to Smithsonian

Whistler's gilty pleasure

The "crown jewel" of industrialist Charles Lang Freer's Smithsonian bequest, the storied Peacock Room is most frequently seen in dim lighting to preserve the rich depth of its pigments. But one afternoon each month, the shutters are opened to illuminate its bold color and opulent gilding. A docent is on hand to tell the remarkable tale of the room's creation in England and its subsequent transatlantic journey.

Sharing James McNeill Whistler's fascination with "the Orient," shipping magnate Frederick Leyland acquired the artist's *The Princess from the Land of Porcelain* depicting a model enrobed in a kimono. He commissioned Whistler to adorn the entrance hall of his London mansion and architect Thomas Jeckyll to design the adjacent dining room. Jeckyll built an intricate system of walnut latticed shelves to display Leyland's collection of Chinese porcelains. Since *The Princess* painting would be mounted above the fireplace, Whistler was consulted on color schemes for the room.

Illness forced Jeckyll to abandon the project. Whistler then began an audacious overhaul of the room beyond the Leyland-sanctioned changes which enchants to this day. Not enchanted however, was Frederick Leyland when he learned of the encroachments. Priceless leather walls were painted over; the spindled shelves and incised framework were gilded beyond recognition of the wood grain. Whistler called it *Harmony in Blue and Gold* and brazenly received press and visitors in Leyland's absence.

Patron and artist quarreled, with Leyland agreeing to pay only half Whistler's fee. Whistler then completed the room with a symbolic mural, an embattled pair of peacocks titled *Art and Money; or, the Story of the Room*. Leyland warned Whistler that he'd be "horse-whipped" if he appeared at the house again, though the room remained unchanged until his 1892 death.

Whistler patron, Charles Lang Freer eventually acquired both *The Princess* and *Harmony in Blue and Gold*. The room was dismantled and installed in his Detroit mansion to house his collection of Asian pottery and stoneware. In 1906 Freer bequeathed his vast Whistler Collection including the room to establish the first Smithsonian art museum. From the opening in 1923 until the 1970s, live peacocks roamed the Freer Courtyard during summer.

ANTIPODES CRYPTOGRAPHIC SCULPTURE ❻

Hirshhorn Museum Sculpture Garden
700 Independence Ave SW
• hirshhorn.si.edu
• 202-633-4674
• Open: daily except December 25: museum 10 am – 5:30pm; plaza 7:30 am – 5:30 pm; garden 7:30 am – dusk
• Metro: Green, Yellow, Blue, Orange, or Silver Line to L'Enfant Plaza

Crack the code

Designed by Washington, DC-born sculptor Jim Sanborn and encoded with ciphers from former CIA cryptographer, Edward M. Scheidt, the intensely-studied sculpture *Kryptos* ("hidden"), in the grounds of the CIA headquarters at Langley, Virginia is in a post-9/11 world no longer publicly accessible. Its appearance on the dust jacket of the best-selling novel, *The Da Vinci Code* and mention in the sequel, *The Lost Symbol* generated worldwide interest in the piece. Installed in 1990, the curved copper sculpture is punched through with four panels of encrypted text. Anyone with an inclination toward code-cracking, from amateur hacks to professional cryptographers have taken a stab it. Three of the panels were deciphered by 1999, the fourth has yet to be. *Kryptos*-related websites, cipher wheels and course curricula emerged in pursuit of the answer. Thankfully for those of us without security clearances, another encrypted work from Sanborn stands in the sculpture garden near the entrance of the Hirshhorn Museum and is open to all.

Antipodes ("diametrically opposite") refers to covert CIA and KGB operations and incorporates text unique to it as well as texts from both *Kryptos* and Sanborn's Cyrillic-language piece, *Cyrillic Projector*. Like the earlier works, *Antipodes* is characteristically curvilinear and perforated with cryptic messages. A length of petrified wood separates the curved copper panels of opposing encoded texts. Though Sanborn cut the *Kryptos* text himself by jigsaw, by the time he created *Antipodes*, a Midwest water jet company did the honors of cutting the text.

Decoded as of September 2003, the KGB/Cyrillic side is solved, but the CIA side is still up for grabs. Get thee to the Hirshhorn, the code-breaker might just be you.

When President Thomas Jefferson sent Lewis and Clark out to explore the Western frontier, he prepared a cipher for Meriwether Lewis, for secrecy of communication. Interestingly, an explanatory letter about the Vigenère-inspired cipher dated April 20, 1803, states: "suppose the keyword to be *antipodes*." A copy of the text is held among the Thomas Jefferson papers at the Library of Congress.

CAPITOL VENTILATION TOWERS

US Capitol West Lawn
Near Southwest Drive off 1st Street SW (or near Northwest Drive off 1st Street NW)
• Metro: Blue, Orange, or Silver Line to Federal Center (closer to the South Tower than the North)

Olmstedian air conditioning

Flanking the West Lawn of the US Capitol like rooks on a chessboard, two stone towers stand mutely in the face of the question, *What are those?* The stately, 30-foot mystery towers date to the 1880s and the noted landscape architect Frederick Law Olmsted's expansion of the Capitol grounds. Designed to house the air shafts of an intricate ventilation system for the Senate and House Chambers, these traces of early air conditioning remarkably still function as fresh air intakes.

Conceived to mitigate outside distraction while Congress is in session, the windowless Capitol chambers suffered compromised air quality. A November 11, 1873, *New York Times* story reported improvements to the existing ventilating system. Notably an underground air duct from the Senate basement out onto the West Lawn would in tandem with existing forcing-fans installed below the perforated Senate floor draw fresh air from the outdoors into the enclosed wing. Declaring the Senate Chamber had become "one of the best ventilated public halls in the country," the *Times* lauded the "ingenious" addition of a vent beneath every desk for each Senator to individually adjust the airflow.

The following year Olmsted received the commission to design the grounds: in his plan, a granite air shaft to the House Chamber. Completed in 1882, its counterpart for the Senate Chamber would not be completed until the decade's end.

NEARBY

THE SUMMERHOUSE

Cloistered in a hillside slope, the Capitol Summerhouse is Olmsted's thoughtful concession to the lack of cooling tree cover and water on the Capitol grounds, a respite. Even with its explosion of color—red brick and tiger lilies in summer—the hexagonal court remains intentionally unobtrusive amid the pale neutrals of the Capitol and air towers. Now purely decorative, its central fountain once supplied spring water to refresh visitors and horses. Today updated drinking fountains provide potable water. Armrests on the stone benches ensure upright resting under the shade of tiled awnings. Beyond a small grille on the eastern face, a serene rock stream and a tangle of wild plant life entice the eye and ear from a secret grotto.

THE AMERICAN VETERANS DISABLED FOR LIFE MEMORIAL ❽

150 Washington Avenue SW
• www.avdlm.org
• Metro: Orange or Blue Line to Federal Center; 32, 34 or 36 bus to Independence Avenue and 1st Street SW

> **Bearing witness to the courage, patriotism and sacrifice of disabled veterans**

Across from the stately Bartholdi Fountain and above the bustle of I-395 is a contemplative space honoring American veterans disabled in military service; a reminder of the cost of human conflict.

Granite walls and etched glass panels envelop the grove of remembrance, punctuated by bronze silhouettes that evoke in mute testimony the experience of our wounded warriors. Centered in the memorial is a star-shaped fountain, from which springs — like hope — a ceremonial flame.

Philanthropist Lois Pope (Secretary of Veteran's Affairs during the Clinton administration), Jesse Brown, and former National Adjutant of Disabled American Veterans, Art Wilson, spearheaded an effort in 1998 to pay tribute to these patriots with a national memorial. Forming the nonprofit organization Disabled Veterans Life Memorial Foundation, Inc. (DVLMF), they sought Congressional approval. To circumvent the standards of the U.S. Commemorative Works Act stipulating that a memorial can be erected only "after the 25th anniversary of the death of the individual or last surviving member of a group," they sought an amendment of the act to include living disabled veterans.

In January 1999, Senator John McCain introduced legislation in Congress to authorize the memorial at no cost to the federal government and designate DVLMF for project oversight from design solicitation and fundraising to construction. President Clinton signed the bill into law in October 2000 and the memorial was dedicated in October 2014.

Landscape architect Michael Vergason's design includes 69 gingko and 23 cypress trees selected for their adaptability in the urban environment to "represent survival under difficult circumstances," he says. The walls, inscribed with quotes, juxtapose granite and glass as metaphors for the strength and fragility of the human spirit. The Bethel white granite Gratitude Wall is hand chiseled by Nicholas Benson with quotes from Presidents George Washington and Dwight D. Eisenhower. Etched by Moon Shadow Glass, Inc. with photographic images and words from disabled veterans, the glass panels are laminated to withstand hurricane-force winds. Larry Kirkland (creator of the Keck Center Lobby, see p. 69) designed the reverse silhouette panels. At each point of the Star Fountain is an emblem from one of the five branches of the U.S. Armed Forces. Water overflows from the fountain to a reflecting pool below, thoughtfully designed at an appropriate viewing height for wheelchair-bound visitors.

BLIND WHINO SW ARTS CLUB ⑨

700 Delaware Avenue SW
- blindwhino.org
- 301-567-8210
- Open: hours vary, call ahead
- Metro: Green Line to Waterfront-SEU

*A pillar
of creativity
for the community*

Anchoring a tiny residential cul-de-sac in Washington's smallest quadrant is an immense brick church surprisingly swathed in an explosion of color courtesy of the muralist HENSE. It is one of few extant survivors of the sweeping mid-century urban renewal initiative which removed most traces of the pre-existing culture of the area.

The Virginia Avenue Baptist Church, founded by former slaves in 1875, commissioned James E. Boyce to build their house of worship in 1886. It would come to be known as Friendship Baptist Church. In 1952, the building was spared the wrecking ball when Reverend Benjamin H. Whiting succeeded in having the "neighborhood bedrock institution" removed from the city's renewal plan. After having served as the spiritual home to various congregations for over a hundred years, it sat, unused and deteriorating after its last congregants relocated in 2001.

The building, at historic address 734 1st Street SW received landmark designation in May 2004. The Historic Preservation Review Board stated, "It was among the earliest independent African-American congregations and despite being relatively early and constructed by a less privileged community, the Italianate Gothic building does demonstrate a certain dignity and architectural pretension."

Seeking to enliven the vacant building while redevelopment plans were pending current owner, Steve Tanner spoke with Shane Pomajambo, Executive Director of National Harbor's Art Whino Gallery who conceived of "an Art Basel-style building wrap" and enlisted artist HENSE to create the dynamic mural. Partnering with Ian Callender, principal of events design firm, Suite Nation, Pomajambo founded non-profit organization Blind Whino "on the principal that art is a catalyst for change in a community, providing inspiration and motivation for those that encounter its power."

The building-as-vehicle for uplift has been restored largely through the creative adaptive reuse of the space. Artists as far flung as DC's Aniekan Udofia to Australia's Meggs have adorned the interior walls of the former sanctuary with a vibrancy that parallels the exterior. A second floor stage provides a performance space and DJ lounge filtered with the glow of stained glass. Callender asserts that "Blind Whino adds an imaginative art incentive" to the once neglected community. The partners are excited by the unlimited possibilities of the space to engage the previously underserved citizens with free access to the arts.

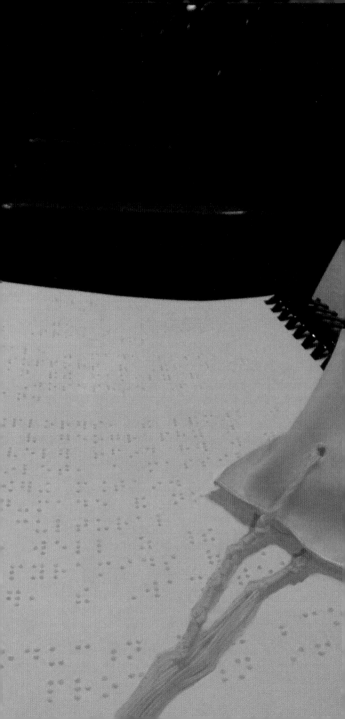

ACCESSIBLE ARTS AT ARENA STAGE ⑩

1101 6th Street SW
• arenastage.org
• 202-554-9066
• Audio Description is scheduled on selected Saturday matinee performances and Open Captioning is scheduled on selected Wednesday evenings for each production in the subscription season; arrange script loan via email access@arenastage.org; for Teletype (TTY), dial 202-484-0247
• Metro: Green Line to Waterfront-SEU

> *Seeing with the hands and verbalizing the visual*

A rena Stage at the Mead Center for American Theater, an exciting element in the revitalization of the Southwest waterfront, has been since its early days as a single Northwest theatre in the round, inclusive and welcoming of all people. As such it has been at the forefront of accessibility in Washington theater, making strides in the best possible approaches to providing access for all patrons. For the blind and visually impaired theater-going public, Arena Stage offers services beyond braille and large-print programs.

Tactile books illustrate through touch what the eye cannot see from fabric samples to hairpieces, immersing the patron in the world unfolding on stage. For a production of *Fiddler on the Roof*, there's a sense of the coarseness and weight of the heavy woolens worn by the villagers of Anatevka. One can imagine Tevye and the other faithful men, the varying lengths and textures of their beards, the sway of the *tzitzit* from their *tallitot* as they dance. Braille notes in the book explain the religious and cultural significance of what the patron is touching.

But what of that balancing marvel audiences thrill to at each performance, the bottle dance? Through audio-described theater, making the visual elements in the performance verbal, audio describers Jo Lynn Bailey or Joel Snyder explain the action: "Two men balance wine bottles in the crowns of their hats. They gently pulse their legs, twirl hands, turn in a circle, sink to the floor with ramrod straight spines…" The carefully timed narration is broadcast live via an inconspicuous FM receiver to the patron's dual headset or single earpiece, allowing for a more autonomous experience by eliminating the need to ask sighted companions for a play-by-play. Blind theater patron, Melanie Brunson, Executive Director of the American Council of the Blind rhapsodizes about audio description, "it enhances my enjoyment of the show tremendously."

Each of Arena Stage's three venues offers accessible seating and the building's open layout fosters ease of mobility. Deaf and hard of hearing patrons may enjoy open-captioned performance, script loan prior to viewing the performance, TTY or assistive listening devices which amplify and clarify the sound onstage.

TO THE BRAVE MEN
WHO PERISHED
IN THE WRECK
OF THE TITANIC
APRIL 15 1912
THEY GAVE THEIR
LIVES THAT WOMEN
AND CHILDREN
MIGHT BE SAVED

ERECTED BY THE
WOMEN OF AMERICA

TITANIC MEMORIAL ⑪

Southwest Waterfront Park
Fourth and P Streets SW
• Metro: Green Line to Waterfront

*Honoring
those men
who put women
and children first*

With head tilted toward the sky above the Washington Channel, a 13-foot granite male figure stands, arms outstretched, eyes closed in what its designer, Gertrude Vanderbilt Whitney declared "an expression of sublime sacrifice." Though designed by a noted sculptor and arts patron in memoriam of the most famous shipwreck in history, it remains a bit off-the-radar due to its location on the Southwest Waterfront bordering the eastern grounds of Fort McNair.

In the months following the sinking of the RMS *Titanic* on its maiden voyage April 15, 1912, women across the US rallied to raise funds to erect a monument to the bravery of the men who sacrificed their lives in the disaster to allow women and children to board first the lifeboats to safety. The initial donor was First Lady Helen Taft. Other society women followed, but most of the funds came from individual one-dollar donations from the grateful everyday woman. Whitney's graceful design was carved from a 20-ton block of granite in Massachusetts by stonemason John Horrigan in 1918. It would be over ten years before a suitably prominent site was chosen along the Potomac River at the end of New Hampshire Avenue and Rock Creek Parkway in Northwest. The memorial was dedicated in May 1931 with the inscription *To the brave men who perished in the wreck of the Titanic April 15, 1912. They gave their lives that women and children might be saved. Erected by the Women of America. To the young and the old, the rich and the poor, the ignorant and the learned, all who gave their lives to save women and children.* Surrounding the pedestal, a 30-foot exedra by architect Henry Bacon, also noted for his final work, the Lincoln Memorial.

The memorial was removed and placed in storage in 1966 to make way for construction of the John F. Kennedy Center for the Performing Arts. Reinstalled at its current site, then called Washington Channel Park in 1966, it now conjures for contemporary visitors a memorable scene from the blockbuster film *Titanic* in which the protagonist stands, arms outstretched, braced by her doomed lover.

CHAMPAGNE FOR THE 1,352 MEN LOST IN THE TRAGEDY

Each year since 1979, a group of dapper gentlemen, The Men's Titanic Society, arrive at the memorial on the April 15 anniversary of the ship's sinking attired in tuxedos and bearing roses. Just after midnight they lift their champagne glasses in tribute to the bravery of the 1,352 men lost in the tragedy.

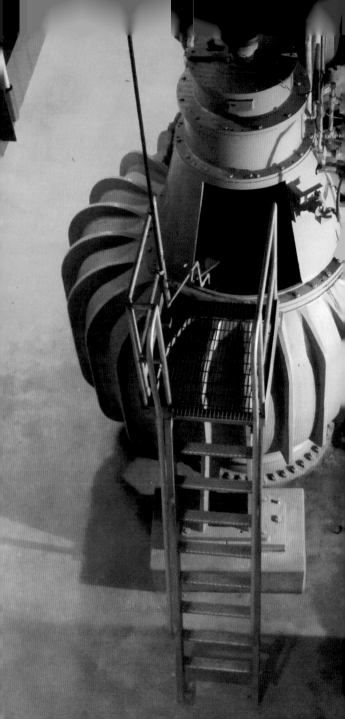

BLUE PLAINS ADVANCED WASTEWATER TREATMENT PLANT TOUR

⑫

5000 Overlook Avenue SW
• dcwater.com/wastewater/blueplains.cfm
• 202-787-2000
• Tours are offered on Wednesdays for junior and high-school students, and Fridays for other interested groups; scheduled to begin at 10 am and lasting approximately 90 minutes; wear closed-toe shoes; hard hats are provided
• Metro: closest station is Congress Heights, but it's best to drive

At the corner of Filtration and Nitrification

O ver a stretch of the Anacostia Freeway, a sulfuric essence hangs in the air. At DC's southernmost tip, gravity pulls the aromatic influent of the District, Montgomery and Prince George's counties in Maryland, and Fairfax and Loudoun counties in Virginia to the largest advanced wastewater treatment plant in the world. The region's sewage undergoes several processes on these 150 acres before discharging, sparkling clean into the Potomac River bordering the site. Approximately 370 million gallons of water are treated daily: enough to fill RFK Stadium. A trip to the Blue Plains plant will leave you mindful of each flush and grateful for the nostril-assailing work performed each day (engineers call it "the smell of money").

In a pristine white conference room evoking cleanliness, guide Yani gives an overview. Blue Plains policies are "among the most stringent in the world," she says, largely to protect the Potomac, a tributary to the Chesapeake Bay, "the cradle of life for this area." She thanks us for our, ahem, contributions, as human waste holds the promise of reuse as compost and even conversion to renewable energy. She implores us, however, to consider our habits: that beyond our biological deposits, we should flush only toilet tissue. This point will be driven home as piles of extracted debris from candy wrappers to condoms pass on conveyor belts in the first phase of separating our region's mass detritus from its water.

Though advised of potential olfactory distress, we waive the option of conducting the tour entirely from the DC Water van and opt for the full-on experience. Given we toured on a cold day, we were spared the emanations say of a humid August afternoon. Eponymous street signage: Aeration Road, Solids Road, and so on are each an unmistakable indicator of the step in the treatment process. Many wastewater treatment plants treat sewage in two multilayered steps—clarification, and sedimentation. At Blue Plains, a tertiary step, making it an advanced treatment facility, removes nitrogen to protect the Chesapeake Bay watersheds. On the vanguard of wastewater transformation, they continue to explore advances in technology.

At tour's end, Yani holds up two beakers; one with DC tap water (a different system) and one with Blue Plains-treated water, both clear. On the banks of the Potomac, the plant's effluent discharge is demarcated, visibly cleaner, from the existing river water.

SOUTHEAST

HIDDEN FORE-EDGE PAINTINGS ❶

Library of Congress Rare Book and Special Collections Reading Room
Thomas Jefferson Building, LJ 239
101 Independence Avenue SE
• loc.gov/rr/rarebook/
• 202.707.3448
• Open: weekdays 8:30 am – 5:00 pm; final book requests at 4:15 pm; closed Saturdays, Sundays, and federal holidays
• Admission: free, but reader card is required (apply on-site)—belongings must be checked into Reading Room lockers and all notes must be taken in pencil
• Metro: Blue, Orange, or Silver Line to Capitol South

Wonders of concealment

Among the many treasures of the Library of Congress Rare Book and Special Collections Reading Room are the secret artworks hidden in their collection of fore-edge painted books. With marbled boards and ornate bookplates the "edgy" beauties are wonders of concealment.

Fore-edge painting, a 16th-century conceit credited to Venetian artist Cesare Vecellio, is the painting of images on the edge of the pages opposite a book's spine. Vecellio turned closed books into canvases for decorative and heraldic art. A century later in England, Samuel Mearne, royal bookbinder to Charles II devised a new method of fore-edge painting by securing the fanned pages of a book in place with a vise, and painting on the angled surface. Gilding or marbling the book edges when dry obscured the painted image from view. The resulting painting was visible only upon fanning the pages. When the book was closed, the image seemed to vanish.

As interest in these books continued, the concealed imagery along their pages became more elaborate with landscapes, portraits, and religious scenes. During the late 18th and early 19th centuries, bookbinders such as Edwards of Halifax employed artists to create fore-edge paintings for their lavishly bound books.

By the 20th century the repertoire of painting techniques expanded to include triple and double fore-edge. A triple fore-edge book utilizes the overlooked top and bottom edges along with the fore-edge pages to create a continuous image around the three sides, viewable on a closed book. However, double fore-edge painted books encompass two distinct paintings viewed from left or right. These astonishing artworks are created by painting two images, one edging the recto pages and the other the verso, for a completely different painting.

With the protracted title *Observations on Several Parts of the Counties of Cambridge, Norfolk, Suffolk, and Essex also on Several Parts of North Wales; Relative Chiefly to Picturesque Beauty in Two Tours; The Former Made in the Year 1769. The latter in the year 1773*, the pictured 1809 book's images presumably represent the two tours.

ODIN

HISTORY OF THE WRITTEN WORD ENTRANCES

2

John Adams Building of the Library of Congress
East and West Entrances
2nd Street at Independence Avenue SE
• loc.gov
• 202-707-9779
• Open: Monday, Wednesday, Thursday 8:30 am – 9:30 pm; Tuesday, Friday, Saturday 8:30 am – 5 pm
• Metro: Blue, Orange, or Silver Line to Capitol South

> **Commemorating the creation of written language**

Many cultures lay claim to the genesis of the written word. How fitting it is that doorways to the "Nation's Library" acknowledge this diversity of creation mythology. The John Adams Building, annex to the Library of Congress, was constructed in 1938, its massive bronze doors sculpted by Lee Lawrie in bas-relief depicting twelve contributors to written language. Some are credited with creating it, others as amanuenses of human destiny.

Installed under the auspices of the Architect of the Capitol, new code-compliant egress doors featuring the Lawrie reliefs recast in glass introduce filtered light and panic bars for millennial functionality. They honor the artistic and historic integrity of the 11-foot originals now conserved, spiffied-up and recessed into architectural niches in their historical hold-open position.

The honored dozen includes Hindu God *Brahma* bearing sacred Vedic texts. Ancient Greeks credited two sources for the modern alphabet: *Cadmus,* who brought Phoenician symbols to Greece, and *Hermes,* for creating letters and numerals. Mayan god *Itzamná* gifted humanity with hieroglyphic writing and the calendar. With his stylus, Mesopotamian god *Nabu* kept the clay Tablets of Destiny. With magic runes from the World Tree of Norse cosmology, *Odin* god of poets, created the runic alphabet. Ogham script, the 4th-century writing system is named for *Ogma*, inventor of Gaelic letters. Writing and books are attributed to *Quetzalcóatl*, the supreme deity of Aztec culture. Persian hero *Tahmurath* coerced the delivery of languages (over thirty) to humankind. Inventor of language, Ibis-headed Egyptian god *Thoth* recorded the judgment of the dead. Inspired by claw marks and animal footprints, four-eyed figure of Chinese legend *Ts'ang Chieh*, created pictographic letters. An indigenous American, *Sequoyah*, the sole mortal represented was born in what is now Tennessee. He developed a writing system for his native language *Tsalagi Gawonihisdi* in 1809. Known as the Cherokee Syllabary, it was adopted by the Tsalagi (Cherokee) Nation in 1825.

For all its beauty, notably absent though, is a female presence. What's Brahma without Saraswati (see page 141), Nabu without his predecessor Nisaba?

"ROBERTA FLACK TRIO" SIGN

③

Mr. Henry's Restaurant
601 Pennsylvania Avenue SE
• mrhenrysdc.com
• 202-546-8412
• Open: Monday to Friday 11:15 am – midnight; Saturday & Sunday 10 am – midnight
• Metro: Blue, Orange, or Silver Line to Eastern Market

A launching pad

Prominently displayed above the bar at Mr. Henry's Victorian Pub is a black wooden sign gilded in calligraphic script, "Roberta Flack Trio," a nod to the multiple Grammy Award-winning recording artist. In the late 1960s, Ms. Flack, the prodigiously talented Arlington, Virginia-bred pianist and vocalist was a music teacher for DC Public Schools by day and with her eponymous trio, the house band for the Capitol Hill boîte by night. So good were her performances, so popular were her sets that owner Henry Yaffe built a performance space for her—complete with church pew seating—on the upper floor of his establishment. In her perfectly shaped Afro, Ms. Flack would share her stage with the many celebrities who rolled through. She even tickled the ivories with Liberace. Impressed with her act, jazz musician Les McCann arranged an audition for her with Atlantic Records.

When the burgeoning star was photographed for the cover art of *First Take*, her debut recording for Atlantic, she staged the shoot at Mr. Henry's. To this day a copy of the album cover adorns the wall next to the cash register.

Though the stage no longer exists, little else has changed in this true neighborhood spot—reasonable prices, super-friendly bartenders and waitstaff, a legendary Sunday brunch and half-price burgers on Mondays. Not a bad way to absorb some pop culture history and due to its location on "The Hill," maybe spot a pundit or two. Political strategist Donna Brazile is a regular who has acknowledged her love for the place to her Twitter following.

Atlantic Records owes a debt to Washington, DC, and not just for cultivating the talents of Roberta Flack. Though introduced to jazz in London, it was in Washington that the son of the first Turkish Ambassador to the US would cultivate his love for music. By needle-dropping at popular record store, Quality Music Shop (later known as Waxie Maxie's) and checking out the acts at the nearby Howard Theatre, Ahmet Ertegün immersed himself in music. Though he attended the toniest of institutions he often said "I got my real education at the Howard." He founded Atlantic Records in 1947 to record the music he'd loved. An early act signed to the label was The Clovers, a group from DC's incubator of musical talent, Armstrong High School (Duke Ellington, Billy Eckstine, and Jimmy Cobb are among its illustrious alumni).

GESSFORD COURT

4

Between Independence Avenue and C Street SE; bordered by 11th and 12th Streets
• Metro: Blue or Orange Line to Eastern Market, get walking directions from there on your smartphone

Alley jazz cats

Scattered throughout the District, many residential alleys, mews, and courts survive Washington's periodic aversion to inhabited alleys. These hidden micro-neighborhoods are found in every quadrant, each with a rich history; their intimate configurations encouraging a deep sense of community.

One of several tucked away in Capitol Hill alone is the easily-missed-if-you're-not-looking Gessford Court. The brick-paved court is home to transitional Hill staffers, longtime stalwarts and its own jazz band, 21 Gessford.

Notorious for the carousing and brawls in two rented frame houses, the court was during its late 1880s incarnation, dubbed "Tiger Alley" by the residents of the surrounding neighborhood. In 1892 prolific Washington builder, Charles Gessford built ten small brick rowhouses along the tiny mews, narrowly missing a Congressional moratorium on new construction in alleys. Directly across from them, Martin Wiegand built two others. Despite the alley's renaming in honor of Gessford after his death in 1894, it is listed as Tiger Alley in the 1900 census. At the time, it was densely populated with an average of six people per household in each small house, all African-American laborers.

THE CONGRESSMAN'S "SLUM"

The dream combo of proximity to the Capitol and seclusion appealed to the congressman from Harlem Adam Clayton Powell, Jr. who, in mid-century, made Gessford Court his home-away-from-home when Congress was in session. His son, Adam Clayton Powell III shared his reminiscences with the *Washington Post* about his father's off-the-radar property. Apparently the elder Powell purchased several properties on the court he called "my slum," renovated them and sold them for a tidy sum. He saved number 16 for himself, its living room as wide as his wingspan, he liked to point out. Secreted from prying eyes (save for a fruitless FBI search of his tiny abode) he held court on Gessford, partying and convening colleagues in a cloud of cigar smoke.

21ST @ 21

In conjunction with the nearby Corner Store Arts Center (900 South Carolina Avenue) David Weiner hosts 21st @ 21, a BYOB jam session/ potluck dinner/community get-together on the 21st of each month in his towering renovated home at 21 Gessford Court.

LIBERTY AND FREEDOM TOTEM POLES ❺

Historic Congressional Cemetery
1801 E Street SE
• congressionalcemetery.org
• 202.543.0539
• Open: daily, dawn to dusk for self-guided tours; check website for docent-led tours
• Metro: Blue Line to Stadium-Armory

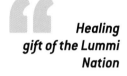

Healing gift of the Lummi Nation

In reverence for the lives lost in the terror attacks of September 11, 2001, Native Americans of the Lummi Nation in Washington state created healing totem poles for each of the three regions where lives were lost. New York (in 2002) and Pennsylvania (in 2003) were each gifted with a single memorial totem. In 2004, Washington, DC received two poles joined by a crossbeam.

Led by master carver and Lummi Councilman Jewell Praying Wolf James, carvers of the Lummi Nation House of Tears carved the *Liberty and Freedom Totem Poles* out of old-growth red cedar legally harvested from Mt. Baker-Snoqualmie National Forest. Timber secured, the painstaking process of creating the totems included peeling the bark from the log; removing the layer of sapwood; shaping a smooth, cylindrical pole; flattening the back; dividing the pole into segments; carving the figures and finally painting them in a color palette of red, black, white, and yellow, representing races in America.

The poles are 13 feet tall, symbolic of the number of the original American colonies and contain images of animals and symbols with spiritual meaning to the Lummi. Bears carved into the poles represent courage and strength. The right pole, *Liberty*, features Bear Mother with Grandmother Moon; the left pole, *Freedom*, has Bear Father holding Grandfather Sun. The crossbar, *Sovereignty*, so named by James because "freedom and liberty are the foundations of sovereignty," is flanked by eagles. The west-facing male eagle symbolizes war; the east-facing female eagle represents peace. Their seven-feathered wings represent American Airlines Flight 77, which crashed into the Pentagon.

Janice Marie Scott was one of the 183 people lost that day. Her husband Abraham rallied for donations to the nearly $60,000 project which included the cross-country journey of the totems from the West Coast to the East, with stops for traditional prayers and blessings from dozens of tribal nations along the way. Installed briefly at the Pentagon, the poles were relocated to the Congressional Cemetery, where they'll stay until the September 11 Memorial Grove opens on Kingman Island.

The burial of pioneering attorney and suffragist Belva Ann Lockwood, the first woman to argue a case before the US Supreme court, near the graves of prominent Native Americans is apropos as she secured a $5 million settlement from the US Government for the Cherokee Nation.

FRANCIS A. GREGORY NEIGHBORHOOD LIBRARY

6

3660 Alabama Avenue SE
• dclibrary.org/francis
• 202-698-6373
• Open: Monday to Thursday 9:30 am – 9:00 pm; Friday & Saturday 9:30 am – 5:30 pm; Sunday 1:00 pm – 5:00 pm
• Metro: W4 bus from either Green Line at Anacostia station or Orange Line at Deanwood station

Adjaye's woodland folly

Enveloped on three sides by the urban glade of Fort Davis Park and fronted by residences in the Southeast neighborhood named also for the fort, the Francis A. Gregory branch of the DC Public Library with its mirrored, geometric-patterned facade reflects both literally and figuratively the surrounding community. As Mary McLeod Bethune once said, "Invest in the human soul, who knows it may be a diamond in the rough." The diamond patterning carried through into the interior with floor-to-ceiling wooden lattice work references not harlequins of the *commedia dell'arte* but rather a jewel box in the green. A "woodland folly," star architect David Adjaye said of his design. He wanted to create a space that would uplift and inspire in the historically underserved community east of the Anacostia River. With local architects Wiencek + Associates, he succeeded.

Colorful Senegalese baskets serve as pendant lamps over a bank of Mac computers, adding a resonant cultural touch for the largely African-American community. The open-plan design and woodland views encourage thinking expansively. Library patrons and employees alike enjoy the beautiful, well-appointed facility. Longtime neighborhood resident and retired veteran, John Henry brings his 9-year-old grandson to the Gregory Library to encourage reading, but admits he enjoys it just as much. "It's great for children and adults. It's a good place to go to chill and read. You can learn something there. For those who don't know how to use the computer, they'll teach you; the staff is very friendly and very helpful," he says. "It's wonderful for the neighborhood."

Though all are expected to use their "inside voices" throughout the library, there are dedicated niches set apart as quiet zones for study. There are even booth-sized "study rooms" with a desk and two chairs each as well as a glass door for the ultimate quiet and privacy.

The branch, once known as the Fort Davis Regional Library was renamed in 1986 in honor of the late Francis Anderson Gregory, longtime Fort Davis resident and the first black president of the Public Library's Board of Trustees. The new, Adjaye-designed building opened on June 19, 2012.

HISTORIC NAVY YARD WATCH BOX ❼

Washington Navy Yard
11th and O Street Gate
• Open: Mon—Fri 9am—5pm; 10am—5pm on weekends and federal holidays
• Free entry
• Guided and self-guided tours upon request. Visitors must have either a Dept. of Defense Common Access Card, an Active Military, Retired Military, or Military Dependent ID, or an escort with one these credentials. All visitor 18 and older must have a photo ID.
• Tel: 202-433-4882 (call to arrange a tour in advance)
• www.history.navy.mil

Final official presidential stroll

Set amid the heavily patinaed bronze guns of Leutze Park stands a porticoed "watch box," erected in 1853-1854 as a sentry post for the Washington Navy Yard, the nation's first home port and naval shipbuilding facility and the U.S. Navy's oldest shore establishment.

With its columned wraparound porch, the small, 13-by-13 foot structure bears the distinction of being one of the last official stops of the Abraham Lincoln presidency. In the late afternoon of April 14, 1865, before his fateful attendance at Ford's Theater that evening, the President passed through

the facility to visit a trusted military adviser and friend, the Navy Yard Commandant Rear Admiral John Dahlgren, and stroll the deck of the naval monitor *USS Montauk*. Ironically, the ship would soon serve as both the autopsy site and bier of slain Lincoln assassin John Wilkes Booth and a floating prison for his alleged co-conspirators.

Until 1905, the tiny "guard shack," situated where the Navy Yard firehouse now stands was manned by Marines who granted or denied access through the Eighth Street entrance to the Washington Navy Yard. A year later, the structure (known also as Building 185), minus its corbeled porch, was relocated downriver to the Naval Support Facility at Indian Head, MD, some 30 miles southwest, where it served various purposes for over a century.

On April 16, 2015, nearly 150 years to the date that President Lincoln passed the gate for the final time, a barge ferried the eleven-ton watch box up the Potomac River and back to the Navy Yard, where an impressive restoration effort returned the centenarian structure to its early 20th-century glory. Based upon historical photos, preservation architects painstakingly replicated the wraparound porch original to the Italianate building and added brick flooring. Stratigraphic examination at 40x magnification revealed 25 distinct paint layers and, ultimately, the original exterior colors.

Since the ribbon cutting ceremony on October 8, 2015, the restored structure, the oldest on the base, now serves as a reminder of turn-of-the-century naval history, a contributing element to the Washington Navy Yard Historic District.

ANACOSTIA COMMUNITY MUSEUM ❽

1901 Fort Place SE
- anacostia.si.edu
- 202-633-4820
- Open: daily 10 am – 5 pm; closed December 25
- Metro: Green Line to Anacostia
- The museum also offers SHUTTLE Anacostia, free seasonal round-trip transportation to and from the National Mall which runs weekends (Saturdays, Sundays, and holiday Mondays) from Memorial Day weekend through Labor Day weekend

> **The only Smithsonian museum east of the Anacostia River**

The words Smithsonian Institution (SI) conjure a grand sweep of the National Mall and an oft-explored group of remarkable museums, but in Southeast is a hidden gem, the Anacostia Community Museum, the only one in the Smithsonian constellation located east of the Anacostia River. Founded in 1967 as an outreach effort to the largely African-American enclave, it was in its early years known as the Anacostia Neighborhood Museum and housed in a former movie theater. As the first federally funded community museum, it became the standard bearer, pioneering the use of special exhibition labels for the hearing-impaired in SI museums in 1982.

By 1987, its hyperlocal focus shifted to a broadened diasporic scope. Its name shortened to the Anacostia Museum, and its location moved from a prominent spot on MLK Jr. Avenue to the parkland of Fort Place.

A 2002 architectural update takes inspiration from multiple African nations. A textural red-brick facade mimics the pattern of woven kente cloth. Accented with a motif suggestive of Malian architecture, the cylindrical forms flanking the entrance evoke the freestone tower ruins of the ancient city of Great Zimbabwe. Presiding over the campus since 2004 is sculptor Allen Uzikee Nelson's *Real Justice*, honoring late Supreme Court Justice Thurgood Marshall.

With the National Museum of African American Heritage and Culture also forthcoming under Smithsonian auspices, the organization returned to a more community-focused mission in 2006. Taking the name Anacostia Community Museum, it now explores aspects of community within and beyond Anacostia boundaries. A recent exhibition explored community empowerment in the KwaZulu-Natal province of South Africa. *Ubuhle Women: Beadwork and the Art of Independence*, is a breathtaking survey of works from the Ubuhle arts organization.

Outreach is comprehensive, with live music, film screenings, lectures, panel discussions, author talks, a variety of workshops, and special programming for the cultural celebrations, Juneteenth and Kwanzaa.

Stroll Good Hope Road for more east-of-the-river culture, at Honfleur Gallery (1241) and the Anacostia Arts Center (1231).

THE BIG CHAIR

2101 Martin Luther King, Jr. Avenue SE
• Metro: Green Line to Anacostia

Looming large

When Charles W. Curtis commissioned Bassett Furniture to erect a Bunyanesque replica of a Duncan Phyfe chair to attract customers to his family's furniture showroom in 1959, little did he know he was creating an enduring Anacostia icon that would bear silent witness to a half-century of change.

In another attention-getting move, Curtis had a 10 by 10-foot glass cube constructed on the seat of the 19½-foot-high, 4,600-pound chair. It was designed as a human fishbowl of sorts; whoever consented to live there, would do so in public view. It was equipped with the basics: bed, curtains, television, telephone, heater and air conditioner and of course, a shower and toilet. Over the objections of her husband, 21-year-old model Lynn Arnold, agreed to move in.

On August 13, 1960, Arnold was forklifted into her transparent home. Advertised as "Alice in the Looking Glass House," she passed the time by reading, watching TV, talking on the phone and waving down to the crowds assembled to observe her every move. Her only in-house visitor was her 14-month-old son, who was hoisted up, as were her meals via dumbwaiter. Passersby hedged bets on the duration of her stay. After six weeks, acknowledging that she was "groundsick," she "decided to return to earth," earning $1,500 for her time.

Though the sixties began with lighthearted publicity stunts, they ended in violence and sorrow. As rioting erupted in the wake of the Reverend Dr. Martin Luther King, Jr. assassination, the chair remained untouched, a fact that deeply moved Charles Curtis. "No one laid a hand on the chair. They had respect for it," he shared with the *Washington Post* at the 2006 unveiling of the new weather-resistant version.

The Curtis family of companies has maintained a presence in the Anacostia community long after the store closing in 1973. The durable mahogany of the Bassett-built chair withstood the elements for decades, but eventually fell prey to rot and was replaced with a detailed copy crafted in aluminum. Purists may dismiss the steely facsimile, known colloquially as "The Big Chair," but most are gladdened by its return; a constant in a city in rapid flux.

FREDERICK DOUGLASS NATIONAL HISTORIC SITE

⑩

Cedar Hill
1411 W Street SE
• nps.gov/frdo
• 202-426-5961
• Open: year-round daily; April to October 9 am – 5 pm; November to March 9 am – 4:30 pm; closed January 1, Thanksgiving Day, and December 25 • Admission: free, house tours by ticket only: reserve online at recreation.gov
• Metro: Green Line to Anacostia: transfer to B2 bus to stop directly in front of the historic site

Enslavement to eminence, the Lion of Anacostia

The east-west vista from Frederick Douglass' final home suggests his trajectory from his 1818 birth into slavery on Maryland's Eastern Shore to the US Capitol where his bronze likeness was unveiled with his descendants in attendance nearly 200 years later in 2013.

Defying a whites-only housing covenant, Douglass bought the hilltop Victorian estate in 1877. Known as "Cedar Hill," it is an emblem of the polymath's exemplary rise from enslavement to eminence as a powerful orator, abolitionist, author, publisher, Trustee of Howard University,

and statesman. During his Washington years, he served as a US Marshal; president of Freedman's Savings & Trust; recorder of deeds for the District of Columbia and consul general to Haiti.

With his wife Anna, he enjoyed life on Cedar Hill, playing checkers in the parlor and croquet on the lawn with their many grandchildren, whom he indulged by letting them braid his white corona of hair. "Family was always central to Mr. Douglass. He'd been raised under the bondage of slavery; his family unit was broken apart. So he knew that family, that the home would be the fountainhead in terms of human progress," says Ka'mal McClarin, curator of the Frederick Douglass National Historic Site.

After Anna's 1882 death, Douglass married Helen Pitts, a white woman twenty years his junior in 1884. They felt "ostracized by white and black alike," but their union survived the controversy. The second Mrs. Douglass rallied to preserve Cedar Hill as a legacy of her husband upon his 1895 death.

Administered by the National Park Service, ranger-led tours of the mansion and grounds reveal Douglass' personal side. See his study with its impressive library. His collection of canes includes one crafted of wood from a house built by John Brown and one which belonged to Abraham Lincoln. Check out the dumbbells used in his exercise regimen and imagine him in his 19th-century backyard man cave, "The Growlery." Taken from the avid reader's favorite author, Dickens, it's an apt name and lair for the man dubbed the "Lion of Anacostia."

> Of his many area properties, 2000 17th Street NW in the historic Striver's Section is now home to the only Japanese grocery in DC.

PANORAMIC OVERLOOK AT OUR LADY OF PERPETUAL HELP

11

Our Lady of Perpetual Help Catholic Church
1600 Morris Road SE
• 202-678-4999
• Open: be mindful that the overlook is private property, access it via the church driveway; Washington's forts are open dawn to dusk every day except January 1, Thanksgiving, and December 25
• Metro: Green Line to Anacostia, transfer to W2 or W3 bus

> *God,*
> *Go-Go and*
> *a glorious view*

A t the apex of Morris Road in old Anacostia, on grounds which rival in their vista the magnificent views from nearby Cedar Hill, converge sacred and secular histories of Anacostia culture. Abutting a Civil War-era fort, this parcel of land long a "those who know, know" spot for Fourth of July fireworks viewing, is owned by Our Lady of Perpetual Help Catholic Church (OLPH). The main sanctuary is of 1970s construction, but the parish was founded in 1920 by the African-American parishioners of St. Teresa Avila, the oldest Roman Catholic Church in Anacostia. A Josephite Church (an order established post-Civil War in 1871 to minister to the formerly enslaved) OLPH today maintains the same mission to serve the African-American community.

The adjacent Church Hall, known aptly as the Panorama Room, has tended to community needs from funeral repasts and civic meetings to fitness classes set to music from gospel to Go-Go. As a performance space, it was possibly the most scenic of the abundant venues in the region to catch a Go-Go show. Chuck Brown and the Soul Searchers, Little Benny & the Masters, Experience Unlimited, Rare Essence and Trouble Funk are but a few bands who have brought the conga-inflected groove there.

NEARBY

EARTHWORKS OF FORT STANTON

In 1860, Washington, then the Union capital, had only one fortification, Fort Washington, which once guarded against enemy ships in the War of 1812. Sandwiched between the Confederate state of Virginia and the slave-holding state of Maryland, the city was vulnerable to attack. Within the next five years, the Union Army built the 37-mile Fort Circle of Washington Defenses with sixty-eight additional fortresses, making the city one of the world's most heavily fortified. Runaway slaves seeking freedom and safety flocked to the city's forts, many settling nearby at the war's end. Built in fall 1861, Fort Stanton stood in defense of the Washington Arsenal (Navy Yard). Today its remnants stand in the parkland at the northeast edge of the overlook, beyond an interpretive marker. As you make your way to the earthworks, you might spot a deer or two in the woods.

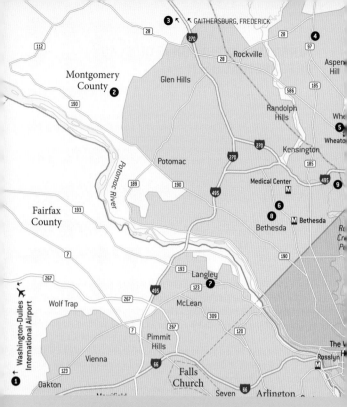

GREATER WASHINGTON NORTH

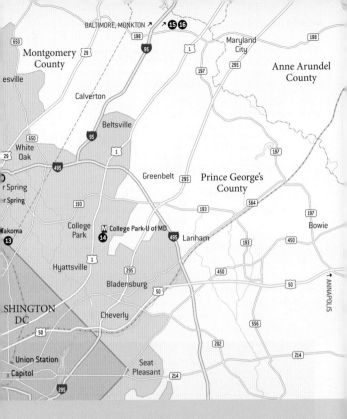

CLOSE ENCOUNTERS ALIEN SPACESHIP MODEL ❶

Smithsonian Institution, Steven F. Udvar-Hazy Center
14390 Air and Space Museum Parkway
Chantilly, Virginia
• Open: Daily 10am—5:30pm, except December 25
• Tel: 703-572-4118
• www.airandspace.si.edu/udvar-hazy-center
• Metro: Silver Line to Wiehle-Reston East station; transfer to Fairfax
Connector bus #983

**Another
Smithsonian,
another
mothership**

Less than an hour away from Washington, the Udvar-Hazy Center, companion facility of the Smithsonian's National Air and Space Museum, houses the model of the alien mothership from Steven Spielberg's 1977 critically-acclaimed sci-fi film *Close Encounters of the Third Kind.*

Master model builder Gregory Jein led the team that executed the director's vision for the spacecraft. He and his team had nearly completed a model when Spielberg returned from India with a new concept inspired by the many lights of a Bombay oil refinery at night.

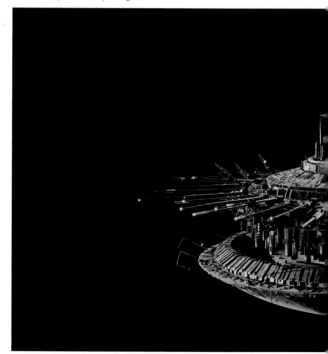

Salvaging some of the materials from the first model, the team went to work, utilizing aluminum tubes, elements from architectural models and model train parts, drilling countless holes for the fiber optic lights to shine through. Jein wanted the spaceship to be densely textured with no blank spaces. The model makers humorously achieved it, adding hidden "inside jokes" that wouldn't likely be visible in the film: a Volkswagen bus, a submarine, a U.S. mailbox, an aircraft, a small cemetery plot. Even R2-D2, the beloved android from *Star Wars* makes an appearance — with a quick eye, one can spy the miniature droid in a scene where the UFO passes Jillian on the mountain.

The photographic legerdemain and lighting effects made the stationary model appear colossal in scale, hovering over the frightened but intrigued earthlings, garnering Jein his first Academy Award nomination for Best Visual Effects.

Though the mothership once filled Steven Spielberg's three-car garage back in 1978, it is now available for close-up public scrutiny, courtesy of Columbia Pictures, which gifted the production model to the Smithsonian.

In *Raiders of the Lost Ark* Spielberg also appears to give a nod to 'droids from his buddy George Lucas's canon; in the scene where Indiana Jones descends into the Well of the Souls, hieroglyphics on the wall include representations of R2-D2 and C-3PO.

GLENSTONE

②

12002 Glen Road
Potomac, MD
• Open: Thur—Sun 10am—5:30
• Due to the fragile nature of the collection, Glenstone welcomes visitors age 12 and above. Service dogs welcome, but no pets allowed.
• Tel: to schedule your visit call 301-983-5001 or go to the website
• www.glenstone.org
• Not Metro accessible

> ## An impressive collection of contemporary art

In tony Potomac, Maryland, forty minutes away from DC's museum locus, the trinity of art, architecture and landscape converge seamlessly in a contemplative environment at Glenstone. Collectors Mitchell and Emily Rales have endowed the museum with an impressive collection of post-World War II modern and contemporary art.

A lovely drive along winding roads leads to the former foxhunting estate, sited on 230 thoughtfully landscaped acres. Every aspect of Glenstone is carefully considered, beginning with the name. Derived from Glen Road, which fronts the property, and carderock, a mica schist stone indigenous to the area, the name conjures a sense of place rather than referring to its founders.

The late Charles Gwathmey's zinc-clad modernist building functions in concert with Peter Walker's beautifully choreographed landscape, presenting

rotating exhibitions from the pre-eminent collection. The purposeful sequencing of indoor and outdoor spaces makes the facility, as architect Gwathmey describes, "an instigator to discovery." From the moment of passing the gatehouse, the experience unfolds in revelatory bursts: a maple allée, rolling hills and monumental sculpture commissioned from Richard Serra and Tony Smith. At the cobblestone entry court awaits water, sleek, oversized umbrellas, and insect repellent for those touring the grounds, while another Serra sculpture invites exploration.

Personable, knowledgeable guides welcome visitors and hover nearby in their gray uniforms, ready to engage should a visitor desire it, yet at a respectful distance, allowing the guest space to encounter the art in solitude. Comprising the Glenstone collection are paintings, sculptures, works on paper, photographs, installations and multimedia works gleaned from critical moments in the artists' careers. Artists in the vast collection include John Baldessari, Joseph Beuys, Willem de Kooning, Felix Gonzalez-Torres, David Hammons, Eva Hesse, Roni Horn, Jasper Johns, On Kawara, Ellsworth Kelly, Barbara Kruger, Brice Marden, Bruce Nauman, Jackson Pollock, Robert Rauschenberg, Fred Sandback and Cy Twombly.

GLENSTONE AT THE NGA

Ruling the roost on the sculpture terrace at the National Gallery of Art's (pg 63) renovated East Building is Katharina Fritsch's matte blue sculptural portrait *Hahn/Cock* (2013) on long-term loan from Glenstone. Enlivening the expansive atrium inside is *Color Panels for a Large Wall* (1978), 18 oil on canvas panels by Ellsworth Kelly, purchased with funds provided by The Glenstone Foundation.

GAITHERSBURG INTERNATIONAL LATITUDE ❸ OBSERVATORY AND MERIDIAN MARK PIER

Latitude Observatory Park
100 DeSellum Avenue
Gaithersburg, MD
• 301-258-6350
• Open: park open during daylight hours year round. During Gaithersburg Heritage Days in late June, interpreters open the building, including the roof, to the public for historical tour and solar observations, weather permitting
• Metro: Red Line to Shady Grove; transfer to Ride-On 55 bus to Frederick Blvd and Summit Ave

Tracking Chandler's wobble

To the east there's Gaithersburg High. To the west, residential quiet, save for the barking of a large dog keeping watch from his backyard onto a fenced-in, oddly louvered, wood frame structure in the adjacent park. Carved on the paved approach from the street is a curious succession of city names along with their longitude and elevation. Carloforte, Italy. Charjui, Turkestan. Mizusawa, Japan. Ukiah, California, Cincinnati, Ohio. But why? Along with Gaithersburg, Maryland, they share the same latitude coordinate, 39° 08' North. In 1898, a network of latitude observatories opened in these cities with a goal to measure the spiral sway of the Earth on its polar axis and the resultant subtle latitude shifts.

For the greater part of the 20th century, data gathered at Gaithersburg's 13-foot square latitude observatory aided understanding of the Earth's rotation and geophysical composition; providing intel that helped pave the way for space navigation. Through the retractable roof, a powerful Zenith telescope precisely measured star positions. Earl Williams wrote of the observatory life in a 1936 report, "I am the variation-of-latitude observer...I work while the rest of the world sleeps, with only the mournful hoot of a distant owl or the incessant call of the whip-poor-will to keep me company."

Now cordoned off by a circular fence, the Meridian Mark Pier 200 feet south of the observatory once provided a crucial step in taking accurate readings—aligning the telescope with crosshairs in the structure.

After an economically-driven hiatus from 1915 to 1932, the station once again functioned until 1982 when satellites and computers supplanted manual observation. Of the five geodetic survey markers scattered throughout the park, one dated 1966 is still used to test new technology for the Global Positioning System (GPS) Receiver.

The Chandler wobble may sound like a dance move, but it's a small nutation (swaying motion) of the Earth's axial rotation, the discovery of which is credited to Seth Carlo Chandler in 1891. A complete wobble occurs every 433 days. The off-kilter movement is attributed to Earth's oblate spheroidal shape: not quite a perfect sphere, but with a bit of a bulge at the Equator.

NATIONAL CAPITAL TROLLEY MUSEUM ❹

1313 Bonifant Road
Colesville, MD
• dctrolley.org
• 301-384-6088
• Open: Saturday and Sunday noon – 5 pm; closed December 24, 25, 31, and January 1; select Thursdays and Fridays (check website); trolley rides offered approximately every 30 minutes
• Admission: age 18-64, $7.00; age 2-17; 65 and up, $5.00; includes unlimited trolley rides
• Metro: Red Line to Glenmont; transfer to Montgomery County Ride-On bus #26 (operates every 30 minutes during museum hours)

A mass transit trove

The much ballyhooed return of streetcars to metropolitan Washington has come after a lull of fifty-plus years. During that half-century interim the National Capital Trolley Museum proudly and with great dedication preserved the streetcar heritage of the region.

For nearly a hundred years from July 1862 to January 1962, streetcars provided public transport to the citizens of Washington, DC and its suburbs. Though the first cars were horse-drawn, the introduction of efficient electric cars in 1888 rendered them obsolete. Atop these new trams, trolley poles connected to overhead power lines—the era of the "trolley car" had begun. "Cable cars" soon followed in 1892 as aerial wires were supplanted by underground cables to power the regional system, the Capital Transit Company. Over the years expansion would carry riders within city limits and into surrounding Maryland and Virginia locales. Transit innovations including taxicabs in 1908 and modern buses introduced by Washington Rapid Transit Company in 1923 would create the competition for ridership that led to the streetcar's eventual demise.

Capital Transit was sold to financier O. Roy Chalk in 1956 with the proviso that he update the system with buses by 1963. The company was renamed DC Transit and the last of the streetcars rolled out on January 28, 1962, one of which resides in the collection of the museum, founded in 1959 and opened to the public in 1969.

Filled with transit treasures, the museum engages every age. The informative exhibits include a working model of Rock Creek Electric Railway set in an idyllic diorama; a compilation of cinematic streetcar scenes and a comprehensive collection of streetcars from those used locally (including an 1899 snow-sweeping car) to international cars such as a 1934 English car designed to look like a boat and a sleek 1971 tram from The Hague.

A PRIVATE TROLLEY RIDE
Uniformed streetcar geeks, all volunteers, conduct 20-minute trolley rides around the wooded grounds in Montgomery County, Maryland. An exclusive, private ride can be reserved for up to forty-five guests of all ages for a very reasonable $150.

WHEATON METRO STATION ESCALATOR ❺

Georgia Avenue and Reedie Drive
Wheaton, MD
• Metro: Red Line to Wheaton

> **The longest single-span escalator in the Western Hemisphere**

With super-steep moving staircases in Moscow, St. Petersburg, Kiev and Prague, Eastern Europe holds the world record for longest single-span escalator, but in the west, Washington, DC's Metro system holds high the flag. A random poll of Metrorail riders may yield the heavily trafficked stations Dupont Circle in DC or Rosslyn in Virginia for holding this superlative distinction, the answer however, is in the commuter suburb of Wheaton, Maryland.

In the 140-foot-deep Metro station, the 230-foot-long escalator travels at 90 feet per minute at a 30-degree angle. That's about 2 minutes and 45 seconds of ascent or descent, plenty of time to ponder other Metro stats. The neighboring Red Line station, Forest Glen, also in Maryland, with its considerable depth—196 feet or twenty-one stories—uses only high-speed elevators for 20-second vertical access between the mezzanine and station platform. In Washington, the Woodley Park-Zoo/Adams Morgan station addresses its 154-foot depth by utilizing two levels of escalators. Rosslyn, on the Blue/Orange Line is the fifth longest at 194 feet. The top four longest escalators in the system are along the Red Line: Medical Center at 202 feet, Woodley Park-Zoo/Adams Morgan at 204 feet, Bethesda at 213 feet, and topping them all, Wheaton.

Upon exiting the station, a 7-foot-tall bronze figurative sculpture, *The Commuter*, by Maryland artist Marcia Billig whimsically acknowledges the area's commuter history. Commissioned by the Montgomery County Arts in Public Architecture Program, the statue depicts a gentleman rushing by on roller skates with newspaper and attaché in tow, necktie flapping in the wind. Adults can relate to commuting frenzy; children love the skates and animated gesture.

A 5-minute, Y8 bus ride away is Wheaton Regional Park at 2002 Shorefield Drive. A must-do for the children is the 12-minute tour of the park's forests and meadows by miniature steam engine train. Make no mistake, it is real, just a scaled-down replica of the 1863 C.P. Huntington, a 4-2-4T steam locomotive, so named for the president of Southern Pacific Company, Collis P. Huntington. Traversing a trestle bridge and passing Pine Lake, the ride is a delightful throwback to the golden age of steam locomotion.

CROSSROADS OF THE WORLD SIGNPOSTS   ⑥

Along the Capital Crescent Trail (CCT)
Bethesda, MD
GPS coordinates 38 57.096N and 77 6.776 W, between mile markers 5.5
and 6
• cctrail.org (Capital Crescent Trail website)
• Metro: Red Line to Bethesda; CCT Bethesda entry is four blocks south
of the station at Woodmont and Bethesda Avenue

Trail surprise

Housed in the Smithsonian National Museum of American History is the original wooden signpost from the set of the TV series "M*A*S*H." Likely the best-known in the country, it features the mileage from the MASH unit near Seoul, Korea to the characters' hometowns in the likes of Boston, Burbank and Toledo. Mysteriously bordering the splendid Capital Crescent Trail somewhere between miles five-and-a-half and six, directional markers point the way and quote the distance in kilometers to Zamboanga, Malindi, and Flåm. You know, just in case you find yourself beset by an inexplicable urge to know where we in the DC metropolitan area are in proximity to the Philippine peninsular city, Kenyan coastal town, and Norwegian fjord village.

Local hearsay attributes them to a chronicle of the owners' world travels, but whose yard is it? The posts stand between an open-ended chain-link fence and a much taller wooden privacy fence; their placement invites exploration but reveals no clues. With a few other global locales, the green signage is nearly camouflaged in a lush thicket depending on the time of year. In summer, they are lost to a tangle of trees, vines, and shrubbery. In fall, they pop against the shifting colors of autumn. In winter's striptease, they reveal themselves completely. Spring is a great time to go, when the temperatures are comfortable, but the burgeoning greenery presents a challenge to an easy discovery.

TREE OF HIPPOCRATES

Thanks to 21st-century biotechnology, an ancient tree lives on in perpetuity at the National Institutes of Health. Legend has it that Hippocrates, the father of modern medicine, taught his students under the shade of a plane tree in Greece. A cutting from its progeny flourished on the NIH campus from 1962 until beset by fungus in the 1980s. The Archangel Ancient Tree Archive, which propagates important old growth trees and archives their genetics, cloned the legendary tree. After planting in April 2014, the sapling thrives at the very site where its forebear once stood. National Library of Medicine 8600 Rockville Pike, Bethesda, MD. Metro: Red Line to Medical Center.

CLEMYJONTRI PARK

❼

6317 Georgetown Pike
McLean, VA
• Open: Daily 7am—dusk, year-round. Carousel open seasonally as
weather permits
• There must be at least one adult present for every eight children.
Bikes, skateboards, and rollerblades are not allowed in the park. No pets
of any kind.
• Tel: 703-388-2807
• www.fairfaxcounty.gov/parks/clemyjontri/

*All are
welcome*

The aerial view of McLean's whimsical and inviting Clemyjontri Park, gives the warm and fuzzies, evoking *The Game of Life* — the board game popular with American kids since the 1960s. Up close and personal, it's even more delightful; a riot of color and inclusion that promises "a place where children who use wheelchairs, walkers or braces, or who have sensory or developmental disabilities, can have a parallel playground experience of fun and exploration."

Clemyjontri Park is the gift and vision of longtime McLean resident Adele Lebowitz, who donated her 18-acre estate to the Fairfax County Park Authority with two stipulations: first, that she continues to reside on the property for the rest of her life (she passed away at 98 in 2014) and second, that a fully accessible playground and park be developed on-site where children of all abilities can play side by side. The unusual name Clemyjontri is an acronym created with letters from the names of Ms. Lebowitz's children: Carolyn, Emily, John, and Petrina.

The two-acre playground is thoughtfully designed to accommodate varying abilities with sensory rich equipment and complete wheelchair access, from the wider openings to the lowered monkey bars to the central, ground level carousel that allows for transfer to a seated position in the spinning teacup. The chariots safely accommodate riders remaining in the wheelchairs.

Four outdoor rooms offer different opportunities for play and learning; the Rainbow Room, with its variety of swings and rainbow archway, teaches about color while integrating sign, Braille, pictures and language; the Schoolhouse & Maze focuses on learning games with maps, globes, time zones and clocks; the Movin' & Groovin' Transportation Area features a race track, motorcycles, planes and trains to teach balance and special skills, stimulate the imagination and simulate true roadway situations; and the confidence-building Fitness & Fun room, with its various jungle gym components, provides progressive challenges for physical strength.

A highlight of the park is the Liberty Swing. It's designed to accommodate wheelchairs and other mobility aids and is the first of its kind to be installed in the United States.

CHERRY TREES OF KENWOOD ①

Dorset Avenue and Brookside Drive
Chevy Chase, MD
• Metro: Red Line to Bethesda

> *Japanese cherry blossoms, far from the madding crowd*

Each spring as the camera-toting throngs descend upon the Tidal Basin for the world-renowned Cherry Blossom Festival those in-the-know will wait for a more peaceful experience just a few days later when the 1,000+ Yoshino cherry trees in the picturesque Maryland enclave of Kenwood reach peak bloom.

The lush landscaping of Kenwood was paramount to its late 1920s development. The flowering trees were planted along its gently winding roads even before the first home was built. In the westernmost section of Chevy Chase, abutting the more populous Bethesda, the planned suburb of some 300 stately homes initially lured homeowners to what had once been farmland with membership in an exclusive neighborhood country club.

A visit to the annual floral profusion is to be charmed. Soft breezes release the confetti of the dense, arching canopy into a limpid brook running through the grassy medians of Brookside Drive. Pink-tinged petals marvelously carpet every step. Benches invite tranquil interlude. Sweet-faced children beckon from their lemonade stands.

"Kenwoodians," as the neighbors in the affluent community once home to the late journalist William Safire call themselves, rally to protect their trees while graciously welcoming visitors to enjoy their bounty. So grab a blanket and some lunch to picnic beneath the blossoms. Just remember to leave the grounds as you found them.

NEARBY

TINY LIBRARY FOR TOTS

With its mansard roof and scalloped siding, the one-room cottage at 10237 Carroll Place in Kensington resembles a gingerbread house, befitting its use as the Noyes Library for Young Children. Opened in 1893, in Montgomery County, Maryland, it's the oldest public library in the DC Metropolitan area. Open: Tuesday, Thursday and Saturday 9 am – 5 pm; 301-929-5533.

The Seneca Valley Sugarloafers Volksmarch Club sponsors a Kenwood Cherry Blossoms and Spring Flowers Walk during daylight hours from mid-March to mid-May. After the cherry trees are past peak, spectacular azaleas and other spring blossoms abound. Grab a free trail map at Starbucks Coffee, 4611-E Sangamore Road, Bethesda at The Shops at Sumner Place.

NATIONAL MUSEUM OF HEALTH AND MEDICINE

9

2500 Linden Lane
Silver Spring, MD
- medicalmuseum.mil
- Open: daily 10 am – 5:30 pm, including weekends and holidays; closed December 25
- Admission: free; photo ID required
- Metro: Red Line to Forest Glen

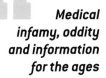

Medical infamy, oddity and information for the ages

There's a sirenomelic fetus, legs fused like a mythic mermaid tail, and an elegant, embossed leather microscope from the 17th century. With a wealth of specimens and objects, far more than are ever on display, the National Museum of Health and Medicine has been making acquisitions since its opening in 1862. In keeping with its Civil War beginnings, it has its fair share of skeletal remains of war dead. US Army Surgeon General, Brigadier General William Alexander Hammond mandated the collection of *"all specimens of morbid anatomy, surgical or medical, which may be regarded as valuable; together with projectiles and foreign bodies removed, and such other matters as may prove of interest in the study of military medicine or surgery."*

Divided into the categories Anatomical, Historical, Human Developmental Anatomy Center, Neuroanatomical, and Otis Historical Archives, the collections cover the gamut offering the what, why, and how of human (and sometimes animal) medicine. Though the museum is public, it is also a research facility available to researchers by appointment.

In the museum's holdings are artifacts from several US presidents including Lincoln and Garfield, as well as their assassins John Wilkes Booth and Charles Guiteau. Delusional job-seeker Charles Guiteau shot President Garfield when his quest for a post was rebuffed. One bullet grazed his arm, another pierced his spine at the 12th thoracic and lodged behind his spine. He survived in agony for a feverish eighty days before his death. It is widely believed today that the injury was survivable if only the doctors had tended his wound under sterile conditions. In 1881, antiseptic practices were not yet commonplace. During the autopsy, museum pathologists removed the vertebrae with the gunshot wound to document it and the resultant sepsis. Guiteau was hanged for the assassination; his skeleton and part of his brain are stored away from view at the museum.

THE GARFIELD BULLET AND AUTOPSY REPORT

30 minutes away at the Historical Society of Washington's Kiplinger Library, the hand-written autopsy report and the bullet that lodged in the 20th president's back sit in archival boxes.

HOLY TRINITY PARTICULAR UKRAINIAN CATHOLIC CHURCH ❿

16631 New Hampshire Avenue
Silver Spring, MD
• holytrinitypucc.org
• 301-421-1739
• Open: tours available after the Divine Liturgy (10:30 am Sunday) or during seasonal bazaars and special events
• Metro: Red Line to Silver Spring, then transfer to Z2 bus, but service is limited—it's best to drive

> *An architectural marvel on the highway to Heaven*

On a 10-mile stretch of New Hampshire Avenue in Montgomery County, Maryland known as the "highway to Heaven," a panoply of houses of worship epitomizes the diversity of religious life in the metropolitan area. A synagogue, a mosque, a Seventh-day Adventist Church, a Cambodian Buddhist temple, a Hindu temple, a Kingdom Hall of Jehovah's Witnesses are but a few of those you'll find within a 10-minute drive.

In a secluded glade near Hampshire Greens Golf Course and Woodland Horse Center is an architectural marvel, the Holy Trinity Particular Ukrainian Catholic Church. A Catholic parish of the Eastern Rite, it is the spiritual home to over a hundred Ukrainian families.

The traditional structure, built over the course of several years in the 1990s, follows the dictates of hundreds of years of Hutsul sacred architecture in the Carpathian Mountain region of Western Ukraine. As Hutsul custom eschews the use of nails, the church is constructed almost entirely of hemlock logs held together with wooden pegs. Ukrainian master builder Yurii Kostiw also observed Hutsul praxis in the traditional cruciform shape symbolizing salvation through Christ, a polygonal dome and distinct roofs. The wooden interior, simple and warm, is enlivened by an altar wall of icons, the iconostasis (a distinctive feature of Eastern Catholicism) painted by Ukrainian artist Peter Andrusiva. Featured among the many are six major icons: Jesus Christ, the Madonna and Child, Saints Constantine and Helena, Archdeacon Phillip, Archdeacon Stephen, and St. Nicholas.

The church hopes to "continue to share our beautiful Ukrainian heritage with the American public," and welcomes visitors. A yearly art show featuring Ukrainian artists is a perennial favorite each November.

As you make your way down the "highway to Heaven," look for the crucifix-topped, gilded domes piercing the sky above the other area Ukrainian church, Saint Andrew Ukrainian Orthodox Cathedral. Every feature has significance. The large central dome represents Jesus, and the four smaller domes represent the four biblical evangelists, Matthew, Mark, Luke, and John. 15100 New Hampshire Avenue.

THE GIANT ACORN GAZEBO

⑪

Acorn Park
1190 East-West Highway at Newell Street
Silver Spring, MD
• Metro: Red Line to Silver Spring

> *Birthplace of Silver Spring*

In a sliver of a park north of DC lies both the promise of love and the promise of a single estate to become one of the largest communities in the state of Maryland. In 1840, *Washington Globe* editor, Francis Preston Blair, Sr. (of Blair House, now the President's Guest House) sought a higher elevation for his summer home to escape the "miasma" downtown. As legend has it, while Blair and daughter Elizabeth traveled north on horseback, his steed Selim lapped at a bubbling spring of mica-flecked water, glinting silver in the sun. Enchanted, he built there, calling his estate Silver Spring.

To commemorate his marriage proposal to wife, Eliza under the shade of an oak tree, Blair hired carpenter Benjamin King in 1850 to craft an acorn-shaped gazebo by the spring. More than a century later, after 1990s sprucing up, the copper-topped dome still stands. An 1894 stone grotto marking the site of the long-gone spring too endures. Murals by Mame Cohalon chronicle Silver Spring landscapes onward from the Blair home.

Though the park is last of the Blair estate, the Blair name remains significant throughout the surrounding area in the nomenclature of Blair and Blair Mill

Roads; Montgomery Blair High School, named for Francis and Eliza's son, and Blair Mansion Inn to name a few.

Underneath the rustic canopy that sheltered the Blairs and reputedly even President Lincoln before you, contemplate the tiny grotto where it all began.

NEARBY

FORMER CANADA DRY BOTTLING PLANT

From 1946 to 1999 the curved glass-block rotunda and ginger ale-colored brick hinted at the product for which the Canada Dry Bottling Plant at 1201 East-West Highway was famous. Its architects Russell and Walter Monroe Cory proclaiming "factories can be beautiful," installed circle-patterned terrazzo flooring at the lobby entrance, suggesting soda bubbles. The spiral staircase seems also to mimic the upward effervescence of carbonation. Through the efforts of the Silver Spring Historical Society, it received landmark status before its conversion to The Silverton Condominium. The interior glazed tiles are restored to their original luster, sparkling, like ginger ale. (Lobby access Monday to Friday 9 am – 5 pm; ring buzzer 003.)

MEDITATION MUSEUM

9525 Georgia Avenue
Suite 101
Silver Spring, MD
- meditationmuseum.org
- 301-588-0144
- Open: Monday - Saturday, 11 am - 6 pm
- Admission: Free, donations are appreciated and tax-deductible
- Metro: Red Line to Forest Glen

> *A museum of the mind*

Launched above a record shop and the traffic bustle of Georgia Avenue in Downtown Silver Spring, The Brahma Kumaris Meditation Museum started as a small, peaceful space to free oneself of the chaos below. Many were drawn to explore the transformative power of quietude. The sliver of serenity has since relocated to a larger facility. Sure, as a museum there are displays, didactic labels, rotating exhibitions, even a small shop, but there's also a tranquil "Quiet Room" for meditation. Spin the wheel of virtues and ruminate on how a particular quality can resonate favorably in your life. Everything here is designed as a catalyst for the inward journey, a return to the self. The museum, a neutral-zone in our politically charged city, offers "non-partisan, non-denominational guided meditation," says its soft-spoken founder Jenna Mahraj, who believes that when accessed through contemplative practice our "intrinsic nurturing qualities can lead towards better diplomacy," effecting global change.

But within the DMV, the volunteer-staffed museum draws a diversity of visitors through its varied programming. From stressed government employees to the city's children, particularly those in underserved communities, meditation offers a survival tool to cope with life's myriad challenges. Its goal, says Sister Jenna, "knowledge of our true selves and our responsibility in bettering our humanity,"

Using the acronym ALGAE, she evokes the concept of freeing the mind of negative thoughts that limit our experience of joy. Through meditation one purges Anger, Lust, Greed, Attachment and Ego.

Sister Gita, Jenna's mother, says "it gives me joy to see someone come in and after a little while you see they really start to blossom." She praises the power of intention. As a cancer survivor, she underwent chemotherapy envisioning it as divine fuel. New initiatives extend the scope of the museum's reach beyond its walls. The "Pause of Peace" phone app utilizes new technology and social media to engage in mindfulness amid the busyness of daily life. Sister Jenna also hosts a radio show, America Meditating. As of 2015, a second Meditation Museum opened in McLean, Virginia at 1984 Chain Bridge Road, Suite 201.

ROSCOE THE ROOSTER MEMORIAL STATUE 🔟

Intersection of Laurel and Carroll Avenues
Takoma Park, MD
• Metro: Red Line to Takoma

*In eternal
strut*

Takoma Park straddles the northern border of Washington, DC and Maryland counties of Montgomery and Prince George's. With historic Districts on both sides of the state line, the 19th-century planned railroad suburb was one of Washington City's first. Its arboreal street names suggested shade from the sun, thus cooling relief from the congestion and heat of downtown. Its location near natural springs promised fresh, potable water. In the 20th century its charming bungalows and grand Victorians inspired a nostalgic maintenance of small town vibe and a live-and-let-live ethos among its progressive residents.

Into this mix strutted, inexplicably, a bantam rooster who, for the next decade (circa 1989-99) would both delight and peeve locals with his cock's crow and fearless wanderings. A fixture in the neighborhood, the vagabond bird was dubbed Roscoe by the grown-ups and Chick-Chick by local kids. When an unfortunate collision with a sport utility vehicle ended his life on February 15, 1999, residents saw fit to hold a service. At the alternately named "Requiem for a Rooster" and "Funeral for a Fowl," many thanked Roscoe for rousing them from sleep each morning. The send-off ended fittingly in a three-cock-a-doodle-do salute.

Neighbor Joan Horn spearheaded a group effort to honor Old Town Takoma's meandering mascot with a memorial sculpture near the site of his demise. Renowned local sculptor Normon Greene crafted a clay model based on photographs of Roscoe and was unanimously chosen by the Memorial Committee above all other submissions to create a life-sized bronze in Roscoe's likeness. The statue was dedicated in 2002 with the inscription:

ROSCOE (AKA CHICK-CHICK) 1989-1999

This free-spirited rooster, who chose to live in our town, was fed and protected by Alan Daugharthy and Alma Keating, and brought joy into our urban lives.

You'll find the commemorative bust on Laurel Avenue, just east of the line of demarcation between DC and Maryland at Eastern Avenue. In the shadow of the modest clock tower, a focal point of the town center, he stands. Chest held high, he keeps haughty watch over the Takoma Farmer's Market each Sunday and various festivals throughout the year. In whimsical homage, the jaunty statue is sometimes adorned: a Santa Claus cap for Yuletide glee, a knitted scarf to cut winter's chill and colorful beads for Mardi Gras.

COLLEGE PARK AVIATION MUSEUM   **14**

1985 Corporal Frank Scott Drive
College Park, MD
• collegeparkaviationmuseum.com
• 301-864-6029
• Open: daily 10 am – 5 pm; closed major holidays; free parking
• Admission: adults, $5; seniors, $4; children, $2
• Metro: Green Line to College Park/UMCP

Celebrating area feats of aviation

Overlooking the approach to its runway, the College Park Aviation Museum celebrates the historic College Park Airport (CPA—see opposite) and the area's aviation heritage. An affiliate of the Smithsonian, the state-of-the-art facility was designed by the same firm as the much larger National Air & Space Museum downtown. A compendious aggregation of aircraft, aviation artifacts and ephemera, the museum maximizes its minimal space with a balanced mix of displays and interactive exhibits to engage all ages.

An animatronic Wilbur Wright welcomes visitors into a recreated hangar leading to the main gallery where ten aircraft arrayed chronologically tell the history of the airfield, from a reproduction 1910 Wright Model B, like that originally used at CPA, to a 1924 Berliner Helicopter No. 5, which made a historic first copter flight on the airfield, to a 1946 Ercoupe 415 D created at the former ERCO Engineering and Research Company in nearby Riverdale, MD.

The Boeing Model 75, known as a "Stearman" was flown for air races and stunts during the airport's heyday. The Stearman pictured has a history of its own. Gus McLeod flew this two-seat biplane in the first open-cockpit flight over the North Pole in April 2000. After a final flight at the College

Park Air Fair that September, McLeod donated the 1941 craft to the museum.

The museum highlights recent history as well, such as the story of 15-year-old Kimberly Anyadike, the youngest African-American female to fly cross-country. With an esteemed Tuskegee Airman Levi Thornhill in the second cockpit chair, the teen flew from Compton, California to Newport News, Virginia, stopping over to great fanfare at College Park. Podcasts available for free download chronicle "feats of aviation" in English, Spanish, or French. Have a listen as a preamble to your visit.

WORLD'S OLDEST CONTINUOUSLY OPERATING AIRPORT

Having remained actively functioning since its 1909 founding, College Park Airport is the oldest continuously operating airport in the world. Known as the "Cradle of Aviation," it began on a 160-acre parcel of farmland adjacent to the B&O Railroad as a training ground for military flight instruction. The US Air Signal Corps contracted Wilbur Wright of the famed Wright Brothers to instruct Lieutenants Frederic Humphreys and Frank Lahm in flying the first US government aeroplane, a Wright Type A biplane. Civilian aircraft soon followed, with the Rex Smith Company taking up residence at the airfield.

The site is a "Field of Firsts." 1909: First woman passenger to fly in the United States and first military pilot to fly solo. 1911: First Army Aviation School and first bombsight test from an aircraft. 1912: First military aviation accident fatality; first test firing of a machine gun from an aeroplane and first mile-high flight by a military aviator. 1918: First US Postal Service was inaugurated after the operations of the US Airmail Service (see page 207) transferred from the War Department to the US Post Office and relocated from the Polo Grounds in Southwest Washington. 1924: First controlled helicopter flight. 1927: First radio navigational aids for "blind" or inclement-weather flying were developed and tested by the Bureau of Standards.

Taking over management of the airport in 1927, George Brinckerhoff during his thirty-two-year tenure taught hundreds of pilots and hosted regular air shows, thrilling the spectators who'd come dressed in their Sunday best. When Brinckerhoff fell ill in 1959, the airport entered an era of decline, but local aviation buffs rallied to save it. In 1973, the Maryland-National Capital Park and Planning Commission purchased it to continue airfield operations and preserve the historic gem. In 1977, it was added to the National Register of Historic Places. In 1981, the College Park Aviation Museum opened on the grounds.

MILLSTONE CELLARS ⓯

2029 Monkton Road
Monkton, MD
• millstonecellars.com
• 443-895-9991
• Open: Friday 4 – 9 pm (Happy hour 4 -6pm); Saturday noon – 6 pm;
Sunday noon – 5 pm»
• Admission: free weekend tours and tastings
• Not Metro accessible; check website for directions

> *Reviving*
> *the brew of*
> *the honeybee*

Winding along Monkton, Maryland's eponymous road, a circa 1960s brilliant red Ford fire truck catches the eye. Immediately after, a sandwich board handwritten in chalk welcomes visitors to Millstone Cellars, father-son makers of artisanal meads and ciders. The refurbished 1840s grist mill-cum-meadery is open weekend afternoons for tours and tastings. Admire the creatively adaptive reuse of the mill with its hefty milling gears extant, sample the honey brews and see how they are made.

Long before grapes' and grains' metamorphic emergence as libation, the nectar-poaching honeybee, buzzing alchemist that it is, transmuted floral nectars into liquid gold. The resulting honey, in tandem with undisturbed rainwater, created the first fermented beverage, as ceramics from Northern China dating thousands of years BCE will attest. Both North and Southern Africa have ancient histories of making honey beverages. Tej in Ethiopia and iQhilika in South Africa from the Xhosa people remain staples.

Madhu, as it was called in the Sanskrit hymns of the Rigveda, was meodu in Old English and has been since some point in the Middle Ages, mead in English. After centuries of waning interest in it, the honeyed elixir is experiencing a recent resurgence in Western consumption. Curt and Kyle Sherrer meet this demand by sourcing unadulterated honey from the best local apiaries to craft their Millstone meads using Old World techniques. But purists the Sherrers are not, adding intriguing, unusual ingredients like local fish peppers for a kick to the traditional mead trinity of honey, water, and yeast. Made in micro batches, they are aged in oak barrels for 6 to 24 months.

THE ORIGIN OF HONEYMOON

That which we call a honeymoon, the sweet vacation newlyweds take as a rapturous beginning to married life, has its roots in quaffing mead. According to medieval custom, couples were encouraged to partake of the ambrosia for the first moon cycle of marriage in hopes of a blissed-out, baby-making start.

LADEW TOPIARY GARDENS   **16**

3535 Jarrettsville Pike
Monkton, MD
• LadewGardens.com
• 410-557-9570
• Open: gardens, manor house and nature walk open daily, April 1 to
October 31 including Memorial Day, 4th of July, and Labor Day;
10 am – 5 pm
• Admission: various prices for the many offerings; check the website
It's in Baltimore County, make a day trip of it—a lovely drive

> ## The enchanted gardens of Harvey Scissorhands

On the scenic drive, vast fields of sunflowers explode in heliocentric motherlode, handsome Holsteins dot the landscape with their distinctive markings, and sinewy horses trot about the sprawling countryside. A lovely prelude to Ladew Topiary Gardens, the legacy of huntsman and topiary enthusiast Harvey S. Ladew's sporting and gardening passions.

Raised in Gilded Age privilege on Long Island and frequent European travel, Ladew's first language was that of his French nanny. His drawing lessons were from Met curators, and his sartorial expression sparked by his maternal uncle, a noted dandy. In his twenties, with a vast inheritance, he embarked on a life of adventure, whimsy and beauty; enjoying a coterie of friends from Cole Porter to Colette; the Duke and Duchess of Windsor to T.E. Lawrence "of Arabia."

As suburbanization supplanted Long Island fox-hunting culture, Ladew discovered the Maryland sporting life suited him and purchased the 230-acre Pleasant Valley Farm in 1929. As the US reeled from the stock market crash, he set out to make the 1747 farmhouse, sans electricity or plumbing, habitable. Over the next decade, he refined the rustic dwelling into a proper English country home, building a magnificent oval library expressly to fit his rare, oval Chippendale partner's desk and house his 1,500 books (look closely for the hidden doorway, Ladew's secret escape hatch).

Outdoors he created fifteen thematic garden rooms. Each has distinct charms; some with statuary, fountains or even a koi pond, some with gazebos, and some ablaze in monochromatic color. They invite enchanted meandering. Susan Snow, on a return visit, says, "It's just amazing. You can come again and again and see things you hadn't noticed before." From the Fox Hunt scene, to the swans floating on the Great Bowl perimeter to the pyramidal fortress at the manor house, the self-taught topiarist's living sculpture enchants. The Tivoli Tea Room is a treasure box. At the end of the breezeway, a Card Room fit for a bridge-playing bon vivant overlooks the sloping grounds toward the new Butterfly House.

To ensure his whimsical landscape would survive him, Ladew created a non-profit foundation to maintain and promote the buildings and gardens for posterity. The manor house is unique in that every item in its fox-and-horse-themed interior is wholly original to Mr. Ladew's occupancy.

Birthplace of fox hunting in America: Robert Brooke emigrated from England to Maryland in 1650, bringing with him a pack of hounds, introducing fox hunting to the New World.

GREATER WASHINGTON SOUTH

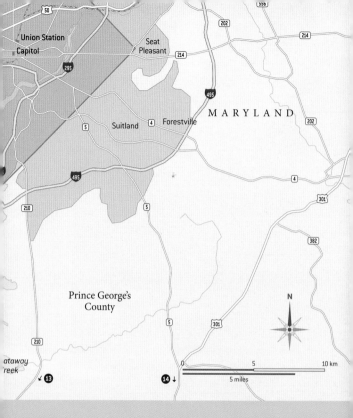

DARK STAR PARK DAY

1655 North Fort Myer Drive, and the adjacent traffic island
Arlington, VA
• rosslynva.org
• Metro: Blue, Orange, or Silver Line to Rosslyn

*Merging
historical
and solar time*

Passing north of the familiar, stilled-in-time silhouette of Iwo Jima flag-raising that is the US Marine Corps War Memorial, a curious sight emerges. Flanked by steel poles, two giant orbs rest on a formerly barren traffic triangle at the junction of North Lynn Street and North Ft. Myer Drive. Below them, permanent asphalt shadows mark the space whereupon, clouds willing, the sun casts its own each August 1 at 9:32 am. Part of a site-specific work from land art pioneer, Nancy Holt, it commemorates William Henry Ross' August 1, 1860, acquisition of the land on which it sits. A portmanteau of Ross and wife Carolyn's names, the urban village is known as Rosslyn.

Created over a period of years from 1979 to 1984, transforming a run-down ⅔-acre parcel, Dark Star Park is the first major commissioned art project in Arlington County. In a groundbreaking approach to public art, Holt did more than design sculpture for the park; she designed the park itself as well as sat on the committee for the architectural design of the adjacent building. The park features two distinct spaces bisected by North Fairfax Drive. North of the open triangle is a green space comprised of a willow oak tree canopy, grass and creeper plantings, reflective pools, and integrated tunnels. Winding walkways mimic the surrounding roads, and strategic placement of the spheres alter their spatial perception from every angle.

The materials used in the sculptural elements relate to the surrounding architecture: Gunite (sprayable concrete), stonemasonry, asphalt, and steel. The spheres, the "dark stars" of Holt's imagination, represent those celestial bodies fallen to the ground, no longer twinkling; the larger cosmos in intimate contact on Earth.

Each August 1st, Arlingtonians in-the-know assemble on the small mound in the 9 am hour to watch in celebration of Rosslyn's historic founding becoming one with solar time. In 2014, the 30th anniversary of the installation, however, cloud cover squashed any shadow alignment; perhaps nature mourning the passing of Nancy Holt earlier that year.

Coincidentally, August 1 is the birthday of Jerry Garcia, founder of the Grateful Dead and "Dark Star" one of their classic songs.

ROOF GARDEN AT FREEDOM PARK

2

1101 Wilson Boulevard
Rosslyn, VA
• rosslynva.org
• Open: Monday to Friday 9 am – 5 pm
• Metro: Blue, Orange or Silver Line to Rosslyn

*Elevated
green space*

During its run as a free interactive museum of news and journalism on Arlington's Wilson Boulevard, Newseum's rooftop Freedom Park housed among other exhibits, segments of the Berlin Wall and a moving tribute to fallen journalists. When the museum pulled up stakes in 2003 to start anew in prime new digs on Pennsylvania Avenue near both the White House and the Capitol, it left an empty domed facility in the Rosslyn Business Improvement District. The space was eventually acquired for use as the arts facility, Artisphere, so named for the structure's iconic dome. Freedom Park became a landscaped urban plaza with benches, trees, ornamental gardens, and a bird's-eye view of the DC skyline across the Potomac River.

The two-block-long park takes its linear orientation from its originally intended use as a commuter highway overpass into the District, drawing comparison to Manhattan's High Line, though a more apt parallel might be the Elevated Acre (see *Secret New York* from Editions Jonglez) in its simplicity.

In this incarnation the space has yet to maximize its fullest potential, but it stands, a welcome, quiet respite from the busyness of the business district below.

NEARBY

THE NETHERLANDS CARILLON

Forged by friendship, forged from steel, the Netherlands Carillon is an expression of Dutch gratitude for US aid to the Netherlands during and after World War II. At the official dedication on May 5, 1960, the 15th anniversary of Dutch liberation from the Nazis, Queen Juliana of the Netherlands spoke metaphorically of the tower's bells from the largest Bourdon to the smallest treble: "To achieve real harmony, justice should be done also to the small and tiny voices, which are not supported by the might of their weight. Mankind could learn from this. So many voices in our troubled world are still unheard. Let that be an incentive for all of us when we hear the bells ringing."

Open 6 am to midnight, the 127-foot, 50-bell tower chimes on the hour daily from 10 am to 6 pm. It plays automated patriotic concerts at noon and 6 pm each day. Carillonneurs perform live 2-hour, Saturday concerts in the summer months from 6 pm to 8 pm. On the quartzite plaza, two stylized bronze lions overlook the sweeping, uninterrupted vistas.

OLD GUARD CAISSON PLATOON STABLES   ❸

201 Jackson Avenue, Building 236
Joint Base Myer-Henderson Hall, VA
• oldguard.mdw.army.mil
• 703-696-3018
• Open: stable tours offered Tuesday through Sunday noon – 4 pm;
official ID required and vehicle search
• Metro: Red Line to Farragut North, transfer to 16Y bus toward Barcroft

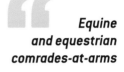

> *Equine and equestrian comrades-at-arms*

The century-old stables at Ft. Myer, while visitable, isn't the spot to get your riding fix. What it offers is a moving glimpse of the symbiotic pairing of soldiers—human and horse. The 3rd US Infantry, or the "Old Guard", is the army's oldest infantry regiment, active since 1784. Its Caisson Platoon, established in 1948, is the last full-time equestrian mounted unit in the Department of Defense. A Civil War tradition of carrying the injured and dead from the battlefield on artillery caissons survives in the Old Guard. The circa 1918 caissons, polished to gleaming, roll out five days a week, bearing the flag-draped caskets of fallen veterans to full honors military burials at Arlington National Cemetery. Two six-horse teams, led by a single horse and rider, move in silence, save for the clopping of hooves at eight funerals a day.

The dedication of the Old Guard soldiers to their steeds and the memory of fellow patriots shows in the exacting maintenance of the facility. They craft tack and maintain the saddles, farrier shop, stalls, wash room, and caissons. When not performing with reverent precision the solemn duty of caisson escort, their equine charges roam the pastures of Fort Belvoir, Virginia.

EQUINE THERAPY
Since 2006, the therapeutic Caisson Platoon Equine-Assisted Program with its "Soldiers helping soldiers" tenet, has paired wounded warriors with horses and soldiers of the Caisson Platoon for riding lessons at Ft. Belvoir. Humans and horses ambulate similarly through the hip, so riding can simulate the familiar motion of walking in veterans who've lost their legs; one of the proven physical, mental, and emotional benefits of equine therapy.

HISTORIC ABINGDON PLANTATION SITE ❹

Ronald Reagan Washington National Airport
1 Aviation Circle
Arlington, VA
• Open: Daily from dawn to dusk
• www.flyreagan.com
• Metro: Blue or Yellow lines to Ronald Reagan Washington National
Airport; take the exit for Terminal B, use the bridge to Garage B/C and
walk through the garage on level two to the site.

Vestiges of a colonial plantation

Centuries of interwoven histories converge on a small knoll engulfed by the parking garages of Reagan National Airport, overlooking its terminals and the elevated Metrorail. Reconstructed ruins of a colonial-era plantation, built in 1998 upon the extant underground foundations of Abingdon, are vestiges of what was once a vast estate.

The area is believed to have been an indigenous fishing village called Namoraughquend before European contact. In 1669, shipmaster Robert Howson received a 6,000-acre land patent on the Potomac for transporting 120 colonists to Virginia. He almost immediately traded it for six hogsheads (massive weighty barrels) of tobacco to John Alexander, whose grandson built the first house on the family property in 1746, and from whom the new city of Alexandria, Virginia got its name in 1749.

John Parke Custis purchased the property he dubbed "Abingdon" in 1778 to raise his family nearer his mother Martha and stepfather, George Washington, the future first President of the United States. His daughter Nelly was born there in 1779. John would die of "camp fever" when his son George was but six months old in 1781. The Washingtons adopted the infant and Nelly. Their mother, Eleanor, remained at Abingdon with her two eldest children and remarried Dr. David Stuart, who would go on to become one of the first commissioners of the new federal city.

The property would change hands through various families and Union occupation. The Hunter family, which bought the property in 1835, successfully sued the federal government to recover the land confiscated during the Civil War. James A. Garfield, another future president, brought the case before the Supreme Court. Railways encroached, industry prevailed, and the property sold to brick companies who excavated yellow clay from the grounds for brickmaking. The George Washington Parkway changed the landscape in the 1920s and the dilapidated house was abandoned. Its wood frame burned to the ground in 1930. Three years later, a preservation society stabilized the ruins and erected a plaque.

By 1941, the western portion of the original estate became Washington National Airport. Public outcry in the 1990s prevented the razing of the historic structures for additional parking. Now preserved for posterity, remnants of the antebellum main house and kitchen are a short circuitous walk from the Metro.

NEARBY:

HISTORIC TERMINAL A EXHIBIT HALL

In the corridor west of the Historic Lobby of Terminal A, travelers can view video presentations and informational text on the histories of the airport and Abingdon, a model of the original terminal, airport memorabilia and artifacts excavated from Abingdon.

FRANKLIN, ARMFIELD & CO. HISTORIC OFFICE ❺

Northern Virginia Urban League Freedom House Museum
1315 Duke Street
Alexandria, VA
• www.alexandriava.gov
• 703-836-2858
• Open: Weekends 1 pm – 5 pm; check website for other dates
• Admission: $5
• Metro: Blue or Yellow Line to King Street; take free King Street shuttle to Payne Street

Triumph over a wretched history

I n a twist of poetic justice, the Northern Virginia branch of the Urban League in 1996 acquired a building that once housed the country's largest slave trading company. Taking very seriously their stewardship of the historic property, they operate the small, but immersive Freedom House Museum in the cellar which once held men, women, and children in bondage. A staircase wall commemorates some of the enslaved. *Phillis $770 18 years old. Ambrose $800 30 years old, tanner. Dennis $770 35 years old, cooper, carpenter, and wheel wright. Betsey and her children $920 25 years old, Clem 9, Ellen 5, Susan 4. Ned and Belina Brown $1500, 21 years old.*

From 1828 to 1836, Issac Franklin and John Armfield ran a lucrative business. After buying the rest of the city block surrounding their Duke Street office, they ringed the property with high walls to secure their investments and obscure their shameful practice. Courtyard "pens" held men on one side; women on the other. The complex featured a slave kitchen, a tailor shop, and a hospital/infirmary. No expense was spared in keeping their human chattel in saleable condition. An on-site horse livery provided overland transport. For moving their captives by sea to Natchez or New Orleans, they even had their own slave ships, a rarity.

While Armfield lived at Duke Street, Franklin manned the Southern offices. George Kephart, the next in a succession of slave dealers to operate there, purchased the property in 1836. By 1858, Charles M. Price and John Cook had set up shop. James H. Birch, who sold Solomon Northup (of 12 Years a Slave renown) from the notorious DC slave pen, the "Yellow House", to servitude in New Orleans in 1841, soon replaced Cook. Price, Birch & Co. prospered until the 1861 surrender of Alexandria. When Union troops seized the abandoned lot, they found one man, still shackled in the basement.

Reverend Henry Lewis Bailey, marched as a boy in a chained coffle from 1315 Duke further south into slavery, went from the whipping post to the pulpit. Freed in 1863 at age 21, he made his way from Texan captors back to Alexandria on foot, found his mother at the corner of Queen and Payne, and became a pastor and community leader.

EDMONSON SISTERS SCULPTURE ❻

Edmonson Plaza
1701 Duke Street
Alexandria, VA
• Metro: Blue or Yellow Line to King Street

Commemorating courage in the darkness of slavery

Old Town Alexandria holds many charms as well as dark secrets. Like the nearby Freedom House Museum (see page 297), the federal-style building at 1701 Duke Street, now a successful realty office, once housed the Bruin's Slave Jail. On the adjacent plaza named for them, sisters Mary and Emily Edmonson, sculpted in bronze, emerge from the shadow of a rock, "the darkness of slavery," says sculptor, Erik Brome.

Though Paul Edmonson was in 1848 a free man, his fourteen children with wife Amelia inherited their mother's slave status. On April 15, led by son Samuel, Edmonson siblings Richard, Ephraim, John, Mary and Emily were among the nearly eighty brave souls fleeing slavery in an organized escape aboard the schooner, the Pearl. The teenaged Edmonson girls became the faces of an abolitionist cause célèbre known as "The Pearl Incident," the largest attempted slave escape recorded in US history.

Paul Jennings (formerly enslaved by President James Madison) hatched a plot with Daniel Bell, a free man who financed hiring the Pearl to secret his own enslaved kinfolk to Northern shores. Under the cover of night, passengers quietly boarded the docked vessel at Washington's 7th Street wharf for the journey on the Potomac River to Chesapeake Bay and finally the Delaware River North to freedom. Strong winds, however, delayed their progress.

Meanwhile, Judson Diggs, a black liveryman, tipped off the slaveowners to the ill-fated plan. They angrily captured the schooner, moored temporarily at Point Lookout, Maryland. The crew faced imprisonment and the seventy-seven escapees were held at slave trader Joseph Bruin's Duke Street business for sale "down south." The elder Edmonsons enlisted the aid of social reformer Henry Ward Beecher to fund the purchase of their children. The girls, whose light complexions were sure to doom them to life as "fancy girls" or prostitutes upon sale in New Orleans, were spared. The brothers eventually negotiated freedom as well, though the fates of the other enslaved parties are uncertain. The crew, after four years in prison, were pardoned by President Millard Fillmore.

The saga inspired the incendiary anti-slavery novel *Uncle Tom's Cabin* by Reverend Beecher's sister Harriet Beecher Stowe, fueling the abolitionist cause. The Beechers educated the girls at Oberlin College, but Mary died within a year, felled by tuberculosis. Emily, grief-stricken, returned to Washington where she married, had a family and made a name for herself as an educator and human rights activist.

QUEEN STREET "SPITE" HOUSE ❼

523 Queen Street
Alexandria, VA
• Private home, exterior view only
• Metro: Blue or Yellow Line to King Street-Old Town; transfer to free King Street trolley to North St. Asaph Street; walk one block east

> *The smallest house in the county*

There are many modestly-sized 19th-century homes in Old Town Alexandria, but none as narrow the blue-painted house on Queen Street near the corner of North St. Asaph Street. At only 7 feet wide, it is the smallest house in the county. According to local lore, in 1830, John Hollensbury, owner of the adjacent house at 525, in a stick-it-to-ya move, built the wee structure in the alleyway between his house and the next to deny passage to his neighbor's outsized horse-drawn carriage. Though no documents substantiate Hollensbury's motives, gouges in the brick walls of the diminutive dwelling suggest that wagon wheel hubs did, in fact, wear away at the surface.

Another theory implies that love rather than spite prompted the construction. Hollensbury, a brick maker by trade is also said to have built the maison miniature for his daughters Julia and Harriett as a play house. It is known that Julia (d. 1901) lived for a time in the house as an adult.

Yet another chink in the armor—or historical record—is that the house extant at 521 wasn't built until 1870. So what was there before to provide the secondary wall of the small house? Was the spite story created in one-

upmanship of New York City's famed 5-foot-wide building erected in 1850 and described by the New York Times as a "freakish revenge structure"?

The house, nonetheless, is worth a pass-by when in Alexandria to check out other Old Town treasures (like page 305) just don't expect a tour of the private home. To see the contemporary upgrades like Sub-Zero refrigeration, do an image search for photographs online.

AN INSURANCE-COMPANY PLAQUE TO ENSURE THAT LOCAL FIRE BRIGADES WOULD EXTINGUISH THE FLAMES

An insurance-company plaque to ensure that local fire brigades would extinguish the flames in the event of fire is mounted above the door, a late 18th-, early 19th-century practice. A 1920s photograph, however, shows neither the fire mark nor the star-shaped anchor plates flanking it today, so it doesn't appear to be original to the building.

UNDER THE STARE MOB DIORAMA   ⑧

Torpedo Factory Arts Center
105 North Union Street
Alexandria, VA
• torpedofactory.org
• ☎ 703-838-4565
• Open: daily 10 am – 6 pm; Thursday 10 am – 9 pm
• Metro: Blue or Yellow Line to King Street; transfer to free King Street
Trolley service down to the waterfront

> *A micro-universe under the stairs*

Yes, it's well established that the former military storage facility on the Potomac River in Old Town once manufactured torpedoes. Yes, the then-Alexandria Art League Director, Marian Van Landingham saw possibility in the dilapidated, infested structure some forty years ago and envisioned a temporary, visual arts center to open in celebration of the city's bicentennial on July 14, 1974. And yes, with over half a million visits a year, the center has grown well beyond those early expectations to become a cherished institution that sparked the revitalization of the Alexandria waterfront with its artists' studios, workshops and galleries. Anyone who knows Old Town knows the Torpedo Factory, but what many overlook is the hidden diorama installed beneath a spiral stair.

In commemoration of the Torpedo Factory Arts Center's 10th anniversary, an appreciative, triply-named artist, one of the first in residence there, gifted the center with a permanent installation crafted of bronze and retrofitted into one of the complex's many staircases.

Scrawled in calligraphy on a fading parchment reads:

(The Under the Stare Mob)
donated to the
Art Center
and the
City of Alexandria
by
Dick Martin,
Dirk Mactin,
or
Dark Mictin
in appreciation
for a good ten years
May 18, 1984

It seems incongruous that Martin, a soundman for CBS News was deaf in one ear. It seems apropos that as a Korean War veteran he should find himself creating art in peacetime from the very place that assembled torpedoes during the time of war. His was a dichotomous life. He survived Korea, but not cancer. Though his larger-than-life persona is gone, his meticulously crafted minutial world remains under a stair of the Torpedo Factory and under the curious stare of all who happen upon it.

STABLER-LEADBEATER APOTHECARY MUSEUM

9

105-107 South Fairfax Street
Alexandria, VA
• apothecarymuseum.org
• Open: Wednesday – Sunday; see website for hours
• Admission: $5
• Metro: Blue or Yellow Line to King Street; transfer to free King Street trolley

The abolitionist apothecary

Formerly the neighborhood druggist to prominent families Washington, Mason, Custis and Lee, the Stabler-Leadbeater Apothecary Museum is a trove of treasures and historical insight straddling three centuries of Alexandria life. Housed in the same location where Quaker apothecary Edward Stabler opened shop in 1796, the building remains remarkably intact. Continuously owned and operated by the same family until bankruptcy forced closure in 1933, the shop was integral to community life. Visionary area residents rallied to preserve the shop, forming The Landmarks Society of Alexandria to purchase the buildings. The contents which were sold at public auction to the American Pharmaceutical Association were donated to the Landmarks Society to establish a museum in 1939.

Archaeological excavations of the cellar conducted in the 1980s yielded thousands of artifacts. Among the discoveries were bottles embossed with such names as Gargling Oil, "a liniment for man or beast" and Witch Cream, for the treatment of acne and to brighten the complexion. A single human molar provides archaeological confirmation of the known practice of tooth extraction at the apothecary site.

The museum tour begins with a brief history of the family from founder and abolitionist Stabler (who would purchase slaves in order to grant their freedom) through his son William and son-in-law John Leadbeater on to grandson Edward Leadbeater who with his sons ushered the business into the 20th century.

The Gothic shelving of the first floor is lined with apothecary jars filled with the contents of the distant past and gilded with words unknown. Oddities on display include morphine potions to calm colicky babies and for the draconian practice of bloodletting, scarificators and fleams.

A note written on behalf of the ailing Martha Washington reads: *Mrs Washington desires Mr Stabler will send by the bearer, a quart bottle of his best castor oil, and the bill for it. Mount Vernon April 22nd 1802.*

Upstairs hand-lettered drawers, boxes, and tins with contents intact, give clues to the *materia medica* of the time: dragon's blood, unicorn root. Herbs such as squaw vine reveal contact with Native American herbal traditions. A trapdoor in the floor reveals an ingenious lift for loading and unloading to the floor below.

The Landmarks Society donated the museum to the City of Alexandria in 2006.

JONES POINT LIGHT ⑩

1 Jones Point Drive
Jones Point Park
Alexandria, VA
• 703-289-2500 (call to request a ranger-led program about the park;
exterior views only, the lighthouse interior is closed to the public)
• Open: park hours 6 am – 10 pm
• Metro: 11Y Mt. Vernon Express Metrobus to Washington and South
Streets; check wmata.com for schedule

> *Where the nation's capital began*

South of Old Town, in the shadow of Woodrow Wilson Bridge, sits the last remaining riverine lighthouse in the Chesapeake Bay area. Due to landfill, its locale at the confluence of the Potomac River and Hunting Creek boasts the only land border between the District of Columbia and Virginia. A glass pyramid on the modest landing reveals a weather-beaten pillar sequestered behind a seawall below. Erected sixty-four years before the construction of the lighthouse, it was placed with much ado as the first of forty boundary markers (see page 117) for the capital city. It is thus the oldest federal monument.

For centuries prior to colonial contact, the riverfront location was a Native American hunting ground and fishing camp. Colonist Margaret Brent, first female landowner in Maryland, lawyer and suffragette secured the first land patent to Piper's Island, VA, requiring her to deforest the 700 acres and plant tobacco, a valuable commodity. Eventually the land would be acquired by John Alexander, from whom the city of Alexandria (surveyed in 1748 by teen future president of the US George Washington) gets its name.

Commissioned by surveyor Maj. Andrew Ellicott, free man of color Benjamin Banneker kept a grueling schedule of astronomical observations to establish the boundaries of a new federal territory with land donated from Maryland and Virginia. The south cornerstone was laid on April 15, 1791.

Creating safe passage while supporting maritime economy, Jones Point Light was built in 1855 to guide the bustling river traffic of the era. It was among

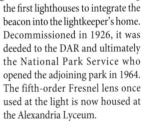

SOUTH ELEVATION

the first lighthouses to integrate the beacon into the lightkeeper's home. Decommissioned in 1926, it was deeded to the DAR and ultimately the National Park Service who opened the adjoining park in 1964. The fifth-order Fresnel lens once used at the light is now housed at the Alexandria Lyceum.

ON THE WATERFRONT

The surrounding grounds have hosted a 19th-century ropewalk, a World War I shipyard, even a 1900s nautical red-light district with floating brothels and gambling barges. Today you can fish, canoe, and play basketball at Jones Point Park.

POPE-LEIGHEY HOUSE ⑪

Woodlawn Plantation
9000 Richmond Highway
Alexandria, VA
• www.woodlawnpopeleighey.org
• 703-780-4000
• Open: Friday to Monday 11 am – 4 pm; tours on the hour
• Admission: adults, $15; senior 62+/active military with ID, $12;
children (K-12) $7.50; 5 and under, free
• Metro: best to drive, but if necessary the nearest station (which is not
close) is Huntington on the Yellow Line; check wmata.com for details

> *The only publicly accessible Frank Lloyd Wright house in the DMV*

On the grounds of Woodlawn Plantation in Alexandria sits a classic example of a Frank Lloyd Wright "Usonian" home, the only publicly accessible Wright house in the Washington Metropolitan Area.

Architect Frank Lloyd Wright as a social reformer believed that well-designed homes created in harmony with nature are key to sustaining an enlightened, democratic society and that these dwellings must be made accessible to the masses. Adopting a turn of the century acronym coined to describe more accurately that which we call "American," he called these affordable residences "Usonian" (United States of North America). From 1936 to Wright's 1959 death, approximately sixty of the dwellings were constructed. *Evening Star* journalist Loren Pope wrote

to Wright in 1939 with an earnest plea: "There are certain things a man wants during life, and, of life. Material things and things of the spirit. The writer has one fervent wish that includes both. It is for a house created by you." Wright responded simply, "Dear Loren Pope: Of course I am ready to give you a house."

Constructed at 1005 Locust Street in Falls Church, Pope's house incorporated "the character of Nature" (Wright's capitalization) bringing the outdoors in. At the entrance, a carport allows the owners to step out of the car and directly into their home. The house, based on an L-shaped single-story plan, uses modest, durable building materials: tidewater red cypress, brick, glass and concrete floors painted in the architect's signature Cherokee Red. Every efficiently designed room from the two bedrooms and bath to the study, kitchen, living, and dining rooms boasts multifunctional features, as does the Wright-designed furniture. Wright ingeniously created small spaces that opened onto larger spaces evoking a heightened sense of expansion. Clerestory windows add visual interest as well as cross-ventilation. Hot water pipes embedded in the concrete floor provide radiant heat.

Bought by the Leigheys in 1946, the property was in 1961 condemned to accommodate the expansion of Interstate 66. Widowed Mrs. Leighey in 1964 donated both the monetary condemnation award and the house to the National Trust for Historic Preservation, who moved it to safety at Woodlawn. Granted lifetime tenancy in her home, Mrs. Leighey resided there until her 1983 passing.

The home, moved yet again in 1995 from unstable clay soil 30 feet uphill is now wonderfully preserved as a house museum. Providing the public an intimate look at the genius of Frank Lloyd Wright, it demonstrates the strength of sustainable development using locally accessible materials.

WORKHOUSE ARTS CENTER ⓬

9518 Workhouse Way
Lorton, VA
• workhousearts.org
• 703-584-2900
• Open: Wednesday to Saturday 11 am – 6 pm; Sunday noon – 5 pm; Workhouse Prison Museum Wednesday to Friday, noon – 3 pm; Saturday & Sunday noon – 4 pm
• Metro: best to drive, though the L Metrobus line services the area from the Pentagon Station (Blue or Yellow Line)

Penal colony to arts enclave

In an interesting bit of adaptive reuse, Washington's former correctional facility in Lorton, Virginia is now a multidisciplinary center for the arts. "A bid at Lorton" once meant serving a prison sentence, but today it could refer to a gala art auction. The journey from prisoner-pitched tents on the banks of the Occoquan River to the Workhouse Arts Center is one of both noble intention and rampant corruption. Prison reform, women's suffrage, Cold War defenses, and decades of imprisonment all played out on the sprawling campus.

Sans fences, cells or locks, Occoquan Workhouse opened in 1910 to counter the crowded, unsanitary conditions at the DC Jail and "rehabilitate and reform prisoners through fresh air, good food" (raised on site) "and honest work." Prison labor provided vocational training and created revenue. In the foundry alone, inmates once forged DC's fire call boxes and hydrants (see page 107) A prisoner-built Lorton & Occoquan railroad provided on-site transport.

Jailed in 1917 for picketing the White House, seventy-two suffragists endured draconian measures such as force-feeding while incarcerated, bringing the women's suffrage movement to critical mass. A walled maximum security prison for "hardened" felons went up in the 1930s. A Nike missile system was installed in 1953 in response to the threat of Soviet nuclear attack. In the '50s and '60s the annual Lorton Jazz Festival hosted top-notch acts like Ella Fitzgerald, Frank Sinatra, and Ray Charles in outdoor concerts for the inmates. By the 1990s it gained notoriety for violence, drugs, and intense overcrowding (44 percent over capacity) undermining the original mission. The complex closed, and its last prisoners transferred out in 2001.

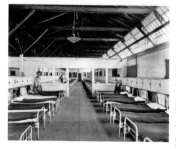

The Colonial Revival architecture, designed in the 1920s to "dispel the suggestion of a penal institution" works well in the new incarnation as arts center. The light-filled studios and galleries immerse visitors and artists in an interactive arts exchange. The Workhouse Museum preserves the dichotomous history of the prison.

A SONG RECORDED VIA PRISON TELEPHONE

During a 1950s bid, Chuck Brown traded cigarettes for a guitar. The rest is Go-Go history. In the mid-'60s, Petey Greene's gift of gab persuaded an inmate to threaten suicide so that he could "talk him down." The feigned heroism earned the deejay an early release, and he pioneered "tell it like it is" activist broadcasting. While incarcerated on marijuana charges in 1985, HR, frontman of seminal punk band Bad Brains, wrote Sacred Love and reputedly recorded the song via prison telephone with the mouthpiece removed for clarity.

GHOST FLEET OF MALLOWS BAY   ⓭

Mallows Bay Park
1440 Wilson Landing Road
Nanjemoy, MD
• charlescountyparks.com/parks/mallows-bay-park
• Charles County Tourism 800 SO MD FUN
• Open: daily, 5:30 am – dusk
• Not Metro accessible; about an hour from Washington

Wildlife refuge amid the wreckage

There is something intensely satisfying about bearing witness to nature lay claim to man's castoffs and repurpose it for her use, as she is wont to do. Like the thriving ecosystem that emerged from the dense flotsam of scuttled hulks in Mallows Bay. On Maryland's western shore, cross-river from Marine Corps Base Quantico, the mile-long bay holds the bones of World War I-era wooden cargo steamships, abandoned fishing boats, log canoes, a circa-1900 four-masted schooner, even vestiges of Revolutionary War vessels. Amid the maritime wreckage, ospreys build their nests, submerged hulls sprout tiny islands, and the turbid waters teem with bass.

The forces of war, economy and ecology converged in this curious corner of the Chesapeake region. As the US entered World War I in 1917, the Emergency Fleet Corporation launched to ramp up shipbuilding for the war effort: 1,000 vessels in 18 months, in anticipation of years of conflict. But the war ended before the augmented fleet was completed. To recoup the monetary loss, Congress sold the ships to Western Marine and Salvage Company (WMSC). On November 7, 1925, WMSC burned and scuttled them at Mallows Bay, salvaging usable parts. However, WMSC went bankrupt in 1931 and "jumped ship." With $200,000 funding from the US Government, Bethlehem Steel, as World War II approached, excavated a marine basin to recover the valuable iron tonnage from the wrecks. They pulled out of the venture, a fiscal failure, in 1943. In the years since, nature has intervened in a different salvage effort.

The quiet cove, save for a single boat ramp added to provide kayak and canoe access in 2010, remains undeveloped. Great blue herons return each February to the Nanjemoy Creek Rookery to nest. Benches on the bluff above the bay overlook the SS Accomac in the distance, a steel-hulled car ferry which discontinued service in 1964 when the Chesapeake Bay Bridge Tunnel opened.

Entranced since childhood by the ship graveyard he christened the "Ghost Fleet," Don Shomette led the exhaustive historic survey of the area and provided the history for the park's interpretive marker.

AMISH COMMUNITY OF SOUTHERN MARYLAND **⑭**

North St. Mary's County Farmers Market and surrounding farms
37600 New Market Road
Charlotte Hall, MD
• visitstmarysmd.com
• Open: weather permitting April to December; closed Sundays; see calendar for exact hours: stmalib.org
• Most Amish prefer not to be photographed; please be respectful and stay on public paths, not private roadways
• Not Metro accessible; about an hour from Washington

Never on a Sunday

Mention the Amish community on the East Coast and thoughts go to painted hex signs and the humble, industrious Anabaptists of Lancaster, Pennsylvania. But in the same Southern Maryland county that hosts many motorsports venues, the speed and vroom of drag racing gives way to the unhurried clip-clop of horses pulling buggies. An insular community of Old Order Amish has had a presence in St. Mary's County since 1939 when the search for plentiful, inexpensive farmland led seven families from Pennsylvania Dutch Country to the 6-mile stretch of Thompson Corner Road (Route 236).

Signs bearing a silhouetted horse and buggy alert drivers to share the road along Route 236 and its byways. Hinting at the residents' humility, modest clothing of subdued color dries on clotheslines. Over 1,000 strong, the cloistered settlement has retained a remarkably self-sufficient culture. Their abiding faith orders their simply-lived lives. Following the *Ordnung*, or unwritten system of behavior, they shun pridefulness, violence, electricity, and cars.

As modernity encroaches, they've adapted slightly, allowing phone use in booths set far from their homes to discourage excessive use. Owning or operating automobiles is *verboten*, but riding in a car is allowed. Hat-clad young men are clean shaven until marriage; single women wear black bonnets. All eschew jewelry, so beards on men and white bonnets on women indicate marital status.

Pennsylvania Dutch (German *Deitsch*) speakers, the Amish refer to all non-Amish people as "English." Selling at local markets or from their homes/farms (only where identified with signage) many families make their livelihoods by farming, canning, carpentry, and quilting. Some of the cutest puppies and bunnies you'll ever see are up for grabs at market, as are delicious jams and pies (try the Shoofly). Quilts made for their personal use are non-boastful and sedate; those made for English sale have no restriction on color, pattern, nor creativity. A quilt auction each November is a highlight of the autumn season.

Nearby St. Clements Island boasts the first colonial landing (March 3, 1634) in the Chesapeake Bay area. It would become *Terra Mariae*, "Mary's Land."

ALPHABETICAL INDEX

ALPHABETICAL INDEX

Acknowledgements

Edward, Loretta & Michele Chatmon
Marielba Alvarez/NPG
Joyce Bailey
Larry Bradshaw
Julia Chance
Harriette Cole
DC Public Library, especially April King and Jerry A. McCoy
Caroline Doong
Lloyd Gayle
Emily Grebenstein/Glenstone
Gregory Hill
Benjamin-Johnson Family
Veda Johnson
Lisa Jones
Valerie Joyner
Lee Lipscomb
Dale and Fred Nielsen
Sabiyha Prince
Ina Ratner
Jacqueline Shepard-Lewis
Angela Wiggins
Alexandra Zealand

Henry Adebonojo
Charusheela Andaz
Jacqueline Berthelot
Isabelle Bulkeley/NGA
Kia Chatmon
Rhea Combs

Carla Garnett
Keisha Goodman/Union Station
Brynda Harris
Historical Society of Washington, DC
Lynda Johnson & Alonzo Wright
Jake-Ann Jones
Yusef Jones
Denise Kerr
National Building Museum
Fleur Paysour/NMAAHC
Susan Burdette Radoux
Toshi Reagon
Dr. Kevin Strait/NMAAHC
Todd Wilson

Texts credits:

All texts by **Sharon Pendana** except pages 112, 113, 148, 149, 150, 151, and 152 (VMA)

Photography credits:

All photographs by **Sharon Pendana** except page 47, Lunder Conservation Center, Smithsonian American Art Museum, photo: Paul Morigi, 2015; page 121, Jonathan Fasano; page 127, Gyrofrog/Creative Commons; page 230, Meditation Museum/Brahma Kumaris; page 254-255, National Air and Space Museum, Smithsonian Institution, photo: Eric Long; pages 256-257, The Gallery, Photo: Scott Frances, Photo credit: Glenstone Museum, Potomac, Maryland; page 260, Fairfax County, VA Parks; page 278, Michele Chatmon.

Historical images courtesy of the following:

Anne Arundel County Public Library, pg.95 1878 Hopkins Atlas. Curtis Investment Group pg.247. DC Public Library Commons, pg.135. Gallaudet Archives, Gift of Reuben I. Altizer, pg.186. George Washington University Museum and the Textile Museum Albert H. Small Washingtoniana Collection, pg. 22-23. Historical Society of Washington, DC, pg.41. Ladew Topiary Gardens, pg. 285. Library of Congress, pg.42 Theodor Horydczak LC-H813-2272-A; pg.97 c.1865 LC-USZC4-1967; pg.107 Jack Boucher HABS DC,GEO,120–3; pg.108 HABS DC,WASH,168; pg.125 LC-USZ62-112436; pg.189 ©Underwood & Underwood LC-USZ62-68318; pg.301 LC-DIG-npcc-32128; pg.307 HABS VA,7-ALEX.V,2. National Air & Space Museum pg.207 NASM (00138840). National Postal Museum, pg.179. Prince George's County Historical Society, pg.281. Scurlock Studio Records/Smithsonian Institution pg.200. Silver Spring Historical Society, pg.227, Willard Ross, c.1917.United States Holocaust Memorial Museum, pg.210, "Oneg Shabbat Milk Can"; Workhouse Arts Center, pg.310-311; pg. 61, Steve Hajjar for Smithsonian Associates.

Maps: **Cyrille Suss** - Layout design: **Roland Deloi** - Cover design: **Coralie Cintrat** - Layout: **Stéphanie Benoit** - Proofreading: **Caroline Lawrence** and **Kimberly Bess**

© JONGLEZ 2018

Registration of copyright: April 2018 – Edition: 02
ISBN: 978-2-36195-219-8
Printed in Bulgaria by Dedrax